Global Political Economy

Global
Political Economy

A Marxist Critique

BILL DUNN

PLUTO PRESS
www.plutobooks.com

First published 2009 by Pluto Press
345 Archway Road, London N6 5AA

www.plutobooks.com

British Library Cataloguing in Publication Data
A catalogue record for this book is available from the British Library

ISBN   978 0 7453 2667 2   Hardback
ISBN   978 0 7453 2666 5   Paperback

Library of Congress Cataloging in Publication Data applied for

10   9   8   7   6   5   4   3   2   1

Designed and produced for Pluto Press by
Chase Publishing Services Ltd, Fortescue, Sidmouth, EX10 9QG, England
Typeset from disk by Stanford DTP Services, Northampton
Printed and bound in the European Union by
CPI Antony Rowe, Chippenham and Eastbourne

CONTENTS

ABBREVIATIONS

DM	Deutschmark
EEC	European Economic Community
EMS	European Monetary System
FDI	Foreign direct investment
G3	USA, Japan and Germany
G5	USA, Japan, Germany, France and Britain
G7	USA, Japan, Germany, France, Britain, Canada and Italy
GDP	Gross domestic product
GFCF	Gross fixed capital formation
GM	General Motors
ICT	Information and communication technology
IFI	International Financial Institution
IMF	International Monetary Fund
IPE	International Political Economy
ISI	Import substitution industrialisation
LDC	Less developed country
MI	Methodological individualism
MNC	Multinational corporation
NIC	Newly industrialising country
NIDL	New international division of labour
OECD	Organization for Economic Cooperation and Development
OPEC	Organization of the Petroleum Exporting Countries
PE	Political economy
PPP	Purchasing power parity
SPD	(German) Social Democratic Party
TFP	Total factor productivity
TNI	Transnationality Index
TRPF	Tendency of the rate of profit to fall

WB   World Bank
WST   World-systems theory
WTO   World Trade Organization

ACKNOWLEDGEMENTS

I particularly thank Carmen Vicos for all her help and sympathy with and during the writing of this book. Many thanks also to Hugo Radice and Anthony Winder for their improvements to the manuscript.

INTRODUCTION

The Outlook and Aims of this Book

This book attempts to provide a Marxist critique of global political economy – that is to say, a critical commentary both on the way the world works and on alternative interpretations of this.

This introduction describes what the book hopes to achieve and how it will try to do this. It is first necessary to explain briefly what is meant by Marxism and by global political economy. There are many different Marxisms, all deeply unfashionable. Even to use the word is to court dismissal. Wise counsel may suggest euphemisms such as 'critical' or 'radical'. Marxism, not for the first time, is pronounced dead. However, the fate of intellectual traditions in the social sciences is not one of simple rise and fall as better explanations prevail. It also reflects changes in the wider social world and is itself a political act. Marxism is often damned by way of lazy caricature and guilt by association. Most Marxists in the West, for example, had disowned the avowedly communist regimes in the USSR and Eastern Europe long before their collapse and few were guilty of the vulgar materialism with which they were collectively charged. The sheer diversity of Marxism attests to a live tradition grappling with what remain real difficulties, steering between materialism and idealism, between overly economic and political Marxisms. Amongst other things the interpretation here, elaborated in more detail in Chapter 4, will argue that the appropriate alternative to determinism requires not simply recognising multi-causality, but working out the relative importance of the interacting parts. Determinism is not an either/or question, but one of degree. Marxism is also a perspective of engaged social science. The perspective here seeks to develop what has been called the 'classical Marxist tradition' (Rees 1998), of Marx and Engels themselves, and followed amongst others by Lenin, Trotsky, Luxemburg, Lukács and Gramsci. It is an activist tradition and I apologise in advance for any formulations absorbed over many years as a committed socialist and repeated without due acknowledgement.

This is not (yet another) book on globalisation. There were indeed important changes to the global political economy in the latter part of the twentieth century, but the premise here is that political economy should be understood 'globally' from the start. So there is no intention to privilege in advance change over continuity or the global over the national and local. The point is to study their interaction.

Global or International Political Economy (IPE) is also an academic discipline, often studied as part of International Relations (IR). IPE developed out of a recognition that interstate politics and international economics could not be satisfactorily understood in isolation from each other. Nevertheless, it often imported the intellectual traditions of mainstream IR and orthodox economics. This produced some rather intractable problems in trying to develop an effective synthesis.

This book therefore engages with existing traditions and tries to develop a Marxist understanding of the global political economy. It is organised into three parts. The first two provide respectively theoretical and historical contextualisations of the longer third part, which deals with contemporary issues. Without anticipating what follows, this content perhaps needs some explanation.

Why Theory?

There is an important empiricist tradition that begins research with evidence. 'What I want is Facts', as the pragmatic factory owner Mr Gradgrind insists in Dickens' *Hard Times*. Undoubtedly there can be something profoundly frustrating about theory that remains abstract and never ventures to discuss real-world problems. For all the difficulties of data and measurement this book takes the view that flawed evidence is better than none. But facts do not speak for themselves. What facts are sought, how they are constructed and by whom all imply prior choices whether acknowledged or not. Empirical evidence is inevitably partial. As Gramsci wrote, 'everyone is a philosopher, though in his own way and unconsciously' (1971:323). So the short answer to the question 'Why theory?' is that knowingly or otherwise we cannot do without it.

However, this means there are innumerable possible theoretical perspectives. Like the facts of which they try to make sense, theories exist in a conflict-ridden social world of competing outlooks in which knowledge is not gleaned from 'outside'; we are never really independent observers, however hard we try to affect a studied objectivity. Even the questions we ask reflect our circumstances and prejudices. As Cox insists:

> Theory is always *for* someone and *for* some purpose. All theories have a perspective ... There is, accordingly, no such thing as a theory in itself, divorced from a standpoint in time and space. When any theory so presents itself, it is more important to examine it as ideology, and to lay bare its concealed perspective. (1981:128)

My choice and characterisations of different traditions of political economy are of course vulnerable to criticisms of selective reading and of caricature. Although I will attempt to indicate where alternative interpretations are available, inevitably much is overlooked and many people would dispute the interpretations. The first three chapters in particular, on liberalism, the state and other institutions, and on critical or anti-rationalist perspectives, do not aim to offer general introductions, but to provide critical interpretations of key claims and assumptions. The fourth chapter, on Marxisms, is somewhat more expository, defending the particular interpretation that informs the analyses that follow, the sort of facts that are discussed and how they are interpreted.

Why History?

Part II provides an introduction to the origins of global capitalism. It condenses the millennia-long processes of social and economic change which preceded the contemporary capitalist system into three short chapters. It is not possible to tell the full story nor to assess properly the complex debates amongst historiographers about how the story of capitalism's origins should be told. However, even at the risk of simplification it seems worth providing some context to contemporary global political economy and some commentary on the way historical change has been understood. How we understand history has implications for how we understand the present (Wood 2002; Hilton 1990).

The world is ever characterised by continuity and change (Lawson 1997) and some historical perspective can help evaluate their relative significance. Historical materialism involves a certain priority in the ordering of the elements of analysis, not a monocausal material explanation. Historical development is a process which is combined and uneven across time and place and in the interrelation of economics and politics. However, these interdependencies are not simply haphazard. It is possible, with the benefit of hindsight, to discern key drivers of historical change and important steps along the path to the current conjuncture. Often, as Marx said, 'the tradition of dead generations hangs like a nightmare on the minds of the living' (1973b:146). The past continues to exert a profound influence. Many practices and structures still bear the hallmark of their origins. Conversely, it is possible to overstate continuity. For some mainstream interpretations, history reveals timeless truths. Generations of economists have accepted, with Smith, a propensity to truck, barter and exchange as something 'natural'. Many students of international relations see Thucydides' *History of the Peloponnesian War* as the crucial starting point for understanding contemporary state strategy. The pursuit of power and plenty are then seen to govern human behaviour in essentially unchanging ways. Understanding the origins of capitalism can therefore also undermine ahistorical and ideological interpretations which 'naturalise patterns of behaviour that are in fact specific to capitalism' (Blackledge 2006a:140). All sorts of institutions, from the nation state downwards, all sorts of practices like competitive individualism and nationalism, can be recognised as relatively recent creations.

It is usually necessary to be a little more concrete to establish whether change or continuity predominates at any particular time. For example, there is a great deal of contemporary talk of transformation, of an era of globalisation and of the decline of the state. Understanding earlier changes can help assess these sorts of claims. Similarly, there is a reciprocal, but not necessarily equal relation between social structures and conscious human agency. What happened in history was never a necessary outcome, but, at least retrospectively, we can identify logics of political and economic power which drove particular processes, which proscribed some outcomes and made others possible. A little historical perspective might therefore make contemporary global political economy appear more readily revocable, but also indicate likely directions of change and inform appropriate political strategies.

Chapter 5 involves a brief discussion of the nature of precapitalist societies, the distinctiveness of European feudalism and the reasons for its supersession. Chapter 6 discusses the emergence of industrial capitalism and the development of imperialism from the late nineteenth century up to the Second World War. Chapter 7 considers the long post-war boom and its breakdown, setting the scene for the discussion of contemporary global political economy in the rest of the book.

Issues, Structures and Agents

Part III begins with separate chapters on contemporary production, trade and finance. These broad areas are the staple of IPE. However, the ordering and the treatment here reflect the priority of work and production and attempt to deprioritise specifically border-crossing activities as the appropriate subject matter. Chapter 8 questions the idea of globalised production and liberal claims that foreign direct investment (FDI) brings economic growth. Chapter 9 argues against a dualist position that advocates either free trade or protection. There is little evidence of systematic advantage or disadvantage brought by trade either for rich countries or poor. Trade's importance for good or bad has to be understood historically and specifically.

Chapter 10 discusses money and finance, their relation to the 'real economy', and argues in particular for the enduring importance of states in reproducing global finance. Chapter 11 considers claims of a 'new economy' and suggestions that this requires radically new social theory. The rise in services and decline in manufacturing has significant economic consequences, but in ways that are much more ambiguous than optimists suggest and quite comprehensible within a Marxist framework. Some of the apparent gains are related to issues discussed in Chapter 12 on the political economy of the non-economic. Many vital aspects of social life are excluded by the emphasis on the money economy; in particular this relegates the use and abuse of the environment, domestic work, exploitation and alienation in paid employment and the ever pressing construction of new wants to absorb capital's relentless expansion.

These global issues provide the basis for the specific discussions of interstate political economy in Chapters 13, 14 and 15. The first of these considers relations within and between rich countries. The second considers poorer countries. These chapters suggest that cooperation and competition between states do to some extent manage and at times moderate the contradictions of capitalist accumulation, but simultaneously create additional layers of contradiction, which produce uneven results that undermine growth and threaten more severe dislocation. Chapter 15 discusses global governance and imperialism in the world economy, rejecting ideas of state retreat, but returning to processes of state construction and its relation to the economy. Finally, the conclusion considers results and prospects. The period since the end of the long post-war boom brought substantial economic restructuring and widespread perceptions that there was no alternative to a capitalist world order. However, capitalism's restructuring has neither achieved lasting economic success nor eliminated spaces for effective opposition at local, national and global levels.

Part I

Theories of the Global Political Economy

1
LIBERALISM

This chapter argues that liberal premises of free markets and individualism cannot adequately explain a world in which free markets are not the norm and in which competitive individualism is only a one-sided and ever contested aspect of social life.

At its worst, liberal political economy can be a crass justification of existing order; crass in terms of how its very narrow focus on what constitutes wealth and growth excludes broader social questions. It can be crass too in adopting models which bear scant resemblance to the real world (corporations, for example, do not behave like rational, competitive individuals) and in its explicit unconcern with this discrepancy. Friedman (1953) notably expressed interest only in the accuracy of predictions, not with the falsity or otherwise of theoretical assumptions. If anything, the implication is often that the world should change to conform to theory rather than the reverse. In recent decades liberalism has been used to justify waves of attacks on labour and the welfare state. It justified processes Harvey (2003, 2005) calls 'accumulation by dispossession' including the seizure of numerous previously uncommodified areas of social life.

However, liberalism need not be the simplistic pro-capitalist theory this suggests. Historically, it emerged as part of the great Enlightenment tradition, contesting very different collectivities than those fought by contemporary 'neoliberals'. Moreover, while the focus here is on economic liberalism rather than the broader tradition, the association between an economy motivated by private profit and individual freedom can still resonate against authoritarian regimes, like the Stalinist states of Eastern Europe. Planning too can be disastrous. And if the marginalist or neoclassical revolution is culpable in dropping the social content of classical political economy and insisting on a more thoroughgoing, but less plausible mathematical modelling, the competition it depicts is often real enough and the models may reveal important if partial truths. Moreover, since Keynes, the same liberal starting points of competitive individualism have produced less individualistic conclusions. Finally, many who regard themselves as liberals do so in a qualified way. Such accommodations can undermine elements of what others insist on as the necessary methodological rigour. However, these things do make liberalism a subtle and diverse tradition, if a somewhat slippery fish with which to deal.

The next section offers only a brief historical contextualisation. Good, critical, introductions to core liberal ideas and key thinkers are available elsewhere (see, for example, Green and Nore 1977; Heilbroner 2000; Fusfeld 2002; Stilwell 2006). The following three sections discuss different interpretations of liberalism's individualist methodology and its normative commitments to self-regulating or free-market capitalism and to only a minimal state. Finally, the chapter introduces some of the ways in which liberalism deals with the specifically international aspects of the political economy and how this further stretches its plausibility.

What Liberalism?

Some contemporary liberals insist on continuity. For example, Wolf (2005) vehemently rejects the prefix 'neo', seeing himself as simply following a long, proud and singular tradition. However, liberalism encompasses a broad range of theorists many of whom have little in common. It is far from clear that Smith would see many contemporary liberals as kindred spirits. Friedman took liberalism in new directions rather than simply developing what went before. A liberal institutionalism (Keohane and Nye 1977) probably has more similarities with the realist and institutional approaches discussed in the next chapter. To understand the diversity a comment on the social and intellectual context seems necessary.

Classical political economy emerged in a rapidly changing Europe in the late eighteenth and early nineteenth centuries. It seems little coincidence that it should develop primarily in Britain or that its most prominent figures were interpreters and advocates, albeit sometimes critical ones, of British capitalism. *The Wealth of Nations* was published in 1776 on the eve of the industrial and political revolutions that would transform the world (Smith 1853). The British political revolutions of the seventeenth century had already established parliamentary power, which helped produce the conditions by which Britain became the richest country. Industrial capitalism then produced even more profound social and economic upheavals, challenges to the old order and to old ways of thinking. Classical political economy was part of a great intellectual tradition that rose to meet the challenges.

Classical PE also reproduced many of the ambiguities of the Enlightenment tradition of which it was a part. For example, Hobbes (1991) had taken atomistic premises to mean that life would be 'nasty, brutish and short' without a Leviathan state. Locke (1993), by contrast, articulated what would become central beliefs on private property and a limited state (Friedman 1962). However, his concern with appropriate government also tempered his attitudes to laissez-faire and individual freedom (Wootton 1993). Smith exemplified both the general optimism in the triumph of reason and order and the belief in social development. His specific characterisations saw stages of society; from hunting to pasturage to agriculture to commerce. Other political economists, like great Enlightenment figures before them (Rousseau 1968) would be more pessimistic, admitting only limited prospects for growth (Malthus 1970; Ricardo 1951; Mill 1994). The commitment to science meant many political economists revealed uncomfortable truths about the emerging society. Smith's world of mutual benefits sat in tension with a society composed of great classes. Where he emphasised harmony between them, it was a relatively small step for Ricardo and of course Marx to reach conclusions of class conflict.

As capitalism passed beyond its youthful exuberance it became impolite to dwell on its many ailments. The industrial revolution transformed Britain's economy and society and the way it was understood. Volatility, polarisation and social struggles, notably those of the Luddites and Chartists, all increased. These provided the context for radical interpretations of PE, most importantly by Marx. In the middle of the nineteenth century the freeing of markets and competitive individualism made decisive advances. The Poor Law Amendment Act freed the labour market, the Bank Act established apparently automatic monetary mechanisms and the repeal of the Corn Laws instigated free trade (Polanyi 2001). There was unprecedented economic growth, with capitalism also spreading first to other parts of Europe, then North America and by the end of the century incorporating most of the world within European empires. By the 1870s, liberalism was established as the ruling ideology in Britain. The neoclassical or marginalist revolution now reasserted a more thoroughgoing (in the sense of more clearly individualist) liberalism against radical challengers. However, it seems little coincidence that with capital's expansion, neoclassical ideas developed more or less independently and simultaneously in several European countries and shortly afterwards also in the United States. Similar ideas had been articulated previously, but ignored in the different social and intellectual climate (Fusfeld 2002). Now the world was ready for an economics which barred discussion of history and society and for which scientific method became the reduction of social relations to physics-like formulae. Neoclassical ideas still battled with alternatives, for example the German Historical School and approaches that continued to stress the social and institutional construction of the economy. However, they eventually established their hegemony over what, now dropping the label 'political', became the discipline of economics.

Thus a thoroughgoing individualism and support for free markets won out even as giant corporations came to dominate national economies and imperial states carved up the globe. However, the victory was never complete. Times of crisis challenged the consensus. The Great Depression proved too great an anomaly for theories that asserted self-correcting markets. In the long post-war boom, what came to be called a neoclassical–

Keynesian synthesis prevailed; any theoretical tensions were largely overlooked. However, by the 1970s the ideas of Hayek and Friedman and a reinvigorated neoclassical orthodoxy in turn challenged Keynesianism. Neoliberalism came to dominate the economics profession and international policy circles, at least for a while. Thus, as the social situation changed, liberalism proved adaptable. What was at the margin in one period moved to centre stage the next. Individualism, support for free markets and the promotion of a minimal state took on different meanings in different contexts, as the following sections will elaborate.

Individualism

Individualism is at once the great achievement and great limitation of liberalism. In the name of freedom it provides an enduring challenge to totalitarianism, past and present. Almost literally inconceivable in earlier, pre-capitalist societies, it captures an important aspect of capitalist political economy and provides a powerful analytical device. It is limited because, taken to its logical conclusions, it precludes discussion of how individuality is constructed, let alone how it might be changed. It reifies a real and important, but historically specific, partial and ever contested aspect of social life under capitalism as the essence of human existence. In positing individual freedom against collective oppression it denies the possibility or desirability of conscious, collective decision making. A thoroughgoing individualism is hard to sustain and in practice interpretations vary.

Individuals and families had long amassed great wealth, but the scope increased in the eighteenth century, particularly in Britain, where entrepreneurs like Arkwright and Wedgwood made fortunes, sometimes from modest beginnings. The intellectual climate changed too. By the end of the eighteenth century, views that economic prosperity was and should be based on individual greed may have ceased to be heresy, but remained to some extent oppositional. Guild regulations were still in place and it took another 70 years before free trade became British government policy. Elsewhere, even limited capitalist versions of liberty, equality and fraternity had as yet made little progress. Thus early liberals' individualism contested the previously dominant religious or absolutist state-based collectivisms, which blocked the rise of new wealth.

Smith's optimism meant he believed that even the poor lived better than had the rich in more primitive societies. Based on 'a certain propensity in human nature ... to truck, barter and exchange one thing for another' (1997:117), his description of the 'invisible hand' became a powerful and enduring metaphor for the way in which the market, left to itself, allowed the free play of individual interests to distribute efficiently. 'It is not from the benevolence of the butcher, the brewer, or the baker that we expect our dinner, but from their regard to their own interests' (1997:119). Thus through the interaction of self-interested individuals, commercial society became the highest and wealthiest form of human organisation. Smith's individualism was, however, qualified. He was aware of class differentiation and that people were shaped by their wider society, by 'habit, custom, and education' (1997:120). Hunt (1992) argues that an ambiguity runs through Smith as to whether harmony or conflict dominates class relations. His faith in competitive individualism sits in tension with a sensitivity to inequality and poverty and with seeing property rights as a defence of the rich against the poor. Individual judgement remained fallible and the object was explicitly *national* wealth.

The tension between individual and class position reflects a real ambiguity in capitalist society. Classes are composed of individuals while individuality is shaped and experienced differently depending on social position. However, analyses were pulled in different directions. Ricardo makes clearer than Smith the opposition between classes in general and wages and profit in particular. Moreover, labour would continue to live at a bare subsistence minimum. Any wage rises above this would depress profits and economic activity, reducing pay. Marx, while rejecting such an iron law of wages, affirmed the basis of capital's wealth as lying in labour's exploitation, but also emphasised the priority of social being over individual consciousness (1973a, 1976).

Conversely, the marginalist or neoclassical revolution of the late nineteenth century would banish class analysis and insist on a more thoroughgoing individualism. It did so in opposition to the subversive direction taken by Marxist political economy, but also in changed social and economic conditions. In many respects these made it still more counterfactual. Capitalism, as Marx anticipated, was becoming more centralised and concentrated, dominated by large firms less easily interpreted (except in law) as rational individuals. Conversely, it may have gained plausibility as conditions did improve for some workers in Western Europe and America. They now had some choices beyond whether to eat or starve and could be depicted as competitive and utility-maximising consumers. There was also an emerging layer of managerial elites, including professional academics, who were the product of an increasingly organised capitalism, but who were nevertheless receptive to ideas of choice and individual achievement.

This new individualism provided the basis for analytical models on which it was possible to develop a discipline of economics as if it were a natural science. Some marginalists like Walras drew explicitly on the earlier liberal tradition of Bentham and 'Utilitarianism'. Bentham advocated what he called a felicific calculus, or psychological hedonism. People try to maximise their utility; they weigh up pleasure and pain and act accordingly. Amongst other things they are naturally lazy. So work is a pain to be avoided, but this can be overcome through wages and therefore pleasure. In the language of economics, people calculate profit and loss. So, for example, drugs may be pleasurable, but are costly in various ways, perhaps with unpleasant side effects. Lectures are boring, but may help bring valuable qualifications. In each case, each person weighs their choices. In allowing these choices liberalism asserts its democratic and anti-authoritarian principles. The state cannot decree, nor can the social scientist ascribe, individual choices as more or less rational or particular commodities as more or less valuable. With preferences equally valid, the best that is possible is 'Pareto optimality', where a change for the better for one person can only be achieved to the detriment of another. On this basis, powerful, 'robust' and suitably detached arguments about the operation of markets were constructed.

However, individual utility provides a fragile basis for economic models. The system can become circular and self-referential. Utility is understood as what makes individuals want particular things – and we know particular things have utility because people want them. Alternatively, a prior philosophy and psychology must be invoked to underpin assumptions of utility maximisation (Dowd 2004). This threatens to undermine the studied objectivity of notions of rationality and choice. The two concepts wear each other rather thin. Most social choices become incomprehensible once they are detached from their social construction. But if social content is allowed back, utilitarianism can have dangerously egalitarian consequences, the last shilling, as Pigou highlighted, bringing greater happiness to the pauper than the millionaire (Stilwell 2006). Marginalism therefore cannot pursue utilitarianism too thoroughly without bringing into question its own assumptions about the equivalence of utility and price and hence undermining its whole framework. There can be no intrinsic rationale for preferring one person's cancer treatment to another person's yacht, poor relief over corporate tax cuts. Individualism has to be separated from the way individual endowments and preferences are constructed (Himmelweit 1977) requiring the highly political act of dumping social content as a precondition for an economics as impartial and objective social science.

Methodological individualism (MI) usually provides the necessary theoretical underpinnings. MI simply insists that the individual is conceptually prior to and independent of social institutions (Ashley 1986:274). People, and only people, have wants, which motivate them to act accordingly. There is nothing 'outside'. This may mean that people act in concert to form institutions, but these have to be understood 'from the bottom up' as no more than the sum of their parts. Social structures are derivative; they arise as the consequence (albeit sometimes unintended) of individual human action. Thatcher famously insisted of society that 'There is no such thing! There are individual men and women and there are families' (1987). This almost, if presumably unknowingly, brilliantly summarises MI. It also provides a window onto some of mainstream economics' contradictions. The last four words are interesting. Economists do usually regard 'the household' as the unit of analysis; tending to rationalise the often subordinate position of women and children within them. This also compromises MI; and if relations within families cannot be reduced to calculating self-interest, what of those within other institutions? People are shaped by diverse institutions, membership of which can have a specific rather than simply generic individuality. MacIntyre gives the example of an army as an institution composed of individual soldiers, which concept already implies that of an army (Thompson 1978). As discussed below, 'the firm' too, is often treated as a rational utility-maximising individual. If firm behaviour is at root the simple sum of multiple individual rationalities (Friedman and Friedman 1980), it is unclear why it should ever act with the singular predictable rationality required by economic theory. Convenient, but similarly counterfactual assumptions of rationality are similarly often made of states in the international system, confirming the methodological chaos.

Liberalism has recently been reasserted with renewed confidence. Once criticised for its failure to engage with the world beyond that of markets, liberal economics indeed now takes an interest in many other fields – in order to colonise them. Methods of explaining and quantifying 'market imperfections' within their own field of study are extended to other fields, most obviously the enduring presence of the state (Mackintosh et al. 1996; Sloman and Norris 1999). 'Game theory' has become fashionable in both economics and political science. Developed on thoroughly asocial and individualised premises, it nevertheless shows numerous circumstances in which individually rational action is constrained by imperfect information and necessarily informed by others' beliefs and behaviour. This means, at the very least, a world in which, as some contemporary liberals acknowledge, individual rationality is 'bounded', choices are socially constructed and, with many games being played simultaneously, outcomes are often unpredictable (Simon 1982; Keohane 2005).

In a capitalist society people do and must act with a calculating individuality. They compete, often in more destructive ways than liberal interpretations suggest. However, liberal economics exaggerates competitive individualism, to insist on a theory of 'everyone, everywhere, all the time, being calculating, rational human beings: no classes, no history, no past, no tomorrow' (Dowd 2004:39). It also overstates the possibilities of anticipating economic behaviour on the basis of such assumptions. Much of human action is not based on calculating individuality, but is imbued by habit and motivated by numerous directly social objectives. To the extent that selfish individualism dominates, the task should be to understand how this came to be – so that it might be changed.

Support for Free Markets

For liberalism, competitive individualism underpins successful free markets. Smith, Ricardo and other classical political economists believed in, even celebrated, the efficiency of the market as a distributive mechanism. However, classical PE again left creative tensions that would lead on the one hand to Marxism, on the other to marginalist economics. Like the individualist methodology on which it depends, characterising markets under capitalism as 'free' masks vital aspects of the real economy; non-price competition, the bureaucratically organised nature of the firm and production, the systematic inequalities of class, economic volatility and the myriad things governments actually do. Markets are not free as the models depict. Support for free markets then means attempting to make the world conform to the theory, belying claims of objectivity and supporting particular freedoms while overlooking others.

For Smith, typically, 'public interest', seen as synonymous with national wealth and well-being, was the ultimate objective. While usually served by competitive free-market capitalism, in principle this was subordinate to wider common goals. State intervention, although like the nightwatchman seldom needed, was legitimate when necessary. Moreover, in classical PE markets do not produce anything. In their more or less consistent ways, Smith and Ricardo instead posited production and human work as the sources of wealth. Indeed, for both, labour as the source of value was literally the starting point of their great works (Smith 1997; Ricardo 1951). Marx, of course, radicalised this and it would be expunged from the canon by the neoclassical tradition. Economics would be redefined, no longer an enquiry into the nature and causes of wealth, but into the distribution of scarce resources. Some liberals have sought to overcome these limitations, for example by extending the models of distribution to account for growth, recalling Schumpeterian (1954) ideas of creative destruction. However, amongst other things, change introduces uncertainties which tend to undermine capacities for rational prediction and thus the original methodological premises. In general, the study (and defence) of market equilibria became the end of economics.

The ideal of marginal utility is powerful – and useful in that it allowed economics to replace the labour theory of value with a purely subjective measure. People simply want more of whatever they consider 'goods', and fewer 'bads'. For each commodity people are all assumed to have declining marginal utility; the more one has of something, the less satisfaction each further increment will bring. A first pair of shoes may be life-changingly important. A second and third pair for different uses may also be welcome, but markedly less so. By the tenth pair any more new shoes are something of a luxury; they do not really make much difference – although some people, of course, have many, many more. They, it should be remembered, and the determined collectors and perhaps the drug addicts are, by definition, equally rational. However, some goods – money and labour are the most obvious – can satisfy different wants; and faced with choices between two or more commodities, what people want depends on what they already have. Whether to buy shoes or beer depends on both the person's relative predisposition and on their prior possession of the commodities. But where the decision lies, at what point someone will choose beer rather than the shoes will vary according to taste. For Menger, if people can achieve satisfaction by spending differently, they will do so until the last dollar, or until 'spending at the margin' makes no difference (Fusfeld 2002). If someone, at least someone with above-subsistence income, has $1000, they do not spend it all on either favourite things or essentials like bread and water. They spend it on a variety of things, some necessities, some treats, in such a way as to maximise their satisfaction. The 1001st dollar makes little difference; it could be spent equally on any of the different wants without much changing utility. If one had no dollars, the first would have substantial utility. If one had $1000, the next 1000 or even 20 dollars might also be significant, but not the last dollar. Similarly, people will work, sacrificing their leisure, only at a certain price. Indeed, we might logically expect them to be on strike for much of the time until they get the right price (Polanyi 2001). That this does not happen merely recalls the underlying inequalities on which this market depends. The models depict a world in which, in the absence of coercion, utility-maximising individuals pursue their different and multiple preferences, which determine levels of price.

Schema of market equilibria had tended to obscure production. Marshall (1961) reintroduced this, assuming it worked on the same principles, effortlessly and instantly responding to price signals (Mohun 1977). This extension exacerbates the conceptual problems. It implicitly ascribes individual psychology to firms; but firms cannot plausibly experience utilities, leisure or other pleasures that are assumed to motivate individuals. The manoeuvre transforms money, which for individuals had simply been a means, into the ends of economic activity. Nevertheless, having done this, an equivalent production function can be derived for the various combinations of inputs needed to produce different outputs. Firms select from the given prices of inputs and finished commodities to maximise their profits. As they increase the use of particular inputs, marginal utility declines as it does for individuals. At some point employing more workers will add no more to the product than is paid in wages, and the firm stops hiring. A similar logic applies to introducing new machinery or employing raw materials. Firms thus continue to employ more inputs until their marginal utility falls and they produce no further profits. This sets the scene for producers and consumers, for capital and labour, to meet as equals in the market place and for each to be rewarded for their contribution. The entrepreneur employs her capital usefully, giving employment and producing commodities. Labour's productivity is a positive utility to capital and is paid accordingly, workers' disutility or disinclination to work is overcome through a money payment equal to the value of the last unit of output produced (Fusfeld 2002). The wages can then buy goods. Capital receives profit as a reward for deferred consumption and everyone is compensated according to their contribution.

The models then depict a smooth and painless adjustment of supply and demand. The basic insistence on market efficiency and automatic adjustment, or Say's Law, is often read simply as 'supply creates its own demand'. Money must be spent somewhere. If at any time supply and demand fail to correspond, the scarce goods become dearer, inducing greater production; while too much supply causes prices and thence profits to fall, forcing firms to cut, or to withdraw from, production and migrate to more profitable lines of business. There can be no general and persistent glut or scarcity. Everything is accounted for. This free play of utility-maximising individuals leads to efficient distribution; therefore attempts to interfere with the market, even to perfect it, are bound to make it worse. The achievement of market capitalism in distributing innumerable goods in great cities, countries and a world of millions of people is remarkable and historically unprecedented. However, there is nothing inevitable about this. It achieves its feats through sometimes dramatic and painful cycles and only with social and political support. The practice, in short, contradicts the theory.

Free-market models are most plausible at the level of individual consumption. People do make choices on the basis of cost and quality. However, even here marketing and product differentiation, corporate size and geographical spread make it very hard to use price alone as a guide for anything but the simplest commodities. Powerful retailers can stop rivals, for example either by temporary price cutting or by lobbying planning authorities (Jones, E. 2005). I shop at the supermarket to which I can walk on the way home from work. Without checking the prices, I know that the time and effort spent going elsewhere would be 'uneconomic'.

The limits of market competition and the implausibility of the models become greater in production. Contemporary political economy is not dominated by butchers, brewers and bakers pursuing their individual self-interest in the market. Corporations do sell outputs and buy inputs. However, pure price relations form only one rather exceptional end of a spectrum of organisational forms including captive suppliers and long-term contracts (Gereffi et al. 2005). General Motors do not scour the shelves of the local supermarkets, weighing the cost and quality of the available screws. Neither is inter-firm competition, therefore, a bloodless adjustment around equilibrium price (Schumpter 1954). Size and corporate power rather than efficiency can beat down the price or beat off the opposition.

Perhaps most fundamentally, the majority of economic activity and decision making takes place within, not between firms (Simon 1991). It is at most indirectly conditioned by market forces. Between the initial purchases and final outputs, most production and distribution is therefore organised and immediately social (rather than the social relation being mediated by money), and not based on competitive individualism. However, production becomes a whole nether world excluded by the liberal emphasis on markets (Keynes 1973; Marx 1976:280).

The apparent equality of markets particularly masks the systematic inequality of class relations. As Robinson says,

> setting the whole thing out in algebra is a great help. The symmetrical relations between x and y seem smooth and amiable, entirely free from the associations of acrimony which are apt to be suggested by the relations between 'capital and labour'. (1964:59)

Workers, in Marx's famous phrase, must be doubly free, able to sell their labour power as a commodity, but also free from the ability to support themselves without paid employment. Workers have traditionally tried to redress the disparity by forming unions, but this may constitute an illegitimate interference in the market.

The models 'produce full employment by assumption and competitive outcomes by the fiat of perfect competition' (Tabb 1999:101). It should be little surprise that the real economy, so far from perfect competition, is wracked by unemployment, and any momentary equilibrium is reached only through painful disequilibria (Marx 1973a). Production is typically a long-term process: corporations need to plan capacity increases often years in advance. Conversely, up to a point, they will continue producing even at a loss rather than simply going under in response to changes in demand (Samuelson et al. 1975). The volatility of creditors' demands and corporate profit can make sheer luck of timing a major contributor to corporate survival (Itoh and Lapavitsas 1999). Meanwhile, saving becomes inherently rational and if incomes are not necessarily spent, Say's Law becomes invalid (Keynes 1973).

In good times claims of market efficiency may seem plausible. The economy works, the theory says it works and there is little reason to worry how closely the two correspond. In bad times the inadequacies of the models and the social costs of making a recalcitrant world conform become sharper. The claim to objectivity evaporates. The market failures and social polarisation of the 1930s made it clear that a consistent defence of capitalism had to abandon assumptions of the efficiency of unregulated markets. Some market freedoms had to be abandoned so that others might be preserved. In particular many who considered themselves liberals accepted that the legitimate role of state intervention and supervision had to increase.

The Minimal State

Liberalism has seldom simply been a simple celebration that greed is good. It also seeks to articulate the right conditions for the inherent goodness of greed to operate, and state intervention can potentially contribute to this. Early liberals supported broad individual freedom, though naturally limited to men and to 'citizens'. The state therefore had to be strong enough to defend rights to individual property and to secure social order.

Individualism and competition must be at least relatively peaceful and orderly. Beyond this there is little consensus. The state should be 'minimal', but exactly where the limit lies is open to different interpretations, some of which look distinctly 'illiberal'. The role might be only that of a nightwatchman, limited to a narrow range of functions and occasional interventions. However, conceptually this legitimises activities in relation to a wider range of 'market failures'. Opposition to state interference is thus a recurring liberal theme, but it is given different interpretations in different contexts. The sphere of legitimate intervention increased from Smith to Mill to Keynes, but fell dramatically with Friedman and 'neoliberalism' in the late twentieth century.

Some, until recently most, liberals accepted that monopolies, particularly 'natural monopolies', need strict regulation if not direct state ownership and control. However, there is a tension between freedom for corporations and the ways in which their existence makes markets less free (Friedman 1962). Some have been tolerant of monopoly and oligopoly (Marshall 1961; Schumpeter 1954). The problem for Schumpeter, for example, was not the existence of oligopoly, but only its ability to bar new entrants. Efficiencies of size may offset any economic losses from monopoly power, which might itself be just reward for innovation. Conversely, Smith opposed monopoly, like any other restriction to economic freedom. He was critical of how 'people of the same trade seldom meet together, even for merriment and diversion, but the conversation ends in a conspiracy against the public, or in some contrivance to raise prices' (1997:232). Indeed if markets composed of competitive individuals are assumed to be optimally efficient, the very existence of sizeable corporations becomes anomalous. Liberal 'new institutionalists' have accounted for this with some deft arguments in terms of market imperfections and the transaction costs they involve, which have to be weighed against bureaucratic inefficiencies (Coase 1937; Williamson 1975). However, even if this is accepted, it confirms that markets and prices fail in the tasks theory assigns to them of providing information (Friedman and Friedman 1980). Moreover, once corporations do exist, they may then generate further market imperfections if their own supply or demand is sufficiently large to alter the wider market. Monopoly or oligopoly might seem to compromise characterisations of neat movement towards equilibrium and efficiency and justify state intervention to ensure that intra-capitalist relations remain properly competitive. Therefore liberal economists may acknowledge corporate size and power as potential problems and accept anti-monopoly or anti-trust laws as necessary to preserve competition. The most 'liberal' of capitalisms in the United States has had some of the strongest such laws, albeit ones that are unevenly enforced.

Public utilities have sometimes been regarded as 'natural monopolies', legitimising state intervention (Friedman 1962). The inherently limited supply of land makes monopoly almost inevitable and various liberals from Mill (1994) to Walras (Kolm 1968) have advocated nationalisation. In the twentieth century few took their liberalism quite so literally. However, the state's role in ensuring the supply of those other 'fictitious commodities' money and labour (Polanyi 2001) has been more widely acceptable. The labour market cannot operate completely freely and states must intervene, for example in education, but also to limit union power. Since Smith, national security has also remained a legitimate sphere of state activity and escalating arms budgets have been compatible with liberalisation. The state as 'bodies of armed men, prisons, etc.' (Lenin 1965:11) shows little sign of retreat in an apparently more liberal world order.

Economists use the term 'externalities' to refer to those effects of economic behaviour which are not priced by market mechanisms (Mackintosh et al. 1996). The preferred solution is to find ways of pricing them, but, failing that, state intervention might be needed (Hayek 1962; Hardin 1968). Negative externalities are 'social costs'. Environmental ones have become topical. For example, overfishing depletes stocks, chemical spills pollute rivers, greenhouse gases threaten the planet, but not the immediate profits of the polluters. The society rather than those responsible bear the cost. In general, liberals would advocate making individual owners protectors of the environment, but state intervention may be needed to prevent, regulate or defray the costs for a greater or shorter time. Other activities produce positive externalities or public goods, which firms are therefore unwilling to provide because others get them free and gain unfair competitive advantage. The common, if historically dubious, example is that of lighthouses; valuable to all shipping, but costly to any one company. Pavements are similarly regarded as a public good, worthless on an individual basis and hard to marketise, but useful if ubiquitous. For Smith (1997), things like transport may also be necessary, but inadequately met by the market. Mill (1994) adds education. However, there is no clear line between the social and the economic. So, for example, equality may be a public good because more conducive to economic growth. Even on narrowly economic grounds it may be necessary to restrain the market.

Keynes and various social democrats built on such possibilities, arguing that various state interventions could increase national efficiency. Keynes's explicit target was the rigidity of neoclassical thinking, which failed to explain – let alone explain a way out of – the Great Depression. He was also trying to save capitalism from itself and the threat of communism, defending liberalism in the older, classical sense against totalitarian alternatives. He expressed doubts about whether individual behaviour could be regarded as rational, describing the 'herd instinct' and 'animal spirits', particularly in financial markets. However, for the most part, he remained individualist in his methodology. He diverged most decisively from neoclassical orthodoxy in describing how individually rational behaviour could lead to socially irrational outcomes. The most well-known example of this is the 'paradox of thrift', whereby saving, which is rational for any one person, may be damaging for the economy as a whole – because it means there is insufficient demand. The Great Depression made it obvious to Keynes (and others) that Say's Law was untrue. Businesses cut back production. Income declined. This then meant that people spent less on goods and services, meaning further cuts in production and in income. The downward spiral continued – however, not indefinitely. As income declined the level of savings fell until it equalled that of investment. This then achieved equilibrium, but at a high level of unemployment – something previously reckoned impossible with efficient markets. The path to recovery could only be affected by government spending to stimulate the economy. Keynes famously suggested if necessary burying bottles stuffed with banknotes for the private sector to disinter, though he preferred more socially useful projects. Such activities would generate multiplier effects through backward and forward linkages to the rest of the economy. The state could then recoup its spending through taxation (Keynes 1973). The necessary minimum level of state intervention is raised considerably.

In practice higher state spending was more or less forced on post-war capitalism by social struggles without which, as even conservative politicians at the time acknowledged, it might not have survived (Kidron 1970; Went 2000). Whether the period can properly be designated 'Keynesian', let alone liberal, remains a matter of dispute (Harman 1984; Heilbroner and Milberg 1995; and see Chapter 7). However, state spending rose, capitalism thrived and voices insisting on neoclassical orthodoxy were marginalised. Rising levels of state intervention appeared neither to be too inefficient nor to greatly trouble liberal consciences.

Liberals, Institutions and the Global Economy

In the post-war period an extension of benign rationality from individuals to states, implicit in Keynes, also informed much liberal theorising about the international economy. This reflected the Keynesian consensus, but also the traditional view of nations as the basis of wealth and states as the agents responsible for securing this.

In general, liberals support free trade for essentially the same reasons they support free markets and a minimal state in the domestic economy. The details of the classical arguments in favour of international trade will be considered in more detail in Chapter 9. Both Smith and Ricardo strongly supported free trade. However, Smith in particular made clear that his support was conditional. He took the priority of national security as given and supported the Navigation Acts by which, amongst other things, the navy protected British manufacturing from the Dutch. The one reference to the 'invisible hand' in *The Wealth of Nations* objects to government intervention because there is already a sufficient natural preference for domestic over foreign produce (1853:198, Magnussun 2004). For Smith it is also clear that a hitherto closed economy should be opened with caution. Even Ricardo's opposition to the Corn Laws was qualified (Fusfeld 2002). A period of European trade openness in the 1860s and 1870s was followed by substantial closure in the nineteenth-century 'Great Depression', with Germany joining the United States in implementing protectionist policies and overtaking Britain in the process. The wars and Great Depression of the 1930s meant further retreat from integration. International competition appeared zero-, even negative-sum. Pessimism regarding international relations was slowly reversed in the post-war period and liberal visions of benign, positive-sum interdependence regained plausibility. The great task of liberalism in the international arena became freeing trade. Latterly, freeing the movement of capital and finance (but seldom labour) has been added to the agenda.

There is a substantial methodological rupture in switching from the individual to the nation state as actor and unit of analysis. If trade theorists consider internal social relations at all, it is usually assumed that the winners can compensate any losers, though the latter might object and obstruct openness for a time (Rogowski 1989). Seeing the state as actor brings IPE liberalism close to versions of state-centred realism discussed in the next chapter (Keohane 2005; Cohen 2008). The similarities are particularly close in the adoption of explanations of increasing openness through hegemonic stability, whereby leading states become providers of the 'public good' of free trade to the world economy (Kindleberger 1973; Gilpin 2001). Latterly, however, powerful international institutions have helped sustain a 'liberal' regime (Keohane and Nye 1977; Keohane 2005). Their importance nevertheless underlines how remote this world order is from the models of free markets and individual sovereignty.

The 1970s crisis and the perceived failures of Keynesianism provided the opportunity to reassert neoclassical theory and practice. The ideas of Hayek and Friedman represented a more determinedly anti-statist and free-market liberalism, reasserting Say's Law and its close relation, the quantity theory of money (see Chapter 10). The principle of monetarism involves restricting the money supply, allowing only steady rises with economic growth; the fight against inflation is deemed necessary if prices are to provide reliable information (Friedman and Friedman 1980). Somewhat ironically this assigns the state an influential role in an area where it has particular difficulty establishing authority. Central bankers have repeatedly acknowledged their difficulties measuring, let alone controlling, the money supply (Galbraith 1995). The practice of conservative, even avowedly monetarist governments in the 1980s and 1990s seldom matched the theoretical models. The closest approximation to monetarism also proved compatible with thoroughly repressive government, notably in Chile where the state also eventually nationalised a collapsing banking system. Elsewhere, despite hyperbole of the retreat of the state, much evidence suggested reorientation rather than decline – even where avowedly free-market liberals came to power. In the United States, state spending shot up under Reagan's Republican administrations of the 1980s. Subsequently, in most countries there were significant shifts in the sources of state funding, with declines in corporate and income tax rates compensated by new or higher consumption taxes (Frieden 1991; Glyn 2006). There were also changes in the direction of spending, with the withdrawal of public services compensated by increased corporate welfare. However, some of these trends have been exaggerated and whether they constitute a more liberal world is unclear. Where dogmatically liberal solutions were imposed on poorer countries, they often proved disastrous (Stiglitz 2002). By the turn of the century the neoliberalism espoused by leading states and international institutions like the IMF was being toned down in favour of a more pragmatic 'post-Washington consensus'. As ever, liberalism proved adaptable.

Conclusion

Liberalism is a diverse tradition, to which a brief critical sketch cannot do justice. However this chapter has outlined how in relation to each of three core liberal views its virtues easily become vices. The rise of individualism, free markets and limiting of state powers all played important roles in overcoming absolutism and establishing the uniquely dynamic system that is modern capitalism. They retain an enduring resonance in opposition to totalitarian interference.

However, these are limited achievements and liberalism's analytical emphasis and normative defence of these produces a one-sided and exaggerated description of contemporary political economy. Competitive individualism is a real but recent and still-contested feature of social life under capitalism. It exists alongside other, cooperative social relations. Markets remain socially embedded and are not the only, indeed not the major aspect, even of a narrowly defined economic life. Long-term planning and conscious organisation pervade the operations of firms and states. If capitalism has brought increased wealth, this has also coincided with rising levels of state intervention. Market capitalism has also always been a world of inequality and struggle. Liberalism systematically overlooks this, despite the importance of notions of competition. This highlights that it is above all a political discourse. It favours atomisation over collective action and market and money mechanisms over conscious decision making.

Many liberals have acknowledged shortcomings in the neoclassical models and qualified their individualism and support for free markets and state retreat. Keynesian narratives and a 'liberal institutionalist' IPE, in particular, offered more plausible interpretations of the world and the basis for a less harsh practice. However, the role they assign to the state compromises important individualist premises most liberals hold dear and, as will be discussed in the next chapter, produces theoretical ambiguities of its own.

2
REALISM AND INSTITUTIONALISM

The previous chapter discussed the liberal tradition and its assumptions and preferences in favour of individualism, free markets and a minimal state. The next three chapters consider alternative perspectives, which in their different ways see individuals as shaped by the society and the institutions in which they live, believe that markets are necessarily embedded in social and political practices and recognise conscious human agency and planning; often as desirable rather than something to be minimised, but at least as an important fact of life with which to be reckoned. This is true of the 'critical' and Marxist traditions to be discussed in the following chapters. This chapter discusses institutional approaches, specifically the economic nationalism and realism which dominate thinking in International Political Economy (IPE) and, more briefly, the tradition of institutional economics.

As in the previous chapter, rather than providing a summary, which is done quite adequately elsewhere (see, for example, Balaam and Veseth 2001; Cohn 2005; Stilwell 2006), this chapter explores some of the difficulties in moving beyond the important recognition that states and other institutions matter – to theorising just how. The path between asocialised but parsimonious theory, mirroring that of neoclassical economics, and mere description can be treacherous. The perspectives discussed here have the singular merit of incorporating questions of power, excised by the liberal tradition. However, the concept of power is itself awkward and contested. As the constructivist accounts discussed in the next chapter emphasise, it has the potential to undermine the best-laid plans to construct a social science. The approaches here also tend to submerge issues of class and power in production, emphasised by Marxism, which this book suggests are a vital element of any analysis of contemporary global political economy. The chapter is comprised of three parts; firstly it considers the tradition of mercantilism or economic nationalism, secondly the political science tradition of state-centred realism and thirdly the attempts to understand the state alongside other institutions in the contemporary global economy.

Mercantilism and Economic Nationalism

As with the perspectives discussed in the other chapters, categorising a single tradition is problematic. It means lumping together what are in many ways distinct strands of thought, often by hostile critics (Schumpeter 1994). However, an understanding of mercantilism as a doctrine advancing national economic interests through extensive state regulation is probably sufficiently wide (Viner 1948). This distinguishes mercantilism or economic nationalism from realist perspectives discussed in the next section, which recognise, but may not support, the power of nation states (Gilpin 2001). It also immediately distinguishes it from a liberal caricature as a simple-minded rejection of trade. However, just as the 'minimal' state advocated by liberals can be variously interpreted, so too can the quantity and nature of 'extensive' state intervention favoured by mercantilists.

The term 'mercantilism' might immediately suggest a paradox, but it is quite a revealing one. Mercantilism is literally 'the policy of merchants'. Merchants trade. Yet mercantilism is often interpreted as a policy of state intervention and of restrictions on trade. Historically relations have changed and there are many tensions between states and private accumulations of wealth; but they have seldom been based on a simple antagonism. As late as the sixteenth century, European societies remained primarily agrarian and marked, in Anderson's phrase, by the 'organic unity of economy and polity' (1979a:19). Lords were rich and powerful. Peasants were poor and powerless. Moreover, a state clearly separate from and relatively independent of subordinate powers was only just developing. Early mercantilism was a policy that played an important part in this process of constructing singular national economies, often against local nobles. It could involve using tariffs to raise revenues, but also a variety of strategies to encourage national industry and agriculture. It typically benefited merchants who maintained through state-backed monopoly higher prices than would have been possible had they competed freely (Hunt 1992). Internationally too, the first European trading empires of Portugal and Spain were conducted either as wholly owned state monopolies or with substantial state support. The Dutch and British East India Companies were private firms, but still enjoyed monopolies and state protection. There were important differences of emphasis over time and between places; different merchants sought different forms of support. However, in general, merchants, like many subsequent capitalists, and states benefited from economic relations that were organised rather than 'free'.

Since Smith, there has been much caricature of mercantilism as a simple-minded determination either to amass gold or to make more money selling goods than was spent buying them (Kirshner 1999). It can be synonymous with import restrictions. Some early writers suggest something close to this. The anonymously published *A Discourse on the Common Weal of this Realm of England* argued in 1581 that 'we must always take heed that we buy no more of strangers than we do sell them; for so we should impoverish ourselves and enrich them' (cited in Rubin 1979:46). The influence appears lasting, with the idea of making profit through trade and of the advantages of a current-account surplus running deep. Contemporary news media almost invariably present surpluses and deficits as unqualified goods and bads respectively.

Locke would later write, 'Riches do not consist in having more gold and silver but in having more in proportion than the rest of the world' (1991:222). This anticipates the idea, which would inform much of twentieth-century political theorising, of international relations as a 'zero-sum' game in which one country's gain is another's loss. However, *A Discourse* suggests that trade surpluses were not to be achieved just by tariffs or by arbitrary currency revaluation, but by making English prices internationally competitive. To achieve this, a young and inefficient capital needed shielding from foreign competition. Britain in the sixteenth century was a backward country compared to the Netherlands or the Italian city states. Britain encouraged imports of raw materials like wool, cotton, linen, dyestuffs and leather, freeing them of customs levies and sometimes even subsidising them. Conversely the import of finished goods was banned or subjected to high tariffs. The reverse applied to exports. Where previously they might all have been encouraged, by the late sixteenth and seventeenth centuries there were restrictions or bans on exporting raw materials. The upshot was that native industry was shielded, to the detriment of agriculture. The imports meant agricultural raw materials prices fell, providing a subsidy (or in the language of liberalism a 'rent') from agriculture to industry (Rubin 1979). Both in theory and practice mercantilism therefore developed an attitude towards 'infant industry' that continues to be admitted as an exception to imperatives to free trade even by textbook orthodoxy (Sloman and Norris 1999).

Even for early mercantilists like Mun, commodities, not money, were the basis of real wealth. Where there were goods there would be money and it was therefore absurd to prohibit the export of commodities or the means of circulating them. To look only at the former was like looking at the farmer only in seed time when he throws good seed onto the ground. Child takes the argument still further, making clear that money is a commodity and so, like others, may be exported to the national advantage (Schumpeter 1994). The particular policy prescriptions varied widely in relation to both domestic economy and international economic relations, but what seems clear is that by the end of the eighteenth century mercantilism had firmly established the state as the basis of economic activity and theory. It is possibly an exaggeration to see Smith as a 'misunderstood mercantilist' (Reinert and Reinert 2005). But he, and most subsequent liberal theorising – at least implicitly – accepted that questions of wealth were henceforth those of nations. As discussed in the previous chapter, by the late eighteenth century the world had changed and what Smith and later Ricardo argued was that relatively free trade now served Britain's national interest.

Britain had become the dominant power and it increasingly supported free trade, albeit somewhat inconsistently at least until the 1840s. The focus of mercantilist arguments shifted to Britain's rivals and figures like Hamilton in the United States and List in Germany. The argument also shifted more decisively from trade to internal development and a broader interventionist policy of economic nationalism. Free trade now threatened the independence of weaker states and their ability to emulate what Britain had already achieved. Pure market mechanisms and standard liberal economics would suggest always buying the cheapest possible goods (for the right quality) irrespective of their origin. Economic nationalists countered that immediate self-interest did not necessarily benefit the whole national society in the long run. Instead of relying on Britain for manufactured goods other countries would do better to build their own industries.

The United States was a vast fertile land (in the language of trade theory it had a comparative advantage in agriculture). Accordingly, for liberals it should have sold agricultural goods and bought industrial products. Against this, Hamilton (1997) insisted that manufacturing would bring many advantages, increasing the division of labour, and hence efficiency, extending the use of machinery (including in agriculture) and increasing the demand for agricultural products. It would increase employment, particularly of women and children, and promote immigration. So the US government should organise the transfer of resources to manufacturing. In addition to appropriate tariffs and trade subsidies, he argued for state support for new inventions and discoveries, for regulation to prevent frauds and to improve quality, and for state provision of financial infrastructure and of transport. Perhaps most significantly, the prosperity of manufacturing would ensure independence and security, which were at least as important as national wealth.

Some 50 years later List (1983) argued similarly, if somewhat more systematically, of Germany and its relation to Britain. Also like Hamilton, he insisted he was not, in principle, against free trade. Within the United States, between the departments of France, within the United Kingdom and the German *Zollverein*, free trade appeared obviously a good thing. Similarly, were there a cosmopolitan world economy, free trade would be appropriate, perhaps at some time in the future. However, List says Smith simply assumed this peaceful cosmopolitanism. It did not exist in the present condition of national relations and British manufacturing superiority. The English had a predilection for their own language, laws, regulations and habits and an interest in supporting their own industry. Therefore, in the absence of such a hypothetical 'universal union and a state of perpetual peace' (1997:51), free trade would have the effect of

> extending the market for English manufactures over all countries ... It would fall to the lot of France, together with Spain and Portugal, to supply this English world with the choicest wines, and to drink the bad ones herself: at most France might retain the manufacture of a little millinery. Germany would scarcely have more to supply this English world with than children's toys, wooden clocks, and philological writing, and sometimes also an auxiliary corps, who might sacrifice themselves to pine away in the deserts of Asia or Africa, for the sake of extending the manufacturing and commercial supremacy, the literature and language of England. (1997:53–4)

Germany and France would be reduced to the level of the poorest countries in Asia. True political science, List suggests, regards such a result of universal free trade as a very unnatural one. Instead, other states should intervene to attempt to build their own domestic economies. Immediate gains in exchange should not be confused with the wealth in productive powers (1983:34–6). These should be cultivated by protecting infant industries, but also developing the three constitutive elements of productive power; nature, matter and mind. Of these, the mental was the most important, capable of almost infinite augmentation which the state should do most to nourish. Here then are already clear anticipations of later arguments for the primacy of education in establishing competitive advantage (Reich 1991; Levi-Faur 1997).

These mercantilist writings made a powerful argument that rich countries climbed the ladder using economic nationalism, then obscured the means by which they industrialised, 'kicking away the ladder' to prevent others from following the same path and becoming competitors (List 1983; Chang 2002). The national focus allowed a longer-term emphasis than it was possible to derive from individual self-interest. State intervention within these economies and the pursuit of something less than free trade eventually proved effective. Both the US and German capital eventually caught up with and overtook their British counterparts. They too then kicked away the ladder.

In the West, mercantilist discourse thus became confined to the margins. Similar ideas were nevertheless articulated in the USSR (Guzzini 1998) and echoed in dependency theory and strategies of 'import substitution industrialisation' (ISI) adopted by several poorer countries. Such policies became unfashionable in an era of neoliberalism. The collapse of communism in Eastern Europe, the singular success of export-oriented economies in East Asia and the retreat of the left in Western Europe and North America saw liberal ideas again predominate. However, a 'new statism' (Cammack 1990) reasserted the importance of the state in economic development (Evans et al. 1985) notably including that in East Asia (Amsden 1989; Wade 1990). Moreover in rich countries, too, several authors confirmed the importance of the state in the different way economic activity was institutionalised in distinct models of capitalism adopted at different times and place (Coates 2000). Free trade became the norm, but no state could afford to be completely laissez-faire with regard to its domestic economy. In practice, capitalism remained inescapably shaped by nation states.

Realism – the Pursuit of Power (and Plenty?)

In mainstream Western, or at least Anglo-American, academia, the separation of politics and economics as discrete domains was firmly established by the early twentieth century. For liberals this separation is something to be celebrated (Friedman 1962; Hayek 1962). Impossible to achieve in practice, theory is left in the lurch. Economics would henceforth discuss individual utility maximisation. Where international issues could not be avoided, the theory of comparative advantage would largely suffice. There was no reason why the countries of the world should not cooperate peacefully and increasingly prosperously. It was left to political theorists (denied tools of socio-economic analysis) to try to understand conflict and war, which clung on rather tenaciously.

In an imperfect world, Morgenthau (1963) thought liberal attempts to perfect it from abstract, rational principles misplaced. International relations should instead be studied though a lens of 'realism', which acknowledged the universality of power-seeking behaviour rooted deep in the human psyche. Power should always be understood as the basic motive, with money only a means to such an end – for states and industrialists alike. States fought for power in essentially unchanging ways, with nationalism bridging any gap between general populations and their rulers. These were powerful if pessimistic ideas, adopted by a long line of social thinkers from Nietzsche to Weber and Foucault. Basing power analysis on individual behaviour makes it something very difficult to disprove, but equally very difficult to use to prove anything else. If drives for power are biological, it becomes impossible to account for sometimes starkly differing behaviour and social structures. Its very generality means that it cannot explain any specific social action. Indeed Morgenthau noted the same biological drives amongst chickens and monkeys, whose behaviour might be thought an unlikely guide to foreign policy (Rosenberg 1994). To anticipate, the pervasiveness of power leaves realism with difficulties distinguishing its claims to objectivity and its status as science from its own role in the world it depicts, its need to 'look over the shoulder' of statesmen (Keohane 1986; Ashley 1986).

Attempting to move beyond this level of generality, Waltz (1959, 1979) argued that there were three interacting 'images'; individual, state and systemic. This reformulated 'neorealism' dissociated state behaviour from biology. The relations between the levels were in principle open to investigation. However, for Waltz the last, the systemic, was decisive in shaping the behaviour of the units. This idea of asymmetrical interdependence of structures and agents is a potentially useful one and the exclusion of questions of internal relations was intended as a theoretical expedient rather than an empirically accurate description (see also Krasner 1999). The internal composition of states was unimportant in the sense of anticipating their external behaviour. Waltz (1979) used the example of the early USSR, which despite its revolutionary rhetoric quickly conformed to the rules and norms of international diplomacy. The 'lower levels' could be excluded as not being the subject matter of IR, which could proceed as if states were independent and sufficiently rational in their responses to systemic influence (Keohane 1986; Rosenberg 1994; Krasner 1999). Disarticulating structure from the units and depicting states as actors in this way provides a powerful simplifying assumption. The costs of too rigid a separation of levels are nevertheless considerable.

Neorealism modelled relations between countries on those of individuals in economic relations as depicted by neoclassical accounts (Guzzini 1998). Also, as in orthodox economics, state behaviour was often understood in terms of 'game theory'. The most well-known game is the prisoners' dilemma, in which imperfect information militates against cooperation. However, states also have to play a range of other games, notably the 'stag hunt', in which any one hunter will risk losing the common but uncertain bounty of the stag for a more certain individual capture of a rabbit (Waltz 1959). As in economic modelling, what are called 'Nash equilibria' mean reproducing what might systemically be sub-optimal outcomes because it is not in one player's interest to change unless others do likewise (Kreps 1989). The recognition of systemic constraint provides a vital antidote to any liberal optimism, but has the conservative implication of predicting continuity rather than anticipating any possibilities of change. IR has often been presented as outlining timeless truths, from Thucydides to the cold war, rather forgetting the centuries when relations were different (Cox 1981). More recently too, the world changed rapidly, with predictions of the durability of the USSR (Waltz 1979), for example, undermining realism's plausibility. Its attempt to constitute a rigorous and parsimonious theory left neorealism echoing some of liberalism's shortcomings, while it created new ones by extending the concept of rationality to the nation state.

The assumption of the state as rational actor is deeply problematic. It 'is a metaphysical commitment prior to science and exempted from scientific criticism' (Ashley 1986:270). It shares with neoclassical economics an asocial and ahistorical assumption of rationality, but adds a second layer of reification by projecting this onto nation states, which are manifestly not rational individuals and are more obviously unequal than individuals (Hobson, J. M. 2007). Justified as an abstraction from the complex social relations within as well as without nation states that determine policy outcomes, the effect is to obscure these social relations (Cox 1981; van der Pijl 2007). State behaviour can, at least in principle, be shaped decisively by domestic social relations. States can build their tanks only if their populations do not insist too strongly that they want hospitals instead. The state centrism also means that other, potentially transnational agencies, of class or even 'humankind', become invisible (Ashley 1986:270).

Earlier realists had questioned the intellectual division of labour between politics and economics, insisting that states pursue both power and plenty (Viner 1948). They intervene in markets while the economy influences states (Rosenberg 1994). As the world changed, particularly in the 1970s, the separation again looked increasingly untenable. Apart from anything else it became obvious that states used economic policy for political ends and that international economic relations therefore had a political dimension (Spero 1982). The field of enquiry should incorporate both states and markets (Gilpin 1987). However, having attributed a rational individuality to states, explicitly modelled on that of orthodox economics, this now became precisely that higher authority over rational individuals within states which orthodox economics denies. The model collapses (Guzzini 1998). Moreover, reconnecting with the economy poses questions of the relationship of drives to power with other supposedly natural propensities to truck, barter and exchange. States can and do seek wealth and military might and (some would add) other attributes like technological capabilities and prestige, which give them power – both over their domestic societies and over each other. There is what Nye (2004) called 'soft power', cultural and ideological influence, as well as hard, military force. Power is thus multi-dimensional. Therefore it cannot be weighed like money on a single scale and it is unclear how different resources can be compared. Their pursuit becomes irreducible to a single, rational, optimal choice (Guzzini 1999). Does a strong ideological commitment and convincing social programme outweigh a planeload of napalm? Ten planeloads? So even were we to consider only nation states and accept that they pursue rational choices according to the rules of game theory, they have to play different, complex games at the same time.

> Even if all the games which all the states play are governed by anarchical rules, we could still not predict the outcomes a priori, since the relative importance to each state of each game at any one time is contingent. (Rosenberg 1994:26)

The reintegration of politics and economics thus questions the models on which they both depend.

Strange (1988) therefore suggests power should be read backwards from its effects. Questions of who gains do indeed often provide a useful starting point. However, they cannot constitute a satisfactory conclusion. If it simply records outcomes, political economy can become a conservative tautology. It becomes impossible, for example, to separate agents from free riders whose success is not of their own making. Luxembourg might not have become wealthy because of its own power (Guzzini 1999). Reading power backwards can also support a conspiratorial view of history – perhaps more plausible than seeing it as pure happenstance – but hardly sufficient. American neocons gained from 9/11, at least briefly, but this does not mean they commissioned the flights. Actions can often have unintended consequences and be undermined by their own contradictions. Perhaps more fundamentally, reading power back from its effects appears to deny any role for politics as the art of the possible. A

Marxist politics of class or feminist politics of gender, which say there are sources of power to change currently unequal conditions, would appear to be excluded.

Finally, power is perhaps a particularly awkward concept for the theorists of power. Once its pervasiveness in ideology as well as empirically observable open conflict is admitted it undermines claims to objective social theory. Moreover if the principal, perhaps sole, wielders of power are nation states, their citizens can do no better than support this. Some realists openly embrace their role as (US) policy advisors (Gilpin 1986). Consequently, as Krasner reportedly remarked, if people from other, weaker states have alternative theories, 'who gives a damn? Luxembourg ain't hegemonic' (cited in Higgott 1991). More critical researchers may enquire into the nature and construction of power, even while forced to recognise the inherent limits to their knowledge (Lukes 1974; Foucault 1980).

As will be discussed below, realism faced further challenges as globalisation, at least according to many observers, weakened the nation state. However, despite conceptual problems, the emphasis on state power and conflict continued to offer an effective counterpoint to liberal views of essentially harmonious cooperation.

State and Other Institutions in an Integrated World

For many authors, including some from within the realist tradition, corporate globalisation challenged a narrowly state-centric view of power (Strange 1996, 1998). Large firms also exert considerable influence. Even leading states are influenced by corporate power; small ones can be dominated. It has become something of a commonplace to present lists of economic entities including both nation states and multinational corporations (MNCs) (Went 2000; Stilwell 2006). The comparison of states and firms in money terms is unsatisfactory. They are not similar entities. Moreover, amongst other things sceptical commentators have insisted on the enduringly national basis of many firms' corporate structure and culture (Doremus et al. 1998). Others characterised a more complex world of rival states and rival firms (Stopford and Strange 1991), with three-way games between states and states, states and firms and between firms and firms (Dicken 2003).

There are also other more or less powerful actors and institutions in the global economy. Acknowledging these complicates analyses and further undermines a narrowly state-centric realism. As will be discussed in Chapter 15, for some commentators it becomes appropriate to describe a regime of global 'governance' or even a 'global state' (Robinson 2002, 2007) although this may operate at multiple levels. Rather than international relations being determined by interstate rivalry, there are also supra-state institutions not reducible to their constituent members and numerous international non-governmental organisations and lobby groups. There are also diverse powers, distinct interests and institutions within states. It becomes necessary to open the 'black box' of nation states to examine its domestic construction (Cohen 2008). Claims of absolute sovereignty look fragile and relations between economic and political power require more than simple addition to account for the different dimensions and different issues around which regimes are constructed (Higgott 1991; Strange 1996). Bull (1977) characterised the multiple and overlapping powers of the contemporary period as 'neo-medievalism'.

The boundary between Waltz's third and second image is transgressed. Nor can that of the first image hold out. Other scholars emphasised knowledge and ideology, either as a means of understanding state behaviour (Katzenstein 1996) or in a wider ranging repudiation of the rationalism of mainstream approaches (see Chapter 3). Strange (1991) advocated seeing the world through four interacting structures, those of security, production, finance and knowledge, each in turn acted on by states, markets and technology. She alternatively suggested that the formula of IPE should incorporate multiple authorities, multiple markets, the variable mix of basic values and their allocation among states, classes, generations, genders and multiple social groups and associations (Strange 1996). Governance is multilayered, not attributable only to states.

Although seldom acknowledged in the IPE literature, much of this thinking recalls older traditions of political economy. Intellectually, marginalism conquered the economics profession first in Britain then elsewhere. However, the resistance was protracted and never entirely silenced. For around 100 years after List, German economic thought was dominated by a historical school that contested neoclassical perspectives in terms of both method and their support for the free play of self-interest in free markets. Substantial rather than minimal state intervention was often favoured. A recurring theme was that theory and institutions were interdependent and historically constituted (Reinert 2005). Better known as a sociologist, Weber was one of the last generation of a long line of eminent theorists.

In the English speaking world, particularly in America, a tradition of institutional economics constituted a significant oppositional current. Veblen (1964, 1998), in particular, described how institutions embody habitual practices and beliefs, evolving through time, but outliving their particular members. He contrasted the instinct of workmanship with the predatory logic of ownership and described the social nature of consumption. Institutions therefore condition and 'govern' behaviour (Hodgson 1993). That capitalism is necessarily 'embedded' in social and political practices has become a common objection to recent strands of dogmatic liberalism (Polanyi 2001). Later institutional economists would focus on the firm as an institution within which, for example, there could be conflict between managers and owners (Berle and Means 1991; Marris 1964). However, institutions are more than formal organisations with permanent staff (Keohane 2005). They are also the diverse habitual practices, which shape behaviour and which precisely undermine presumptions of individual rationality, instead raising questions of how it is constructed.

Strange's structural typology has close similarities with the approaches and structures identified by avowedly Weberian sociologists like Mann (1986) and Giddens (1991). The re-emphasis on ideas similarly echoes the Weberian tradition

(Weber 1930). The broader understanding of institutions and their significance has significant similarities with Veblen. What all these perspectives highlight is that even to attempt an evaluation of alternative powers it is necessary to abandon a perspective which a priori treats states or markets as primary.

However, a recurrent criticism of institutional economics was that it failed to produce a hard science and was better regarded as a descriptive economic sociology. So although institutional economists sometimes offered profound insights, these 'descriptions' were inevitably insufficiently rigorous, scientific and mathematical to be accepted by mainstream economics. The new approaches, too, tend to suggest description more than analysis. Beyond states and firms one can add ever 'more actors – labor unions, social movements, and nongovernmental organizations of all types. The cast of characters is potentially endless, all crowding alongside the state and clamoring for attention' (Cohen 2008:140–1).

In the extreme, apparently frustrated with the failure of mainstream attempts to bring order to the complex and apparently chaotic social world, some authors advocate an openly 'eclectic' political economy. This can be read as a plea for academic tolerance, as a defence of the relatively open nature of PE and IPE against attempts to fit the world to the doctrines of 'grand theory'; be it liberal, realist or Marxist orthodoxy (Strange 1991; Anderson 2004). Formally, of course, to be eclectic means to borrow freely from different sources. It has been used as something of a term of abuse against those who use mutually incompatible perspectives more or less knowingly. In practice few seem to exercise a thoroughgoing theoretical anarchism (Feyerabend 1988), instead simply favouring multi-causal explanations of complex social phenomena. However, in whichever way it is interpreted, theory is not so easily escaped. The absence of explicit theory leaves intact all sorts of implicit assumptions about how the world works and the explanatory priorities. As argued in the introduction to this book, everyone can be regarded as a philosopher, and while it is useful to show the limits of conventional understandings of the world it remains necessary to construct more satisfactory alternatives. The selection of elements and their ordering even of a multidimensional analysis imply prior choices. The next two chapters will outline different attempts to confront this.

Meanwhile, it may have become hard to defend thoroughgoing 'state as rational actor' realism. Nevertheless, even Marxists can insist on an enduring realist 'moment' (Callinicos 2007). What states do, and the theoretical and practical problems of confronting their power, continues to matter. Against the hope of liberals and globalisation enthusiasts the world continues to experience, or to suffer, the actions of powerful states. Much of international economic relations remain just that, relations between discrete nation states (Hirst and Thompson 1999), which struggle to gain competitive advantage over each other. What they can do may have changed over time, but Levi-Faur (1997) identifies a direct mercantilist lineage from List to Reich's (1991) *The Work of Nations*. Reich, who was soon to become Clinton's labor secretary, advocated a policy based on education and a high-tech, high value-added route to international competitiveness. This was necessary because of, but remained possible despite, a world which had become thoroughly globalised. Similarly, insights on the asymmetries of power stressed by dependency theorists have been developed (if inverted) by 'new' or 'strategic trade' theories to suggest that there may be advantages for rich countries in supporting their monopoly industries (Venables 1996; Gilpin 2001). States are seldom laissez-faire in their domestic economy, and many, including the most powerful, engage in industrial policy on an extensive scale (Weiss 1998). Several authors have argued that the apparently chaotic global financial regime should be seen as 'Bretton Woods II' or the work of a 'Wall Street–Treasury–IMF complex' accomplishing US state interests (Gowan 1999; Hudson 2003; Panitch and Gindin 2005; Arrighi 2005a, 2005b). Some of these claims are problematic, as will be discussed in more detail in Part III of this book. It is also necessary to understand the state and other institutions not simply as containers of wealth and power, but in their distinctively capitalist forms. However, there are reasons to be cautious of claims of state retreat.

Conclusion

The world is shaped by more than the rational self-seeking individualism played out in free markets. It is influenced by relations of power, both overt and covert. It is shaped by powerful institutions; institutions both in the sense of formal organisations like states and corporations and in the sense of habitual practices and social structures. These make liberal depictions of a harmonious world implausible. However, systematising the power relations of diverse institutions has proved difficult, leading some scholars to abandon the attempt. The approaches discussed in the next two chapters acknowledge many questions of power and of the complex interdependencies identified by the realist and institutionalist traditions discussed here, but suggest different ways of making sense of their relations.

3

CRITICAL APPROACHES TO IPE

Since the 1970s many scholars have identified significant shortcomings in conventional theories of the global political economy and offered a variety of alternative formulations and constructions. Making no claim to be comprehensive, this chapter discusses constructivist, feminist and green approaches. Each of these challenges conventional interpretations and questions what exactly it is that needs interpreting. At the most elementary level they rightly assert that ideas, issues of gender and gendering and of the wider ecology are essential (but of course not sufficient) to any adequate understanding of how the world works.

Each of the 'schools' discussed here is broad and any characterisation risks caricature. To begin with a sweeping generalisation: recognising interdependence in opposition to crude materialist structuralism, although a useful first step, does not provide a convincing theoretical challenge nor is it capable of guiding action to change the world. Worse, it often tips into an equally one-sided idealism. The next chapter will argue that, properly understood, Marxism provides important signposts for moving forward and building on these insights. Nevertheless these perspectives provide important challenges to the mainstream and raise issues with which any purportedly radical international political economy must engage.

Constructivism

Rapid changes in the global political economy in the 1970s and 1980s, from the end of the long boom and the US defeat in Vietnam to the collapse of communism, undermined much of conventional IR thinking and helped open the space for broader conceptions of IR and IPE (Lapid 1996; Ferguson and Mansbach 1996). Both the liberal and realist or 'neo-utilitarian' schools (Ruggie 1998) tended to predict stasis and were weakened as the world changed rapidly. The confounding of realist predictions of stability were discussed in the last chapter, but liberal expectations of peaceful interdependence, and in the extreme of the end of history (Fukuyama 1992), also soon appeared premature.

Constructivists were able to posit that changing systems of belief had the potential to undermine material constraints. The weight of ideas provided a force to break down structures in the global political economy and a materialist structuralism in theory. At least in the United States, constructivism quite quickly established itself as the principal opponent of the dominant paradigms. Also contributing to this was the dearth of other perspectives offering fruitful lines of critique. In particular, the Marxist tradition was weak, both numerically and in the predominance of relatively strongly structuralist interpretations. Relatively free to deny or appropriate Marxist insights (Teschke and Heine 2002) constructivism could appear as the alternative to conventional wisdom. Condemning both liberalism and realism for their rationalist assumptions, the focus turned to the construction of rationality, to ideas and ideology.

Constructivist IR and IPE also drew on earlier philosophy and psychology that emphasised that the world was not independent of human understanding (Kant 1993). The starting point for the constructivist critique was that notions of rationality cannot be taken as given. Norms and values matter. So for constructivists nonmaterial things influence people's identities, which in turn influence their interests, which in turn influence how they act. Therefore if the object of social theory is to explain social action 'all the way down', material structure is not enough. People may be defined as rational in their own terms, but this does not help us to understand the world if they nevertheless behave differently in response to similar stimuli. 'Interests' become a matter of perspective and cannot be reduced to narrow, empirically determined criteria. Nor are differences settled in a free market of ideas or of prices. If the IMF tells Uganda it would be in its interests to privatise its education system, or Bolivia to privatise its water supply, we are not surprised when people say they would rather have free education or free water, irrespective of what the IMF deems economically rational. If Marxists believe it would be in the interest of workers to overthrow capitalism, most workers have thought otherwise. They have been interested in other things. As Thompson (1968) insisted, we should see 'interests as what interest people'. Constructivism similarly reintroduced ideas of human consciousness and agency. As discussed in the previous chapter, realists acknowledged different dimensions of power, for example prestige alongside wealth and military power. Liberal institutionalists incorporated the role of ideas – for example, the Keynesian 'consensus' and the significance of its breakdown – in their understanding of 'regimes' (Keohane and Nye 1977). However, once ideas are socially constructed and manipulated, this undermines assumptions of rational self-interest, whether posited as the property of individuals (by liberals) or of states (by realists). The construction of interests is not pre-given, but is worth investigating.

Ruggie borrows from Foucault the idea of '*epistemes*' as 'a set of shared symbols and references, mutual expectation and a mutual predictability of interest' (1998:55). Behaviour differs in apparently similar situations so cannot be reduced to material conditions or ascribed sets of interests. Consider the famous prisoners' dilemma. It is easy to show that prisoners kept incommunicado can be offered material incentives to 'default' on their accomplices, to their mutual detriment. But it is equally easy to imagine social situations in which the shame of 'default' would outweigh any additional penalty. Notions of solidarity – or of honour amongst thieves – are sufficiently widely accepted to make the game theory of orthodox IR and economics, which overlooks these motivations, often seem deeply perverse on first encounter. More concretely, Wendt (1999) describes Cuba and Canada, medium size powers close to the United States, but whose relations and attitudes to it are completely different. Katzenstein (1998, 2003) and Berger (1996) both give the examples of Japan and

Germany to show how over time different cultures and attitudes developed towards terror and national security. Or we might consider how Anglo-American entrepreneurialism developed in contrast to a Scandinavian model of corporatism or social democracy. Therefore, as the title of an influential article by Wendt (1992) maintained, 'Anarchy is what states make of it'.

Finance has proved a fertile ground for constructivist reinterpretation (Best 2005). Notably Sinclair's (2005) work on ratings agencies shows how ideas of companies' value itself can profoundly influence that value. Lukes (1974) anticipates some of these arguments. We can see power where there is open conflict and clear winners and losers. However, there can be less overt second and third dimensions of power in setting agendas and (still harder to prove empirically) in ideas and ideology and unconscious accommodation. Agenda setting can be seen in institutions like the WTO where despite formal equality some countries are excluded as others decide what will be discussed in the 'green room' prior to the open sessions. It is also at least plausible to suggest that ideological consensus can be manipulated. The vast sums spent by corporations on advertising confirm that they believe in this possibility at least as much as Marxists who maintain that the liberal/conservative voting worker has been duped.

This also has implications for those sets of ideas called theory, undermining the positivism of mainstream IR (and mainstream social sciences in general). We cannot just measure wealth or count tank divisions. We can intuit power relations not only when people take up arms against each other, but as something all-pervasive; present in our acceptance as much as in our defeated opposition to authority. Social scientists themselves are 'inside' the social system and the ideological constructions they describe. What they see is affected by who they are and how they look. Pretensions to scientific objectivity evaporate and both liberalism and realism are revealed as thoroughly policy-oriented.

Ideas matter in an interdependent relationship with the world they describe. However, without addition, this does not help us to get at the nature of the relationship. Constructivists have interpreted it in different ways. In principle most constructivists advocate an interaction of ideas and institutions, of structures and agents. Even Wendt (1987, 1999), perhaps the most 'hardline' of IR constructivists, in principle insists on a reciprocity, an interest in both ideological and material interests. Structures and agents are mutually constituting. He borrows the term 'structuration' from the British sociologist Giddens (1979). Structures are composed of individuals, pursuing their 'rational' self-interests, as methodological individualists would insist. States and markets are not 'real' empirical things in the world. But conversely, social structures do affect the individuals who comprise them. Institutions continue when the individuals who established them are long dead. Values and ways of doing things persist beyond any one individual. They constrain particular forms of behaviour (in a negative sense) and positively condition others. We make our own world as it makes us (Marx 1973b; Onuf 1997). In practice notions of interrelation can lead to a woolly sociology of mutual interaction and if pushed towards parsimony the constructivist preference is to see the world as primarily structured by ideas. Smith, for example, maintains that 'the fundamental division in the discipline is between those theories that seek to offer explanatory accounts of international relations, and those that see theory as constitutive of that reality' (cited in Burch 1997:1). Values, if not always so narrowly those of the social theorist, tend to be emphasised and material concerns downplayed.

There are, of course, varieties of constructivism. Reus-Smit (2001) suggests a three-way categorisation. Wendt (1999) advocates a 'systemic' constructivism. This shares with realism an emphasis on states and how they are conditioned by the interstate system. He remains similarly uninterested in domestic political economy. He also shares with realism the intention of developing a parsimonious theory. In the tradition of Occam, it is best to explain events as simply as possible. The addition of ever more variables leaves theory behind and approaches mere description. The values of the individuals are ignored in ascribing values to states. In Wendt the focus is thus on international 'socialising principles'. Ideas may be transmitted through international organisation, by which they conform to norms of 'civilised behaviour' (Hobson 2000). For example, states accepted limits to their sovereignty in adhering to the Geneva convention. With the focus on state behaviour, Wendt and other constructivists can then also defend a positivist methodology. The data, if not the interpretations, of conventional accounts may be accepted rather uncritically. This means that systemic constructivism reaches very different conclusions from other constructivisms and from the interpretive anthropology and sociology with which it appears to share its epistemology.

In contrast, a unit-level approach typified by Katzenstein (1998, 2003) focuses on how domestic social and legal norms are developed (Reus-Smit 2001). Here there appears to be potential to situate the construction of ideas in their social and economic contexts. While the next section will discuss attempts to do this with respect to gender and gendering, issues of class and of race (Hobson, J. M. 2007) have tended to warrant less attention. The state has typically been afforded a high degree of autonomy over its domestic society. State interests may themselves be 'derived from normative statecraft and changing actor identities' (Hobson 2000:158). The question becomes how national interests are defined, not how they are defended. Typically, however, the state still tends to be conceived as a 'thing' that acts in particular ways, though motivations are now rooted in values rather than material interests and the 'methodological nationalism' remains intact (Cohen 2008). States have effectively constructed national identities, but in particular historically conditioned ways; shaped by different actors and institutions within the state, but also under social pressures from within and without their borders (Anderson 1991; Hobsbawm and Ranger 1984; Hobson 2000). In as far as constructivism assumes differences in ideology rather than investigating their social origins, it repeats the realist reifications of the state.

Finally, a 'holistic' approach allows more variables (Reus-Smit 2001). In this vein Ruggie has discussed questions of grand shift, of the rise of sovereign states, and Kratochwil recent changes like the end of the cold war. This moves away from grand theory closer to earlier traditions of Durkheimian and Weberian sociology of multi-causality (Ruggie 1998). These are perspectives that are more historical and practice-oriented. Some critics see constructivism and Weberian international historical sociology as more or less synonymous, and familiar difficulties of sociological interpretation reappear (Teschke and Heine 2002). Many constructivists 'confine their ambition to providing compelling interpretations and explanations of discrete aspects of world politics' (Reus-Smit 2001:222). Ruggie attempts to 'engage in what Geertz termed "thick description"' (1998:2). This is a reasonable way of responding to postmodernist rejections of metanarratives (Lyotard 1984). However it appears to provide at best an 'analytical framework' rather than a theory (Reus-Smit 2001).

An alternative reading reproduces a rather strong idealism. Weber's most famous book, *The Protestant Ethic and the Spirit of Capitalism*, ends by insisting that it was not his 'aim to substitute for a one-sided materialistic and equally one-sided spiritualistic causal interpretation of culture and history' (1930:183). However, like much of contemporary constructivism, it is hard to read in any other way. In the extreme, this approach mirrors the rationalist structuralism it sets out to criticise. There is no more indication why ideas should spontaneously change than should political and economic structures. In particular, it often appears that states are simply moulded and remoulded by norms, which are the autonomous, independent variable.

Problems raised by constructivists associated with structures and agency and the position of the theorist are well known to those familiar with Marx and Weber (Teschke and Heine 2002). It is not clear that the recent theorists provided more satisfactory answers to some ancient problems. They nevertheless presented a substantial challenge to many mainstream assumptions and amongst other things helped provoke an atmosphere in which other critical perspectives could prosper.

Feminism

Feminism has perhaps had less impact on IPE than some other social sciences. This may itself reflect a particularly masculine and male-dominated discipline. However, there has been an increasing awareness of this and of the gendered nature of the global political economy and some significant attempts to develop more thoroughgoing feminist accounts.

There is a very long tradition of resistance to the oppression of women and of support for gender equality. What has been described as the second wave of feminism emerged in the 1960s and 1970s. Arising alongside and often associated with other radical perspectives, including Marxism and movements for black liberation, it also identified how within these other movements the position of women could be ignored or even explicitly subordinate. Feminists identified structures of patriarchy, of male power over women. These might operate alongside, but separate from, other structures of oppression, such as those of class, or in a more or less awkward conjunction with them (Delphy 1977; Hartmann 1981; Walby 1986).

Even as the radical movements of the 1960s and 1970s went into decline, feminist theory was reinvigorated (and taken in new directions) by the postmodern and cultural turn in social theory. The works of Foucault, in particular, described a pervasiveness of power and explicitly engaged with questions of sex, gender and sexuality. No longer separate or specialist concerns, these were deeply implicated in every aspect of social life. In a similar spirit, post-Marxist writers like Laclau and Mouffe (1985) saw hegemony not as something material and structurally determined, but as diffuse and therefore allowing multiple sites of potential resistance. Influenced by such perspectives, much contemporary feminist theory has therefore sat somewhere close to (certain interpretations of) constructivism in its holistic ontology and anti-particularistic methodology. Indeed, feminism is sometimes seen as one of many perspectives sheltering under the broad umbrella of constructivism (Sylvester 2002; Wendt 1999).

The most obvious achievement of feminist accounts has been to draw attention to the enormity of gender differences in the global political economy and the way in which they have been overlooked by other perspectives. For example, Pettman writes: 'women are half the world's population and one-third of its official workforce, do two-thirds of its productive work, earn one-tenth of its income and own less than one-hundredth of its property' (1996:171). The numbers may be contestable, but they emphasise the scale of economic inequality. Gender inequalities in political power are similarly well documented both in parliaments and in unelected authorities like the judiciary and military. Contemporary change, in the form of 'globalisation', is also substantially gendered. Women's participation in the paid labour force rose in rich countries (OECD 2005) while 'global factories' in the South were more likely to be staffed by women than those in the old industrial heartlands. Amongst people moving across a supposedly shrinking globe, the business people are disproportionately men, the service workers women; the sex tourists are men while it is women who are traded (Whitworth 2000). The 'retreat of the state' – particularly of its 'left hand' (Bourdieu 1998) – and the privatisation of functions concerned with welfare increase women's double burden of unpaid domestic labour and low-paid employment. Moreover, Coleman suggests 'neo-liberal development and the violence attendant on it is legitimised and made possible through the mobilisation of hierarchically ordered gendered identities' (2007:205). She is writing about Colombia and how a 'hypermasculine' militarisation and a feminised 'protection' work to similar ends. However, there might be a wider validity in terms of the ways restructuring both uses and re-establishes a thoroughly gendered political economy. Despite its supposed preoccupation with global inequalities, mainstream studies in IPE seldom discussed these gendered fault lines. Therefore feminism is both 'deconstructing, revealing the discipline and its key constructs as male; and reconstructing, making women and gender relations visible' (Pettman 1996:viii). Revealing such inequalities and more accurately characterising a gendered world may thus for some authors constitute (at least the core of) a feminist PE.

However, the problems may run deeper, the invisibility of gender to mainstream theories being more than mere oversight. So although most authors now at least pay lip-service to inclusivity, for most feminists something more is needed than inserting women or gender into analyses that otherwise remain substantially unchallenged. Something is more fundamentally wrong (Runyon and Marchand 2000; Squires and Weldes 2007) and there are significant reasons why the incorporation of gender into PE often proves difficult. The classic IPE understanding of the world as one of states and markets (Gilpin 1987) almost by definition excludes many of the important and interesting questions of gender inequality.

States and markets are masculine constructs (Pettman 1996), through which a male-dominated discipline talks about male activities. For example, differentiation by gender (as well as by class or ethnicity) remains hidden to conceptions of the world which see it in terms of *international* economies and inequalities. Divisions within the nation are obscured even while states actively construct the public/private distinction which excludes and/or differentiates by gender (Hobson 2000). However, feminist accounts also point towards a powerful critique of reified notions of sovereignty which posit states as the sole legitimate authorities over their territories. Patriarchal authority might be reinforced by, but has little to do with, nation states per se, yet it pervades society. The great brouhaha in so much contemporary social science around the end of state sovereignty thus becomes something of a non-question. Similarly, market activity is a privileged masculine arena and a market-oriented economics is profoundly limited by its ability to measure wealth only in dollar terms. Domestic work and subsistence agriculture are excluded from consideration, failing to 'measure up' to the masculine criteria of rationality and efficiency, and so are undervalued (Gibson-Graham 1996). Therefore neither mainstream economics nor politics are easily assimilated by feminist accounts. The accepted ontologies of the disciplines are riddled with dualist binaries of international/domestic, outside/inside, and public/private (Squires and Weldes 2007). The game-theoretic approaches of both are 'the opposite of relational and context dependent' (Fierke, cited in Sylvester 2002:14) and a marriage of feminism with positivist standards is likely to prove unhappy (Sylvester 2002; Squires and Weldes 2007). States and markets thus involve a typically male, top-down approach to power, constraining human action, but leaving little room for agency. A feminist political economy – as opposed to one which merely acknowledges gender – therefore requires a thoroughgoing critique and reconstruction of the nature of knowledge (Goldstein 1997).

The term 'patriarchy' has been used widely and variously. At one extreme it characterises a biologically driven male power and implies a determinist structuralism. More common have been approaches stressing either the ideological or multidimensional construction of gender. Even the existence of physical differences between men and women becomes controversial. These may seem obvious, but at least since the availability of relatively effective birth control much of what is often ascribed to physical difference on closer examination proves to be ideologically or socially constructed. Women's nimble fingers or men's strength have been desiderata for employers, more excuse than material requirement. Many social scientists therefore insist on a distinction between gender, which is socially ascribed, and sex, which is biologically given. However, even this has been challenged; overtly through sex change operations, but perhaps more fundamentally in the way men and women are perceived as separate (Butler 1990).

Writers influenced by the earlier socialist and Marxist feminist traditions have long seen gendering as primarily a social construction. It may have roots in biological differences, but it persists through diverse social practices and institutions. Capitalism, while ever contested and changing, benefits from a dual (gendered) labour market and the extra unpaid work women spend reproducing labour power. Ideology can be important to this, both reinforcing and itself reinforced by social relations that confirm gendered patterns of work and behaviour. However 'objectively' irrational, there is a material basis to women's subordination in its utility, perhaps necessity, for capitalism, which must therefore also be challenged to achieve sexual liberation.

Many recent feminist accounts have been critical of such approaches, condemning a perceived materialist functionalism to re-emphasise the importance of ideas and ideology. Gendering works through pervasive norms about what constitute acceptable social roles. These influence people's conceptions of themselves and their interests and hence their actions. Masculinity is associated with strength and rationality, femininity with weakness and emotion. Differences and inequalities become naturalised, for example in relation to unequal times or types of work. Men's and women's roles are inscribed by pervasive assumptions about gender performativity (Butler 1990). Much constructivist feminism extends this to repudiate not merely a crude materialism, but any 'materialist underpinnings' (Marchand and Runyan 2000:8). The demand for a dialectical understanding now flips over into a rather thoroughgoing idealism. As discussed above, if ideological structures alone exist in the world, they would appear to be just as restrictive and immutable as material ones. If ideology alone sustains gender, it appears to leave little room for feminists to step outside the gendered categories. Some feminists accordingly celebrate their 'feminine' roles as mothers and wives. Alternatively, idealist strategies can be reckoned necessary to overcome established gendering.

Most feminism therefore remains anti-essentialist; concerned with multiple sources of social power. It deconstructs other pretensions to primacy. Gibson-Graham (1996), for example, argues that if the United States is described as a capitalist society, this both exaggerates and naturalises the power of capitalism and downplays other elements of social power. We might equally describe it as a Christian and heterosexual society, which it similarly is, if similarly not entirely. This anti-essentialism is also used to challenge views of contemporary change as ineluctable product of restructuring. Family structures, for example, should not be seen as merely passive victims, but as actively engaged in reshaping social practices. Therefore feminism, in common with other critical approaches, sees change as an ever contested social process and reinstates human agency (Marchand and Runyan 2000).

However, this anti-essentialism means that although feminism can insist that everything is gendered, gender cannot play a unique explanatory role. Some feminists do understand or 'appropriate' other oppressions under a rubric of gender, ascribing masculinities or femininities. For example, there is 'a line between the White

Man (elite white men) and women (colonised people/nature) all of whom are feminised' (Pettman 1996:163). More typically and perhaps more consistently, gender itself constitutes only one, however important, aspect of social power relations. There are 'multiple forms of economy whose relation to each other are only ever partially fixed and always under subversion' (Gibson-Graham 1996:12). This anti-essentialism also has implications 'inside' gender analysis, as it were, undermining gendered categories. Masculinity and femininity are themselves not unitary. Women may be almost universally disadvantaged in relation to men, so that even royalty suffer from primogeniture. However, this does not imply any universal sisterhood, that the queen is likely to have much common feeling with her female subjects or they with her. Some feminists have accordingly suggested that elite, white feminism can parallel the sexist Western philosophy which generalises from white men (Tickner 1996). There are therefore many feminisms – liberal feminism and socialist feminism amongst others – sometimes articulating diametrically opposed social policy. Questions of class, of work (both paid and unpaid) and of wealth, form a vital component of any understanding of the patterned nature of gender oppression. States, markets, ethnicities all matter. Thus if feminists complicate analyses of political economy by asking questions of their implications for gender, feminism too is complicated by asking 'which women and which men' (Runyan and Marchand 2000:226).

Green IPE?

Green critiques of political economy – critiques both of the existing capitalist system and of prevailing understandings of it – are invaluable in their own right. In recent years it has become something of a commonplace to insist against liberalism that the economy is 'embedded' in wider social relations (Polanyi 2001). Green IPE would add that there is a deeper level of embedding within the biosphere, or what Berry called the 'Great Economy' (Helleiner 2000). The failure to value this leaves political economy – again both capitalism and prevailing understandings of it –

fatally flawed. However, there are parallels with what has been said above about the limits of constructivist and feminist critiques. This section highlights two ambiguities. Firstly, some authors see green solutions as achievable within capitalism. What is needed is either to price that which is not yet priced or to regulate that which is not yet regulated. This repeats the faith in markets or states criticised above, and can be contradictory even from narrowly ecological perspectives and have unfortunate social implications. However, advocates of a more fundamental transformation can still leave awkward tensions in terms of what is wrong and how anything better might be achieved. There can be dualisms between idealism and materialism, positing people's independence from, or determination by, their external environment and of pitting people against nature, 'anthropocentrism vs. ecocentrism' (Foster 2000:18). The identification of the physical limits to economic growth, most obviously and reasonably in the using up of fossil fuels, can tip into some rather vulgar determinism, for example, in the invocation of absolute thermodynamic laws or into the pseudo-science of Malthusian demography. This can be accompanied by some utopian visions of how to affect change. Ecological critiques thus draw attention to vital issues that have been overlooked and highlight the limitations of conventional understandings, but may fail to construct convincing alternatives.

A wide range of ecological issues have become topical and pressing. The environment suffers both from subtractions – as resources are depleted – and additions – the dumping of wastes. The most well-known contemporary problem is global warming and its potential to produce catastrophic planetary effects. Many other issues are familiar; the exhaustion of fossil fuels, deforestation, the destruction of natural habitats and species extinction, atmospheric and oceanic pollution. The long-term effects of some new innovations remain unknown and perhaps unknowable, whether in the disposal of nuclear wastes or the introduction of genetically modified crops. Innumerable local issues may be equally serious for those who experience them; from the destruction caused by logging and mining to depletion or degradation of water supplies.

Many of these issues have important consequences even in narrowly economic terms. The depletion of resources pushes up prices, the costs of cleaning up mount ever higher even as they are deferred. Minimally, all but a few hardcore sceptics (see, for example, Lomborg 2001) acknowledge that ecological issues present an important practical challenge. They also present a conceptual challenge, undermining ideas of the environment as something external to human society, simply a resource to be drawn upon at no cost. Moreover, limited environmental damage appears to be a 'good' to conventional understandings of wealth. If resources are spent both damaging and repairing the environment, these all appear on the credit side of measures of GDP (Kovel 2002). This might suggest a rethinking of economic categories.

However, the dominant approach to environmental problems mirrors the typical neoclassical demand to liberalise the world into conformity with its unrealistic models. Much of the world remains uncommodified. This means that it can be grabbed for free or destroyed without cost. Economists here talk of 'free riders' and in terms of 'public goods' and 'externalities'. The mill owner can use a river as a power source and to take away waste. The sea provides fish and the great plains buffalo to all who can kill them. Of course, the rivers then become polluted, the fish stocks depleted and the buffalo near extinction. This is what Hardin (1968), giving examples of pollution and population, called the 'tragedy of the commons' – the tragedy being the inevitable ruin as everyone pursues their self-interest. The benefits of the invisible hand and natural selection cannot be assumed. Where possible, as is usually the case in terms of resources, the market can be introduced; where it cannot, coercion is needed.

The example of buffalo shows that the solution should be to privatise that which was common. While the buffalo headed towards extinction, privately owned cattle multiplied (Block 1990). The idea of marketising the environment and its destruction also lies behind ideas like carbon trading. There are some rather obvious objections to this approach. It is not clear how broadly applicable it can be. Some things are hard to privatise because hard to quantify. If scientists have reached no consensus on the long-term effects of global warming, genetic modification or nuclear waste, it is hard to see how economists could do so and price them accurately (Martinez Alier 1994). In practice, like so much of the market economy, this privatisation only works because the state underwrites markets and preserves the fiction of competitive individualism. So, for example, it can be good business to take on unknown risks, but only because the legal system is structured to limit the downside dangers. There are huge potential profits from accepting risks, while the worst that can happen to a company is that it goes out of business. There is no real suffering; except of course to the victims of any accident, damage or long-term degradation.

Perhaps more fundamentally, the accentuation of the processes of competitive commodification is precisely what lies behind so much of the environmental damage. So Norway can buy carbon credits with wealth amassed from oil exports and put itself at the forefront of the fight against climate change with offsets bought on international markets. The logic of such schemes both relies on and entrenches inequality. Just as liberal perspectives turn people into 'human capital' and social relations into 'social capital', now environmental destruction presents an opportunity to commodify nature and put a dollar sign on it as 'natural' or 'environmental' capital. Profits can be made from a rationalised environmental destruction (Kovel 2002), and it is conveniently assumed (indeed specified as an economic law – 'Hartwick's rule') that an equivalent quantity of other forms of capital can replace that which is lost (Mackintosh et al. 1996). The commodification continues to treat nature as an external resource to be used by people. That there might be something intrinsically desirable about *wild* buffalo does not figure, any more than the future of species for which humans cannot find a commercial use. Many ecological thinkers acknowledge that the specific destructive rationale of capitalism produces fundamental problems. For example, rising salinity is killing the flora and fauna in Australian rivers and reducing the quality of the farmland. Rather than retreating from the destructive agricultural techniques that caused this, farmers must intensify their land use to survive in the worse conditions (Pilkington 2006). Capitalist competition must prioritise short-term profit. Methodological individualism, inherently incapable of looking beyond individual gain to future generations, seems a particularly appropriate philosophy in this context (Martinez Alier 1994). Thus capitalism is the cause of environmental crises. It may retrieve itself from these, but perhaps only 'through mechanisms and measures that cumulatively tend to worsen the damage' (O'Connor 1994b:54).

It may instead be necessary to look to collective regulatory solutions. Some legislation has indeed been effective. The London smogs were lifted and many polluted rivers have at least partially recovered. Even at an international level, the Montreal Protocol proved largely successful in cutting CFC emissions – if not as yet in repairing the damage they caused to the ozone layer (Dauvergne 2008). However, this was exceptional, and the difficulties of legislating at an international level remain considerable, as evidenced by the failures to ratify or implement the limited and probably inadequate provisions of Kyoto with respect to global warming. Environmental legislation that leaves capitalism in place can quickly be undermined. Laws requiring catalytic converters to reduce pollution from cars, for example, are negated by the inexorable rise in the number of vehicles. What Hayek implicitly acknowledges in condemning the 'totalitarian social engineering' inherent in ecological critiques (Martinez Alier 1994) is that challenging environmental destruction necessarily challenges capitalism. States can face similar competitive pressures to those experienced by businesses, and extensive state regulation of national economies has been entirely compatible with environmental destruction. Whereas in the early 1970s leading states had acknowledged 'limits to growth', such ideas receded in the face of intensified interstate competition and liberalism's ideological victories. The tragedy of the commons is played out again as things like deforestation make economic sense to heavily indebted poorer countries. However, at the international level, there is no coercive authority.

Many ecologists have therefore argued that there is something more fundamentally wrong with humans' interaction with nature.

Some have posed the problem as one of 'anthropocentrism', which posits people as separate from, and striving to 'overcome', an external nature. Humans see themselves as superior to other species, which can then be used to satisfy our wants. Therefore rather than starting from premises of mutual interaction and necessary sustainability, prioritising growth undermines its own basis, destroying the external environment and the prospects for the future. However, the split between people and nature, which opposition to anthropocentrism seeks to avoid, can creep back as anti-humanism. Opposition to anthropocentrism turns into its opposite. Humans are the problem and – as Malthus had it – should be judiciously destroyed. Hardin (1968) argues something similar, with coercion needed to stop people breeding (see also Ehrlich 1968). 'Wilderness' should be preserved even at the expense of indigenous inhabitants, who may actually have created the conditions Western capitalism now deems to be wild. At its worst, seeing an undifferentiated humanity as the problem leads to an invocation of superhuman agency to effect change. For Heiddegger this took the form of support for fascism (Kovel 2002). This, of course, is an extreme example, but it does signal the need to defend some version of humanism.

Humans are indeed a part of nature who just happen to have found a particular evolutionary niche. To imagine they are somehow intrinsically 'higher' than other animals, or plants for that matter, is essentially theological. Causing needless harm to other species epitomises the objectification of nature produced by capitalism. However, as humans, it is impossible to live without prioritising our species. It is surely not necessary to attempt to prove that cannibalism is worse than eating other species: apples, for example. Of course, there is no need to eat meat, or to club seals or to use ivory billiard balls. But it may be conscionable to prioritise human health over that of rats or fleas or the parasites they bear. Safe blood transfusions until quite recently relied on using reagents (called anti-human globulins) that could only be produced in other animals. Many would baulk at using laboratory animals for other purposes, but, for example, testing cosmetics instead on humans either in clinical trials or without them might not be preferable. These present difficult choices, but not ones in which humans and animals can be treated indifferently. There is something unique in the way people are not simply passive witnesses, but have the potential to consciously transform and to live sustainably with nature.

Similarly, it is clear that there are physical limits to economic growth, which can be self-limiting and environmentally destructive. However, there are dangers of stating too strong a determinism. Many green scholars invoke entropy and the second law of thermodynamics to highlight the mismatch between 'the equality of inputs and outputs in brute energy and material terms, and the qualitative irreversible changes in entropy and ecological terms' (O'Connor 1994a:7). Unlike the first law, of energy conservation, the second law is directional. Entropy increases over time. It is a law of increasing disorder and guarantees that eventually we will all be long dead in an icy universe. However, the processes through which entropy increases are themselves patterned. Otherwise something as complex and ordered as life on earth would never have been possible. So perhaps some environmental problems (global warming being the most obvious) can be understood under this rubric (as a particular, temporary, human-mediated consequence of the sun's cooling). However the sheer inexorability of the law makes it an unlikely guide to action.

If material laws condemn us, the response is often flight to idealism. This can mean siding with nature, seen as possessing its own 'capriciousness' against a predatory humanity (O'Connor 1994b). Such expressions are often useful metaphors. However, they appear to be taken rather literally by many environmentalists, particularly those influenced by stronger versions of 'Gaia' or Schumacher's Buddhist economics. The idealism can also be reflected more practically in attempts to live 'outside' or alongside the structures of capitalism without challenging them. For example, 'small is beautiful', in Schumacher's phrase, can inspire attempts to build specifically localised economies (Hines 2000). This may underestimate the expansionary and globally destructive capacity of capitalism. It also leaves awkward problems in defining localities and policing boundaries (Kovel 2002).

Achieving sustainable ecology is tied up with broader human transformation, though how this might be achieved can remain vague. Even avowedly Marxist ecologists may insist that 'there is no privileged agent' (Kovel 2002:218). Beck provides some justification for the realisation of a common situation, depicting a 'boomerang effect', whereby environmental destruction comes back, in one way or another, to those who pollute. 'Poverty is hierarchic, while smog is democratic' (1992:36). However, as Yearley (1996) highlights, neither in its causes nor in its consequences is environmental destruction usually egalitarian, and motivations for wanting to achieve changes and the price reckoned worth paying for them are likely to differ. This points towards integrating social and ecological concerns.

Environmental destruction is not exclusive to capitalism. Other societies have met catastrophic ends: for example, in Mesopotamia and on Easter Island (Dauvergne 2008). However, its unique competitive and accumulative dynamic makes capitalism particularly destructive. Better ecological futures therefore depend on wider social transformations. Foster proposes 'transcend[ing] the idealism, spiritualism and dualism of much contemporary Green thought, by recovering the deeper critique of the alienation of humanity from nature that was central to Marx's work' (2000:19–20). Technologies are merely tools that can be used in different ways. It may, for example, prove possible to develop ecologically sustainable and efficient fuel sources. Within capitalism, the likelihood is that they would simply be used to extract more resources. Reduced commodity costs would require more sales to simply stand still in economic terms (Kovel 2002). Were it possible to overcome the fetishism of exchange values, many resources might be shared with no real diminution of the use value. Innovations might be compatible with both reducing environmental impacts and raising living conditions. Long-term planning rather than short-term profit might predominate. Society will probably always confront serious problems in trying to live sustainably, including difficult decisions weighing current against future consumption armed with insufficient information. However, replacing the individualised competitive nature of capitalism and accepting an ongoing metabolism between humans and the rest of nature seems a necessary starting point.

Conclusion

The perspectives discussed in this chapter address familiar problems of political economy in quite different ways to mainstream approaches. They also address different problems, of no less importance. It is perhaps a sign of intellectual advance that few would now restrict the study of the global political economy to that of states and markets. More complex interdependencies are involved. These lead some critics to reject the possibility of identifying conceptual priorities, effectively admitting theoretical defeat. Other constructivist, feminist and green theorists summon idealism against materialist structuralism. The questions these perspectives raise remain pertinent, but the next chapter will argue that these are not necessary conclusions.

4

MARXISMS

This chapter advocates a materialist, but anti-determinist Marxism. It does this in three ways. Firstly, it offers an exposition drawing on Lenin's characterisation of the three component parts of Marxism. In particular it distinguishes Marxism from the caricature as vulgar materialist determinism. Secondly, it discusses the transformation of Marxism after Marx, with a brief critical commentary on the 'orthodoxies' of the Second and Third Internationals. Finally, it considers the recovery of anti-determinist Marxism. It suggests that it is necessary and possible to move beyond notions of interrelation (and to overcome what appears to be a fear of relapse into vulgarity) to recapitulate a more adequate historical materialism.

Three Component Parts of Marxism

Lenin (1950) suggested that there were three sources or component parts of Marxism: German philosophy, British political economy and French socialism. This can be misleading. Marxism is more than the sum of these parts, each of which is changed by Marx's critique. Nevertheless, it offers a convenient framework for presenting important features of Marx's outlook and a 'first cut' at explaining the interpretation advocated here.

Marx was a radical democrat in the tradition of the extreme left of the French Revolution, in favour not just of universal suffrage, itself rare enough at the time, but also of a thoroughgoing democratisation of society. It is perhaps easy to imagine what Marx would have made of contemporary parliamentary systems, in which alternative business-sponsored parties replace each other every few years. That this should have become so widely accepted as the essence of democracy is perhaps harder to comprehend. Marx's vision of proletarian dictatorship was one in which for the first time in history a majority could transform and then run the world in its own interests.

The proletariat, according to Marx, could not challenge existing private-property relations only to institute alternative ones. It was a class with 'radical chains', capable of fighting (and only capable of fighting) and controlling society collectively, so that its separation from private-property ownership under capitalism could turn into its opposite, collective ownership, under socialism (see, for example, Marx and Engels 1974). This was necessarily self-emancipation; not simply because the working class could not overturn the old order except through concerted action, but also because there was a necessary process of self-changing achieved through such struggles. Marx's vision of exactly what workers' power would look like and how it might be achieved changed over the course of his lifetime as struggles and organisation developed. A key event was the brief Paris Commune of 1871. Principles of direct democracy and immediate recall showed the possibilities of a state in which the dictatorial elements were qualitatively different from all previous instances in which minorities had ruled. Marx also insisted that even this state would in any case wither away (Engels 1934; Lenin 1976).

Marxism's commitment to radical democracy also underpins a practical rather than scholarly understanding of the world. Theory is directed towards the development of what Poulantzas described as 'concepts of strategy' (1978:24), while revolutionary practice in turn tests theory. Through practice, Marxism seeks to overcome the dualism between subject and object and to become self-critical. 'The coincidence of the changing of circumstances and of human activity or self-changing can be conceived and rationally understood only as *revolutionary practice*' (Marx 1975:156). This cuts through many of the epistemological agonies of mainstream social science, even if it does not entirely assuage them. Experience teaches that it is possible to practise without learning to change either theory or practice (Althusser and Balibar 1970). The commitment to practise does also mean that Marxism always lives somewhat uncomfortably within academia. On the one hand, universities hardly constitute vital arenas for revolutionary action and theory testing. On the other hand, Marxism struggles against the norms of studied objectivity (or becomes compromised in failing to do so). Nevertheless, despite being repeatedly written off, Marxist theory and socialist practice have, with varying results, continued to reinforce each other and to contest both the world and mainstream characterisations.

The radically democratic outlook also informed Marx's appropriation and transformation of German philosophy, particularly that of Hegel and the later young or 'left' Hegelians. Here the relationship between Marx and his predecessors is complex and contested (cf. Althusser 1969; Lukács 1974). Hegel's philosophy began and ended as a thoroughgoing idealism and a defence of the absolutist Prussian state. However, even leaving aside Hegel's own early explicit radicalism, also inspired by the French revolution (Avineri 1972), his philosophy remained one of change and one in which a system's parts had to be understood within the whole. The *Philosophy of Right* (1991), in particular, was not concerned merely with ideas, but also with their relation with the social world. However, for Hegel social and historical analysis served only as a 'middle term' for the advance of spirit or ideas in the world. For Hegel, unity is achieved 'in thought', and 'the entire movement ends with absolute knowledge' (Marx 1975:393, 384), albeit an understanding, he pessimistically concludes, that is reached only 'at dusk' (Hegel 1991).

Marx described an 'inversion' of Hegel and of extracting the rational kernel from his thought (1976:103). These are ambiguous metaphors, but they convey some of the sense in which Marx tries not simply to replace Hegel's idealism with the equally one-sided materialism of the young Hegelians, but to reconstruct a historicised account of change, incorporating an understanding of the 'whole', of ideas and social being, of agency and structures. Nevertheless, despite their interdependence, from the beginning Marx, the historical *materialist*, makes clear that he seeks to reverse the priority of 'thought' and 'reality' in Hegel (Marx 1975:80, Draper 1977). This changes both the form and the content of the dialectic. For Marx, the beginning and end of the process is the complex social world, with thought the middle term. Marx has been much criticised for too strong a materialism, memorably asserting that it is 'social existence that determines ... consciousness' (1970:21). However, this 'social existence' should be understood as an already complex material, institutional and ideological interrelationship, not a claim that class location directly determines thought (Avineri 1968). At particular historical conjunctures, the immaterial might matter decisively. There is a necessary subjective moment, understanding the world in order to transform it. However, the outcome of action remains 'open'. Marx suggests a method of movement from the abstract and general to the concrete, but each specific moment has its own particularities that need to be investigated and established empirically. The more concrete phenomena are often strongly conditioned by, but cannot simply be deduced from the more abstract. Marx undoubtedly used many methods, rejecting the notion of a royal road to science (Smith 1993; Althusser and Balibar 1970). This has helped fuel the controversy of what is the 'real' Marxism; but it can also be interpreted as reflecting an open, practical engagement with necessarily complex real-world problems. Marx admits numerous possibilities rather than articulating a closed teleology. What was indeed a grand narrative in Hegel is (or need be) nothing of the sort in Marx.

The radical democracy and the philosophical critique in turn influenced Marx's attitude to British classical political economy. Here too, Marx's relation with figures like Smith and Ricardo is controversial. Marx both extended and rejected elements of what went before. As discussed in Chapter 1, it seems clear that Marx forced a break and that neoclassical counter-revolution eschewed exactly those parts of the classical project, particularly the labour theory of value and attempts to historicise capitalism, in which Marx had been most interested and which he had developed furthest.

Marx's starting point (as it had been for Smith and Ricardo) was human work. However, labour has a deeper epistemological significance for Marx than it did for classical political economy. Marx and Engels wrote that 'men can be distinguished from animals by consciousness, by religion or anything else you like. They begin to distinguish themselves from animals as soon as they begin to *produce* their means of subsistence' (1974:42). Social labour is the essence of humankind and the key presupposition of a materialist conception of history (Rubin 1973; Carver 1975). This underpins Marxism's preoccupation with class. The argument is that questions of exploitation, production and distribution should inform the research project, not that they have some preordained determining character (Blackledge 2006a). Marx's understanding of the contradictions of capitalism develops through the interplay of different levels of the system. Certainly particular political and institutional forms may prove crucial. The point is simply that the specific can be understood in the light of the general in a way in which the inverse is not true; conceptually labour and its social form under capitalism as wage labour in relation to other fundamental classes can precede and make sense of more specific investigations (Marx 1973a). To understand any society it is useful first to understand what is produced, how, and by and for whom.

Historical materialism thus begins by attempting to understand the development of relations between what Marx called the 'forces of production', people's capacity to produce, and the 'relations of production'. These last include relations between exploiters and exploited, but also (if more controversially) relations within the respective classes (Molyneux 1995). Marx's critique of political economy, most notably in the three volumes of *Capital* (1976, 1978a, 1981), then understands capitalism as a historically specific mode of production. Exploitation becomes masked by the apparent equity of market relationships. Labour power, the ability to work, is itself reduced to a commodity, which can be bought and sold. Its value, like that of other commodities, is determined by the work needed (to produce the commodities needed) for its reproduction (but see Chapter 12 for a discussion of the problems with this formulation). So in a sense workers do receive a 'fair wage'. Of course, even market relationships between capital and labour are iniquitous; workers have no choice but to work for capital, while capital's ability to draw on a reserve army of unemployed workers exerts downward pressure on wages. Conversely, workers' organisation can ameliorate exploitation. However, the fundamental inequity and exploitation comes in production, as workers can be made to work longer or more intensely than is needed to produce goods equivalent to the value of their labour power. Exploitation in production creates surplus value, which can become profit for capitalists.

Exploitation, in capitalism as in any other class society, is the necessary basis for the production of surplus. However, relations between capitalists are hardly less important, providing capitalism with much of its contradictory dynamism. Marx's arguments cannot be adequately summarised here (see Fine 1984; Fine and Harris 1979; Clarke 1994). In brief, he describes how a fundamentally anarchic system, in which the immediate goal of each producer is simply to make profit, contains within it the ever present possibility of crisis. Competition between capitals drives an imperative to accumulate, to produce more and more cheaply than competitors. This impels exploitation, but also innovation. The productive powers expand relentlessly, but equally continually disrupt any momentary equilibrium between supply and demand. Competition also produces a concentration and centralisation of capital; the scale of production increases as the unfortunate and inefficient go to the wall or are taken over. Ever larger firms tend to dominate. Amongst other things this makes Say's Law an almost worthless abstraction, and movements back towards equilibrium are likely to become less smooth and more painful. As Volume 2 (1978a) makes clear, a delicate and ever changing balance must be established and sustained between production and consumption goods. However, even this is not sufficient. The demand for particular consumer or producer commodities are themselves discovered only after the event (Clarke 1994). Meanwhile, as Volume 3 (1981) describes, the continual imperatives to innovate mean a constantly changing weight of human labour and machinery and raw materials in the production process. Capitalism involves displacing workers, as living labour the ultimate source of profits, with machines, 'dead labour'. Marx describes a rising organic composition of capital and a concomitant tendency of the rate of profit to fall, itself countered by various features, including the cheapening of labour and other means of production. Perhaps most fundamentally, there is no 'invisible hand': what is good and rational for each individual capital may be irrational for collective capital. With surplus ultimately directed to accumulating more surplus, not to satisfying human wants, what works at one time may at another be the cause of instability, of over- or of underproduction.

Thus, although Marx is developing much of what had been said by earlier classical political economists, he transforms and radicalises it. He also sees capitalism as only one, historically specific, form of production. There is nothing 'natural' in the individualist propensities it generates. What may seem fair and inevitable actually represents a transitory form of exploitation. Capitalism, a recent phenomenon, also contains within itself the seed of its own potential downfall.

The various 'component parts' thus contribute to the materialist conception of history. In this there was no necessary progress. Or as Engels put it, 'each advance in organic evolution is at the same time a regression, fixing a *one-sided* evolution and excluding the possibility of evolution in many other directions' (cited in Foster 2000:234). There was always the possibility of advance or the 'common ruin of contending classes' (Marx and Engels 1965:33). This contrasts with the common charge, even from avowedly sympathetic critics, that Marxism is a structuralist 'grand theory' (Anderson 2004). Critics can find examples, particularly from later followers, to support their contention. Metaphors of base and superstructure (Marx 1970:20–1) are certainly unsatisfactory if taken literally. Marx (1978b) also notoriously described how the hand mill produces feudalism, the steam mill capitalism. He wrote of people's social relations, established in conformity with material productivity, producing 'also principles, ideas and categories, in conformity with their social relations' (1978b:103). However, read as a whole, Marx's work is very hard to interpret as economic reductionism. From his earliest writings, for example the

1844 Manuscripts, to later work like the *Eighteenth Brumaire* and the *Civil War in France*, Marx is full of ambiguity, contradiction and political contingency. Even the comment on hand mills and steam mills is followed by an insistence that nothing is inevitable, that progress is characterised by 'bloody struggle or death' (1978b:170), and an apparently crude conformity between material circumstances and ideas is posed in explicit opposition to the notion that 'everything happened in the *pure ether of reason*' (1978b:108). There is no need for extensive textual exegesis here. There is an abundant literature (albeit one of which anti-Marxists seem strangely unaware), which rather thoroughly debunks the idea of a determinist Marx (Avineri 1968; Lukács 1974; Carver 1975; Draper 1977).

Marx does nevertheless suggest that there is a tendency to develop the forces of production, human material capabilities. This is not automatic; it can stall, even regress, 'fettered' by social relations. The formulations may be imprecise, but Marx articulates a complex interaction of economic and political forces, of structures and agents. In particular, revolutionary change is needed to realise the material potential, the development of which becomes obstructed by previous social structures.

Marx's critique of political economy saw capitalism as a complex and contradictory social system. It created enormous material advances, yet because it did so for private profit, it did not necessarily produce any general social improvements. As witnessed in the twentieth century, technological advance is compatible with social catastrophe, wars and mass murder. However, in also creating enormous numbers of exploited proletarians, capitalism was creating its own potential gravediggers (Marx and Engels 1965). Knowledge of the circumstances, not of their own choosing, provided the basis for effective social action in which people could then make their own history (Marx 1973b). Marx and Engels (1974) envisaged the realisation of working-class potential only as a protracted decades-long process of struggles necessary to change both the world and the workers themselves. Even this, of course, proved hugely overconfident.

Marx and Other Marxists

Marx's vision is thus one of contests and contradictions, of incessant but open-ended conflict between labour and capital and of anarchic and unstable inter-capitalist relations. The accusation of vulgar economic or material determinism is a caricature of Marx, which relies on a grossly one-sided reading. Of course, he left unresolved problems and tensions. His critique of alternatives is often clearer than what he established positively. His metaphors are sometimes insufficient and the ambiguities leave room for different interpretations. Even before his death, Marxism was being pulled in different directions, and at one point Marx was moved to comment, 'All I know is that I am no Marxist' (cited in Callinicos 1983:9).

With hindsight, the avowedly revolutionary tradition of 'socialism from below' (Draper 1966) was probably always in a minority. However, as Luxemburg (1989) emphasised in her polemic with Bernstein (1961), the revolutionary, radically democratic and gradualist evolutionary approaches were not merely different roads to a common socialist goal. Reinforced by the experiences of the 1905 revolution in Poland and Russia, Luxemburg (1970) reasserted the centrality of mass spontaneity and workers' self-emancipation. Attempts to impose socialism 'from above' not only lacked the means, but denied the popular democratic ends so central to Marx.

The early twentieth century saw a remarkable flowering of revolutionary Marxism. This coincided most obviously with the movements at the end of the First World War. In political economy, particularly in relation to imperialism, Marxists produced analyses that continue to provide at least a useful point of departure (Luxemburg 1963; Hilferding 1981; Bukharin 1972; Lenin 1965). It also saw innovation in philosophy (Gramsci 1971; Lukács 1974). The avowedly revolutionary current could hardly avoid engaging with questions of structure and agency. Luxemburg and Lenin, for example, disputed the role and nature of party organisation in the revolutionary process. However, for both, determinism made little sense. As Lenin insisted, 'intelligent idealism is closer to intelligent materialism than stupid materialism' (Lenin 1961:276). Trotsky's (1969) notion of combined and uneven development, first developed in relation to the Russian revolution of 1905, articulated an anti-teleological and anti-determinist, but still a recognisably historical materialism. Trotsky suggested that, rather than having to progress through discrete stages, the revolutionary process in Russia, under the impact of capitalist development elsewhere, could combine the bourgeois and proletarian revolutions. The theory thus already implicitly had geographical dimensions, a conception of the world as a whole, the relative advance of which then impacted on other, more 'backward' parts like Tsarist Russia (Barker 2006). Moreover, the state played a distinct role in mobilising resources, particularly in response to military competition. What it could do was conditioned both by the domestic social relations on which it stood and its international relations; but there is not a hint of economic determinism. However, by the late 1920s, Lenin and Luxemburg were long dead, Trotsky was in exile and Gramsci in prison. Most fundamentally, the mass movements on which this revolutionary Marxism was based were in retreat and it was soon marginalised.

The great schism in Marxism only became obvious, even to those involved, in 1914. Almost all the (Marxist) socialist parties supported their own countries' war efforts. Kautsky (1983), who (since Engels' death) had been seen as the leading Marxist theoretician, initially supported the war, on the basis that the defence of the national state was essential as an arena for workers' organisation and power. Opprobrium has subsequently been heaped on Kautsky, as an advocate of an unsubtle mechanical materialism. Some of the criticisms may be exaggerated (Blackledge 2006b). However, even before the war Kautsky's theoretical acceptance of revolutionary process coincided with an increasingly reformist practice, both in the German Social Democratic Party (SPD) in particular and more generally in the Second International, of which it was the leading constituent. Crudely put, teleological ideas of inevitable progress and evolutionary advance were comforting to a party adapting to, and becoming adept at, working in the difficult conditions of Wilhelmine Germany. Revolutionary adventurism was condemned in theory and later, when social democratic governments were elected, brutally repressed. Marx's critique of political economy was reconceived as a tool for better managing capitalism, a task for which it was never designed, as was confirmed by the miserable experiences of the great theoretician Hilferding as German finance minister in the 1920s. The SPD retained a formal commitment to Marxism until 1959, but its practice had long since been similar to other European socialist parties, which had never been, or had long ceased to be, Marxist.

By that time, however, the main interpretation of Marxism was that espoused by the USSR-supporting communist parties. In the twentieth century Marxism became the official ideology of some brutal dictatorships, and this sad history becomes a big stick which opponents wield with relish. As Chomsky (2003) has written, these regimes also regarded themselves as democracies, yet few dismiss democracy on that account. This attack on Marxism is intellectually superficial, but pervasive and often effective. In Russia, the early post-revolutionary democracy and ideological creativity soon dissipated under the impact of civil war, foreign invasion, backwardness and isolation. This is not to deny that its early rulers made some egregious political and theoretical mistakes; but it is more important to understand how the interests of the surviving ruling elite supported a particular reinterpretation of Marxism, which served the interests of the USSR state and its rulers. This justified material advances, for example in iron and steel and tank production, irrespective of the human cost. The state was defined and defended as the essence of workers' power. A unilinear vision of progress was reassuring and useful against potential criticism. A reductionist 'orthodoxy', devoid even of the mild oppositional content of the Second International, therefore emerged out of a unique political and economic conjuncture. Alternative traditions, which placed much greater emphasis on agency and contingency, were more or less successfully exorcised, irrespective or perhaps because of their theoretical consistency with Marx's method. However tenuous its

Marxist provenance, the apparent success of the USSR in narrow material and economic terms provided a forceful alternative to Western capitalism, both to many intellectuals and to the rulers of newly independent states in the post-war period. This helped to establish a determinist Marxism as 'orthodoxy'.

The focus on growth and on states as institutions capable of driving this also inspired a range of more or less Marxist 'dependency' theory. This made many important criticisms of mainstream theories of development and international relations, highlighting systematic inequalities and exploitative relations between nations (Dos Santos 1970; Frank 1970; Wallerstein 1974). The theories owe something to Lenin (1965), who had suggested that the gains from imperialism produced an 'aristocracy of labour' within the rich countries, and to Luxemburg (1963), for whom the exploitation of a non-capitalist exterior remained vital. They have the obvious attraction for scholars of IPE in that they deal explicitly with global relations. However, unlike in the earlier Marxist traditions, there was little sense of differentiation or of potential class agency within poorer countries (Cardoso and Faletto 1979), and exploitation within production tended to be downplayed (Brenner 1977). Although for many writers in this tradition revolution is necessary to break the chains of dependency, there is seldom a sense of socialism as workers' self-emancipation.

Marxism is thus interpreted in different ways. The USSR and its supporters in the various communist parties around the world did establish something of an 'orthodoxy', which was relatively crudely materialist and deterministic. However, the hegemony of this interpretation waned after 1956, with many communists repudiating association with the Stalinist regimes and the theories they espoused. Today, 'orthodox Marxism' persists largely as its opponents' caricature and easy object of derision: it has virtually no known adherents. Chinese communism bore many practical similarities to its Russian counterparts, but was justified instead by some (absurdly) voluntarist reformulations. Even Althusserian Marxism, perhaps the last intellectual gasp of the communist parties, was strongly structuralist, but contested *economic* reductionism. Dependency theories became more nuanced even as they lost influence. This has not quietened a long-standing anti-Marxist tradition of denouncing 'grand theory' and materialist determinism (see, for example, Weber 1930, 1968; Popper 1961, 1962). The 'postmodern turn' is the latest iteration. Amongst other things, this critique firstly insists (perfectly correctly, if rather obviously) that there are multiple sources of oppression and resistance, that it is not 'all about class'. But secondly (and this does not follow) it continues that there can be no analytical or practical priority. Class is either nothing special, a complete irrelevance, or even theoretical fiction. The next section will argue that an anti-determinist Marxism can easily accept the first proposition while rejecting the second.

The Recovery of Anti-Determinist Marxism

Very few Marxists now articulate anything close to the supposed 'orthodoxy'. Yet the term lives on. Not least, 'vulgar' Marxism appears to provide a yardstick against which anti-determinist critics can demonstrate their sophistication.

Recent anti-Marxist critiques have reinforced and been reinforced by a long-standing academic Marxist literature, which takes the accusation of crude determinism to heart. Not discussed in the previous section, an earlier tradition of non-revolutionary Marxism argued rather more subtly. The early Frankfurt School or 'Western Marxist' tradition of Horkheimer and Adorno probably owed as much to Weber as to Marx and articulated a correspondingly pessimistic view of the prospects of emancipatory social change. Abandoning any commitment to practise, such Marxism could then become but one strand in a more broadly conceived 'Critical Theory'; critical mainly of other more or less esoteric theories (Held 1990). However, it would also inform a more practically oriented 'New Left', which emerged after 1956 articulating various if sometimes contradictory strands of anti-determinist Marxism (Anderson 1979b). Unfortunately, as Thompson suggested, 'the correction to historical materialism too often assumed its guilt without scrupulous enquiry into its practice' (1978:212). Appearing to read Marx through the filter of Soviet Marxism or of hostile criticism, the mud of 'vulgarity' appears to have stuck. The result was sometimes a sanitised and indeterminate Marxism, which, while never likely to satisfy the sensibilities of mainstream social science, is simultaneously unlikely to inform strategies of social change.

A strongly anti-determinist version has recently been articulated by advocates of 'Open Marxism'. This reasserts the role of agency and individualism against an essentially static and ultimately disabling structuralism. It insists that subjectivity cannot be adequately achieved simply by 'adding on' the role of ideas to otherwise structural models. Following Lukács (1974), the appropriate method is to emphasise totality and dialectical unity. Structure and agency, theory and practice have to be conceived together. The necessary and contingent cannot be understood through their juxtaposition, but 'taking into account the internal relation between the two' (Psychopedis 1995:19). 'Society is not merely object, but at the same time subject' (Backhaus 1992:57). 'Economism' is a particularly egregious sin, against which Open Marxism stresses workers' subjective, subaltern perspectives and active involvement in shaping the world (Bonefeld 2004). All of this is perfectly valid, if not, without addition, terribly useful. Authors associated with this tradition have produced many telling critiques. However, this militant anti-determinism can topple into something close to its opposite. Some Open Marxists refuse to offer any 'objective' political economy and openly disavow historical materialism (Gunn 1992). Backhaus lauds Schumpeter's apparent insistence that 'matters of fact ... are wholly uninteresting' (Backhaus 1992:75). Holloway pushes this reassertion of ideas and agency further than most, insisting on the priority of experience and that when understood in a 'practical–genetic sense ... the symmetry of subject and object disappears ... it becomes clear that there is no object, there is only a subject' (1995b:170). Holloway is perhaps now an atypical if still prominent exponent. However, the aversion not simply to empiricism, but to empirical evidence does appear conducive to a certain reluctance among some Open Marxists to move beyond abstract philosophising.

An alternative school of anti-determinist 'critical economy' or 'neo-Gramscian' Marxism developed largely out of opposition to mainstream international relations theory. The primary structuralism contested here was that of realism. Nevertheless, drawing on Gramsci (1971), but also on other critical Marxists like Thompson (1968, 1978), they too rejected 'orthodox Marxism'; they too emphasised notions of reciprocity and interrelation against determinism. Cox's (1981) now well-known triangulations sought to explain on the one hand the mutual interaction of material capabilities, ideas and institutions and on the other hand the state, social forces and world order. Other authors have expressed similar thoughts slightly differently, but they typically allow a strong emphasis on ideological autonomy and contest, on civil society and on notions of hegemony. Cox's triangulations seem broadly compatible with the dialectical method advocated by Marx and Hegel, incorporating notions of totality and interrelation, allowing contradiction and movement. Again there is a willingness to engage with other traditions. Cox embraces a methodological pluralism and draws on Vico and Ibn Khaldun (Sinclair, in Cox 1996). He sees Weber as a better guide to understanding the spatial, Marx the temporal, aspects of society (2002:28).

Cox's (1987) and Harrod's (1987) work on labour were early examples of a tradition that has been more prepared than its Open Marxist counterpart to combine such diverse theoretical insights with detailed empirical investigations. However, without addition a framework of interdependence offers little to guide how to conduct such studies, and perhaps predictably neo-Gramscians have been reprimanded for both idealism and economism (Bieler and Morton 2004; Burnham 1991; Bonefeld 2004). Perhaps the appropriate emphasis is always in the eye of the beholder, and these accusations may reflect instead the prejudices of their critics. However, it is not difficult to find one-sided formulations. Cox (1987), for example, (following Weber) sees class as objectively heterogeneous, but then appears to posit an 'intersubjective content' as rather strongly determined. Perhaps more typically, Gramsci's perceived corrective to an overly economist Marxism sometimes leads contemporary followers into a more radical downplaying of the economic and to a strong emphasis on ideas (Rustin 1989). The concept of 'hegemony' is used in various ways, but often appears to take a particularly decisive role. Gills (1993), for example, insists that the material only sets limits to the range of what is possible. Neo-Gramscian work is diverse, and many try to steer carefully between idealism and materialism (Bieler and Morton 2004). The point here is simply that recognising interdependence is only a precondition for a Marxist analysis.

These brief paragraphs indicate that accusations of determinism directed towards contemporary Marxism are misplaced, but also highlight the difficulties of sustaining notions of interdependence. They suggest that the challenge remains to avoid a vulgar determinism without regress to an 'open' and ultimately useless eclecticism. Of course, explanations need to be multicausal. Of course, an absolute one-to-one determinism is as silly as the abject indeterminism characteristic of more extreme versions of contemporary postmodernism. People no more behave like pre-programmed robots than float around choosing what to do irrespective of their social and economic conditions or conditioning. However, between such poles there is a vast spectrum of pluralist possibility. Marx similarly makes plain his frustration with 'the dialectic balancing of concepts, and not grasping the real relations' (1973a:90). Mediation can slip into reciprocity and on into circularity (Carchedi 1986:222).

Therefore, Marxism needs to move beyond grasping the multiplicity of determinants in their unity to identifying conceptual and practical priorities (Carver 1975). Stressing the interconnectedness of things, that the parts can only be understood in relation to each other and to the whole, is only a first step. It is also necessary to grasp where to start and how to advance (Arthur 1997). Some things have a greater relative influence. 'Claims for primacy,' as Sayer writes, 'have at least to be nuanced' (1987:9) and justifications for any such priority have to be established. There are always corollaries and qualifications (Storper and

Walker 1989). Nevertheless, there is no inherent 'democracy of determinations' (Foley 1986) and the attempt to identify those of greater moment is a significant distinction between Marxism and liberal pluralism.

Although it seems to trouble some social theorists, this 'asymmetrical interdependence' has become a commonplace in IPE (Cohen 2008) and seems obvious in many areas of social life. Neither the United States and Denmark nor the factory owner and the worker confront each other as equals. We can acknowledge an interdependence of ideas and material circumstances, but recognise at the same time that we are more products of our environment than able simply to wish it away. We can have a two-way street without the traffic flow being the same in both directions. As Wright comments, it is possible for there to be interdependence yet 'an asymmetry between allocative and authoritative resources' (1983:33). Recognising a dialogue of concepts undermines determinist monologues, but need not require each party to be equally articulate.

Marx sketched what he considered 'The Method of Political Economy' in his introduction to the *Grundrisse*, stressing the need to move from the abstract to the concrete (1973a:100–8). Specifically, he thought:

> The order obviously has to be (1) the general, abstract determinants which obtain in more or less all forms of society ... (2) ... Capital, wage labour, landed property. Their inter-relation ... (3) ... the form of the state ... (4) ... international relations ... (5) The world market and crisis. (Marx 1973a:108)

This ordering is not obvious and not even necessarily right. However, it highlights the principle that to understand things like the world market and crises it may be necessary to already know something of the world of work, of labour and capital. This does not mean that the more concrete determinants can simply be deduced from the more abstract. Each has its own relative autonomy and specific empirical character, but these can be better understood in the context of the more general features. Moreover, structure and agency remain interconnected. The vital role of practice and experience in Marxism implies a prior climb up to particular abstractions before it is possible to move back down to the earthly concrete. There is always a two-way process, but not necessarily one of either conceptual or practical equality. Identifying how socio-economic forces exert strong constraints and pressures towards particular sorts of action remains a vital starting point for understanding the world and for developing strategies to change it.

Conclusion

It is possible to interpret Marxism in very different ways. However, a blanket characterisation of it as structuralist grand theory is inaccurate to the point of deliberate falsification. It misrepresents both Marx and most Marxisms articulated today. It is hard to avoid the conclusion that opponents find it is easier to rely on a few decontextualised quotes passed down by generations of anti-Marxists, or to find Marxism guilty by association with Soviet communism, than to engage seriously with a challenging, contested and ambiguous tradition. Marxism is not determinism, as so many Marxists have now stressed for so long.

Nor is Marxism indeterminism, a vacuous sociology of 'everything influences everything else'. Marxists use different tools and in that sense Marxism is an 'eclectic' approach. It cannot claim a monopoly of truth, can engage with and learn from critics and new theorisations, and remains open particularly in the sense of necessarily being an unfinished and ongoing project, committed to learning from struggles and an ever changing world. This has to be understood as a complex and historically constructed social whole. However, within this, the world of work and production remains of prime importance, lying at the root of capitalism's growth and volatility. A materialism which is properly historical and dialectical withstands many of the misunderstandings and calumnies directed against it and can provide an effective basis for understanding and changing the world.

Part II

The Origins of Global Capitalism

5

THE TRANSFORMATION OF EUROPEAN FEUDALISM

This chapter deals schematically with an enormous time-span and controversial debates. Any exploration of the origins of capitalism is forced to investigate a series of anterior questions about the nature of the society that preceded it and the processes that contributed to its genesis. In an absolute sense, these are unanswerable. Modern capitalism came after and was built upon at least elements of almost everything that went before. The extent to which any of these was essential, or conversely how different the world might have looked without any of them, is impossible to prove. The intractability of these questions seems to have contributed to an ahistorical or even anti-historical turn in much social theory. Nevertheless, there are important reasons for including at least a brief summary. Capitalism emerged out of various, still imperfectly understood processes. Considering these nevertheless helps to contextualise the contemporary global political economy and perhaps to understand general processes of social change. These chapters do not attempt to provide a history of the world (cf. Harman 1999). The already ambitious objective is to outline the origins of capitalism in Europe. However, even a thousand years ago European society should be understood in its global context. There were always mutual if sometimes very unequal interactions, and the establishment of capitalism in Western Europe would then decisively shape the rest of the world. Other places would have developed differently, but in ways we cannot know, had they not been stamped, and stamped upon, by European intervention. However, with hindsight it is possible to discern distinct features, both in Europe's internal social structures and in its wider connections, that shaped its unique trajectory.

The next section describes pre-capitalist societies in very general terms. The following one discusses the specific character of European feudalism and why it had an unusual tendency to change. This was a very slow and fragile process, with apparent 'progress' frequently reversed. Growth was also overlain with huge swings, and the chapter goes on to discuss the role of these demographic crises – how they were shaped by and in turn shaped class struggles, how their outcome exaggerated tendencies towards commercialisation in agriculture, how the importance of trade and urbanisation increased and finally how the early modern state transformed domestic economies and established intercontinental empires. However, even where this chapter ends, at the dawn of the industrial revolution, there was still little reason to anticipate what lay ahead.

Characterising Pre-capitalist Societies

For most of human existence people lived in conditions Marx described as 'primitive communism'. They did not know competitive individualism and some, at least, possessed no concept of war (Harman 1986). They lived a very basic hand-to-mouth egalitarianism, sometimes with a basic division of labour based on gender and age. The changes wrought by the coming of class societies remain enormous. The first agrarian revolution of about 10,000 years ago made it possible to produce surpluses. Some people could live off goods produced by others. However, the establishment of class societies remained exceptional, only an apparently fragile possibility. Mann suggests that 'Most of the prehistory of society saw no sustained movement towards stratification or the state. Movement toward rank and political authority seems endemic but reversible. Beyond that, nothing sustained' (1986:67).

Oppressive rulers could be overthrown. Perhaps more significantly, the option of flight seems to have allowed escape from the worst of exploitation. Archaeologists have uncovered evidence of several lost civilisations, many apparently superseded by more 'primitive' and less hierarchical societies. Only where flight was socially or geographically difficult – in Mesopotamia, the Nile valley, the Indus valley and in north China – do the great hierarchical societies seem to have endured and gradually spread their influence (Mann 1986).

However, over the millennia, numerous agrarian class societies emerged around the world. Many of these would fit Hilton's definition of feudalism as 'an exploitation of servile peasants by a landowning class' (1990:1). These were marked by direct forms of exploitation, with little or no separation of political and economic power. There was no 'automatic' mechanism of distribution like the market in modern capitalism (Wood 2002). Nevertheless, both the nature of exploitation, whether surrendering part of the produce or performing demesne labour on the lords' estates, and the political, judicial, military and customary power used to affect it, took a wide variety of forms.

The Dynamism of European Feudalism

It is common to see European feudalism, like other variants around the world, as stagnant. Feudalism was conservative and inert compared with capitalism and was eventually put out of business by it. Feudal social relations undoubtedly limited the incentives and abilities to apply new technologies. Lords did not have direct control over the labour process nor was there the motor of competitive accumulation that makes capitalism so dynamic. Why would lords innovate when gains were more easily, more cheaply and more certainly achieved by squeezing the peasants harder or by stealing from rivals? Why should peasants, with so few spare resources, innovate when lords could grab any gains? Investments therefore tended to be in breadth rather than depth, in more land and in strengthening coercive power rather than in increasing productivity (Wood 2002; Postan and Hatcher 1985). However, this picture has to be qualified. Questions of lordly power and peasant 'servility' were always relative and potentially contested (Hilton 1985b). European feudalism was never entirely static (Dobb 1976).

In 1000 Europe was poor. Its population had barely increased in a millennium and its income had fallen. However, it then grew. Figure 5.1 shows that this growth was incredibly slow compared with rates later achieved by industrial capitalism. There were huge swings, not steady improvements. Nevertheless, as Harman (1989) and Hilton (1990) in particular have emphasised, over the centuries slow growth transformed Europe and distinguished it from other parts of the world.

Feudal Europe's propensity to change might in part be explained by 'privileges' or 'advantages' of backwardness (Trotsky 1977; Gerschenkron 1962). Europe was able to appropriate technologies and ideas from more advanced societies in Asia and the Middle East. Even medieval Europe was already situated within a global (or at least Afro-Eurasian) process of combined and uneven development (Trotsky 1977; Rosenberg 2006). Europe was not outward looking as it would be in the last 500 years of the millennium. Nevertheless, the geographical links forged in antiquity did not disappear and the Asian, African and Arab worlds continued to exert an influence, for example on Europe's consumption, languages and technology. Advance was gradual, uneven and precarious. However, Europe did – over centuries – utilise innovations made elsewhere. There was a slow spread in the use of the heavy-wheeled plough, of fertilisers, the scythe and the haystack, and progress in crop management; for example in the use of new crop rotations (Maddison 1991; Harman 1989). Windmills and watermills, the spinning wheel and the compass were introduced in the twelfth century. The shoulder harness multiplied horse power around the same time. The rudder replaced the steering oar in the thirteenth century. Later, 'pedals, cranks and lathes' were amongst the 'human engines' which came from either India or China (Braudel 1974). Of other Asian imports, examples like gunpowder and printing are well known, but the wheelbarrow was probably at least as important. In terms of ideas, innovations in science and the classical tradition, kept alive in the Islamic world, could return to Europe in the Renaissance.

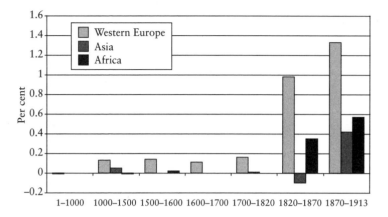

Figure 5.1   Average annual GDP per capita growth rate (per cent),
regional averages
Source: Maddison 2003

Notions of 'advantages of backwardness' may seem perverse,
but the different social situations in which technologies were
introduced produced different results (Brenner 1985b). Significantly,
European society was distinguished from its counterparts by its
fragmentation, including the cross-cutting authorities of lords,
kings and churches. Braudel (1995) suggests that Europe's position
at the fringe of a greater Eurasian continental society contributed
to the relative weakness of centralised authority. Its differentiation also reflected its specific geography, for example variations
in soil fertility, ease of communication (Mediterranean sea routes
were easiest), island isolation which for a time cut England off,
but also later helped secure kingly power. Its differentiation
also reflected its specific history. Any general regression from
classical antiquity was uneven, with the strongest continuities
in Italy. Cities like Florence and Genoa remained important and
relatively wealthy centres of urban economy and it was here
that the Renaissance flourished and where the more advanced
ideas and innovations from the East were most readily received.
Significant elements of Roman urban life also continued in the
eastern empire, particularly Byzantium, at least until it was sacked

by the Crusaders in the thirteenth century. Meanwhile Britain and Germany became relative backwaters, with few towns. However, rural as well as urban elites continued to enjoy at least some of the luxuries of Roman nobility.

For whatever reason, neither the forces nor the relations of production were monolithic. There was competition and some incentive to change. That is probably particularly obvious with gunpowder. The success of the Chinese central authority meant that for thousands of miles it faced no significant enemies. Europe, in contrast, was awash with warring feudal fiefdoms and gunpowder had immediate uses. Military competition in general gave lords an interest in raising productivity (Harman 1989:54). Davidson (2006b:149) identifies interstate competition and the need for thousands of skilled shipbuilding workers. Inequalities within Europe meant, for example, that peripheral England could take technical resources from the richer French while being able to escape its fossilised feudal relations (Bois 1985). Even within England, it was in the most backward north and west that serfdom as direct labour services disappeared earliest (Dobb 1976). Competing authorities also left some room for dissent and intellectual development (Braudel 1995). Many important Renaissance, Reformation and Enlightenment figures enjoyed periods of sanctuary. Landlord–peasant relations also varied. The sheer number of peasants meant that lords' control was never complete (Hilton 1985b). Peasants may have been able to keep at least some of any returns from improvements and so had some incentives and possibilities to innovate. Again, by contrast, China by the seventh century had largely solved the problem of subsistence crises (Hutton 2006) while in Europe improved output might still be a matter of life or death. Some of these features were no doubt found elsewhere in the world. The point here is merely that European feudalism was complex and changeable.

Any growth was slow and reversible. 'Natural' and social disruptions like feudal wars could be devastating. Wood also criticises as circular accounts which presuppose technical improvements (2002:4). Undoubtedly a proper history would need to show in detail how innovations were transmitted and utilised.

Nevertheless, whatever the ultimate causes, the crucial point here is that wealth increased. Feudal relations were not something 'stable' into which it is necessary to inject an exogenous cause to conceive their transformation (Hilton 1990). With change, and particularly with increasing agricultural productivity, it became possible for more people to do other jobs, in trade, in industry and in other less productive occupations. More could live in towns. Increased supplies of basic foodstuffs diminished the risks of specialisation and relying on others' produce. This made commercial farming a more attractive proposition (Brenner 1985b). This propensity to change provides the context for the apparently crucial role of demographic crises in Europe's development.

Demographic Cycles and Feudal Class Struggles

Orthodoxy once held that feudalism's demise was the consequence of a demographic or Malthusian crisis. Malthus (1970) wrote how population tended to increase exponentially, food resources only linearly. With birth control an abomination against God, the remedy for lower class lust was therefore that the poor should be judicially destroyed that few be absolutely starved (Tabb 1999:61). Ricardo's argument to the same end describes how increasing population forced people onto new lands, which were harder to farm; the returns, the productivity decreased. Population growth thus puts ever more pressure on resources. As mentioned in Chapter 3, similar arguments persist, usually directed towards populations in poorer countries, but, fortunately, they have become less fashionable. Malthus' ideas are now generally reckoned to be not just deeply unpleasant, but also profoundly mistaken. Already wrong in his own time, the theory was proved consistently and emphatically so by the subsequent 200 years' experience. Agricultural improvements meant an ever declining agricultural workforce fed an ever growing population increasingly well. Famine and pestilence still blight many parts of the world, but a population six times greater than in 1800 has no absolute food scarcity. However, before the nineteenth century, demographic pressures were important. It is perhaps less clear why they brought collapse rather than stagnation, but questions of the material conditions in which people live, of their natural environment and what people do to it, are not secondary, whether in relation to global threats today or to understanding human history. Ecology has profoundly affected the development of human society, limiting and conditioning what people can do. For most of our existence as a species, people lived a precarious existence.

Demographic pressures do appear to have underlain a series of cycles in the Middle Ages (Postan and Hatcher 1985). Even Brenner, advocate of a strongly 'politicist' interpretation of the transition from feudalism, insists that his 'explicit point of departure was precisely the two-phase grand agrarian cycles of non-development bound up with demographic change' (1985b:217). Periods of prosperity and growing population were followed by collapse. Ladurie (1985) identifies two large agrarian cycles, each of ebb and flow, the first from 1100 to 1450, the second from 1450 to 1720. The crisis of the mid fourteenth century was the most drastic and for many scholars was crucial to the collapse of feudalism (Postan and Hacher 1985; Ladurie 1985).

As populations rose, land scarcity increased lords' power. The abundance of land after crisis made landowners more willing to sell it or to pay those willing to work it; important if not sufficient spurs to capitalist farming. Of course, demographic cycles were not simply natural phenomena either in cause or effect. These were not amorphous 'populations' which rose and fell, but already class societies, with complex and contested relations between lords and peasants and of organisation amongst the peasants themselves. Lordly power and peasant servility were functions of each other. If lords grabbed perhaps half the produce and employed large numbers of unproductive retainers, this obviously contributed to peasant poverty and conditioned the dynamic of cyclical crisis (Brenner 1985a; Harman 1989). Far from 'natural', birth rates were already less than any biological maximum, influenced no doubt by Christian morals, but also by knowledge of contraceptives and abortifacients (Maddison 1991; Epstein 2001). Different balances of power and property relations thus led to 'overpopulation' at very different densities, at lower levels in France, for example, where Brenner (1985b) suggests that the small parcellisation of land provided a greater barrier to innovation than in the much more mountainous places like Italy (Cooper 1985). Bois suggests that the problem with demographic accounts like those of Postan and Ladurie is therefore not too much discussion of the economic and demographic factors, but not enough: 'stopping themselves mid-stream and ... not integrating the demographic factor into the all-embracing whole that is the socio-economic system' (Bois 1985:117).

Crises were similarly uneven in their consequences. They wiped out huge swathes of population and the Black Death killed across the social spectrum (Postan and Hatcher 1985). However, they increased the power and wealth of the surviving peasants. Braudel writes that 'between 1350 and 1450, at a really bleak point in the graphs of European growth or lack of it, there was a sort of golden age in the daily life of ordinary people' (1985:87). In Languedoc, for example, 'the peasant and his patriarchal family were masters of the abandoned countryside' (Braudel 1974:3). Crisis could dramatically reduce feudal levies, unless lords were able to reassert authority and limit peasant freedom. This produced bitter struggles (Brenner 1985a; McNally 1988).

Brenner's (1985a, 1985b) argument is that the outcome of these was decisive. In France, in particular, results tended to favour the peasants. Effectively organised communities reduced feudal levies and redistributed land so that peasant smallholding became the norm. This meant a proliferation of subsistence farming and agricultural stagnation. In Eastern Europe, reaction led to the 'second serfdom', and doomed the region to relative backwardness for centuries as landlords adopted a policy of 'anti-mercantilism', encouraging industrial imports from the West. Even between East and West Germany different outcomes reflected significant differences in peasant organisation.

In England results were more ambiguous and commercial agriculture could emerge in the space between peasant freedom and unfreedom. The great peasant rebellion of 1381 was crushed. However, lords were unable to re-enserf the peasants. Ongoing resistance and the more favourable demographic circumstances still allowed peasants to improve their lot. The search for novel ways out of the crisis increased commercial forms of rent extraction and the letting out of land to peasant 'copyholders'. The size of manors shrank, that of peasant holdings grew (McNally 1988). The differentiation within the peasantry also increased and thus produced the classic three-tier agrarian structure of landowners, rent-paying tenant (yeoman) farmers and agricultural labourers. This separation of the direct producers from their means of subsistence, though only definitely established with the later political revolutions, according to Brenner (1985a), then provided the basis for self-sustaining growth and for later industrialisation.

Thus on both upswing and downturn, across places and over time, the outcome of demographic cycles varied. Capitalism was not the inevitable result of anonymous processes of economic change, either the contradictions within feudalism or of challenges of commerce coming from without. Capitalism, according to this 'political Marxism' can only be understood as the unintended consequence of class struggles under feudalism (Brenner 1985a; Wood 2002).

This analysis has been challenged. It is not clear that the path was yet set fair for capitalism. In particular, by positing a rural capitalist class as 'already dominant not only in society but also in the state' (Wood 2002:119) this 'politicist' reading of change has the curious implication of denying the significance of those most political of events – the great bourgeois revolutions. Serfdom may have disappeared from England by the fourteenth century, but there was a long and turbulent path to the industrial revolution five centuries later. Some dispute the historical picture, questioning the idea of a clear distinction between the prior organisation of peasants, either east and west of the Elbe (Wunder 1985) or between France and England (Croot and Parker 1985). In France 'where rents tailed off, this was largely due to the inability of the peasants to pay, rather than to their capacity to resist' (Croot and Parker 1985:84). Even amongst those who broadly accept the history, if the struggles had such different outcomes in England, France and Eastern Europe principally as a result of different struggles and levels of peasant organisation, this suggests regress to questions of why these differences existed. 'Brenner appears ... to explain the balance of class forces in terms of itself' (Croot and Parker 1985:90). The context of class conflict remains to be explained (Hilton 1985a; Harman 1989). Commercialisation may in fact have been cause as much as consequence. Hilton suggests that '[t]he most advanced peasant gains were made in those areas where peasants were producing the most important and marketable cash crop of medieval Europe, wine' (1990:47).

The Rise of Commercial Agriculture

Crisis boosted commerce, but it magnified already existing tendencies. Feudalism has been characterised in terms of the non-separation of politics and economy. However, just as the separation in capitalism is often more apparent than real, neither was the identity absolute under feudalism. In the early Middle Ages most crops were produced locally for subsistence or lordly consumption. However, luxury goods like wines, spices, furs and silks were imported throughout the medieval period. England already imported 2.5 million gallons of wine from France in 1242, more than a gallon a head (Heaton 1948). More commonplace necessities like iron and salt might also be unavailable locally. To buy these, even subsistence farmers had to sell surpluses to raise some money income (Hilton 1990; Takahashi 1976). As productivity and surpluses tended to increase, there was potentially more to be sold, increasing the importance of markets and merchants and of commercial relations of rent and wage labour. Crises then improved peasants' position and their ability to produce surpluses which, even at reduced prices, could be sold.

Money rents also had a long history. Hilton (1990) suggests their scope was already rising in eleventh-century Carolingian France. This did not imply modern landlord–tenant relations. Rents were extracted by 'extra-economic' compulsion, legal and military actions backed by the state. However, their monetary form increased the scope of commercialisation and gave peasants a further incentive to produce cash crops or handicrafts, different from their subsistence produce. Demographic crises simultaneously increased the willingness of lords to accept money rents and to sell their land, and created more potential buyers or tenants. By 1500 most English land was held on payment of money or produce. This received a massive boost in England through the sale of monastic lands under Henry VIII, when something like a quarter of England's land was sold (McNally 1988). Such sales, of course, presuppose the existence of potential buyers.

Commercialisation also increased polarisation within the peasantry (Hilton 1990). A few could become relatively wealthy. The gradual development of the English yeoman is the archetype, renting farms of up to 200 acres, far beyond subsistence needs. Others struggled to produce enough and faced ruination by debt. Wage labour became a necessity. Again the antecedents are long. The Doomsday book lists 32 per cent of England's population as *cottars* or *bordars*. These were people with insufficient land to support themselves. Some were tradespeople like blacksmiths and carpenters. Most would have had to work, at times, as agricultural labourers (Heaton 1948). Again the scope increased. Most labourers would have had some land of their own and feudal obligations. They were still doubly unfree, not modern proletarians, but it now paid the yeoman to employ wage labour and to innovate. Yeomen would also be prime movers of enclosure, which pushed the poor further towards proletarianisation (McNally 1988). Large farms gradually displaced smallholdings in grain production by the sixteenth century and on these it paid to innovate (Brenner 1985b).

England's population rose from 2.2 million in 1450 to over 5 million in 1700, the same level as that before the fourteenth-century famine. But average wealth was also rising and now there was no famine despite perhaps half the population being engaged in non-agricultural pursuits (Brenner 1985b). As such employments expanded they in turn affected agriculture. Some supplied tools that increased productivity. Merchants, workers and soldiers all provided a market for food. Many peasants remained self-sufficient, selling only their surpluses, but there were more markets and the importance of money and money rents expanded. Many of these developments therefore reinforced each other. Wood argues that a new capitalist logic had begun to operate 'before industrialization and was a precondition of it' (2002:65). However, the rise of commercial agriculture was also linked to the wider rise of trade and commerce. If commerce grew in the 'interstices' of feudalism, these were not ready-made gaps or outsides, but spaces created as commercial wealth and power developed within the old system.

Markets, Trade and Urbanisation

At one time, even for many Marxists, the growth of markets and trade was the crucial solvent of feudalism (Sweezy 1976). There were several elements to this. Braudel writes:

> Far in advance, there were signs announcing the coming of capitalism in the rise of towns and of trade, the emergence of a labour market, the increasing density of society, the spread of the use of money, the rise of output, the expansion of long-distance trade or to put it another way the international market. (1985:620)

As merchant activity and wealth increased it exacerbated the tensions within the old mode of production. It was merchants who brought the goods and innovations to Europe from the non-European world (Sweezy 1976:41). The rise of trade may also have developed moves away from agriculture – for example, into handicraft manufacture. Artisans could then make goods better than serfs on the manors (Sweezy 1976:42). Wolf suggested that the notion of merchant capital is misleading. If capital is concerned with production, this applies to merchants in only a very narrow sense (Rosenberg 1994). Trade, organised on capitalist principles, was an ancient pursuit, without previously or elsewhere leading to the establishment of a wider capitalist society. Wealth could also allow successful merchants to dissolve into the feudal ruling class, most conspicuously with the purchase of noble titles in France. However, others would continue to pursue and extend the methods of the new system (Harman 1989). Merchants themselves could become 'factors' in production, either though the 'putting-out' system, or, as in places like Florence, gathering large numbers of increasingly dependent workers in single manufactories. Alternatively, great financial houses like the Fuggers could begin as manufacturers and then diversify as merchants and financiers. While she does not see this as a sufficient explanation, Wood acknowledges that 'capitalism did emerge within a network of international trade and could not have emerged without that network' (2002:63).

Similarly, urbanisation contributed significantly, but not sufficiently to explain the rise of capitalism. In 1000 there were few notable towns. From the twelfth century, towns and the money economy within them became more important. Still around 1300 Europe had only five cities of 100,000 inhabitants or more: Constantinople, Paris, Milan, Venice and Florence (Heaton 1948). There were more and larger cities elsewhere, notably in China. Even in 1500 only 5.6 per cent of Europe's population was urban (Horlings 2001). But this was very uneven, with much larger concentrations in the Low Countries and northern Italy. Many towns were commercial or administrative centres rather than centres of industry, but even these provided important and growing markets for agricultural products (Hilton 1990:72).

Many European towns did become important centres of production. Braudel goes so far as to suggest that 'the whole panoply of forms of capitalism – commercial, industrial, banking – was already deployed in thirteenth-century Florence' (1985:621). In 1330 the wool guild had 200 workshops supporting 30,000 people. Around the same time, in Ghent there were 4000 weavers (Harman 1989). These industries cannot necessarily be read as 'capitalist'. 'Neither urban artisans nor merchants tended to function as capitalists' (Brenner 2006:144, Dobb 1963). Instead they operated through guilds and chartered monopoly companies. For Polanyi, 'the two meanings of the word "contain" perhaps express best this double function of towns, in respect to the markets which they both enveloped and prevented from developing' (2001:65). Moreover, each apparent industrial advance could prove ephemeral. The Flemish cloth industry declined after the late fourteenth century, that of northern Italy a century later.

From 1500 to 1800 wealth per head in Italy hardly grew. Dutch capitalism had great success in the seventeenth century, but then fell back. Thus Florence and the Dutch republic did not produce capitalism (Wood 2002). Similarly, '[m]any of the once industrialised English provincial towns were, by the late fifteenth century, simply becoming regional markets for agricultural produce and food-processing centres for local institutional buyers' (Hilton 1985b:136). The auguries of capitalism in Europe might have come and gone, as they did elsewhere – in India and China, for example. Commercialisation was ubiquitous (Brenner 2006). The market, Polanyi suggests, 'was fairly common since the later Stone Age [but] its role was no more than incidental to economic life' (2001:45). Wood therefore criticises models of commercialisation as tending to 'read back' the success of capitalism, seeing it as having existed 'in embryo' from the dawn of history (Wood 2002:14). However, for Harman these 'were embryos of a new mode of production, and ... like many other embryos they were often aborted' (Harman 1989:61).

In Europe, there were nevertheless significant survivals. The Italian cities remained, as somewhat diminished centres of production and of wealth that would help finance industry and empire elsewhere. Flemish cloth production declined, but left its impact on commercial wool production in England. 'English landowners could never have started their conversion to commercial agriculture without the market for wool in Flemish towns' (Anderson, cited in Wood 2002:48). The French state recruited skilled workers from the fourteenth century, and similarly British mercantilism would recruit artisans from Antwerp and the Netherlands to the early protected cloth industry. Dutch finance in the seventeenth and eighteenth centuries would back both the British East India Company and the Bank of England (Heaton 1948).

Finally, towns were also political centres. The German aphorism that 'town air makes you free' may underplay the unfreedom of many early urban feudal societies. But many towns won considerable freedom and city dwellers escaped some of the feudal repressions (Dobb 1963). As centres of industry and innovation they also became centres of ideological transformation.

Mercantilism, Slavery and the Rise of Capitalism

The modern 'nation state' and the interstate system are relatively recent innovations, of only a few hundred years' standing. Nevertheless, they preceded capitalism; and the emergence in many places in Europe of singular nation states – the rise of 'absolutism', of centralised monarchical power – represented a break with feudal political forms. Through economic intervention both domestic and foreign states contributed, perhaps crucially, to capitalist development.

Even before Britain's revolutions of the seventeenth century, the relatively coherent national state played an important economic role. It was suggested above that it contributed to the peculiar resolution of demographic crisis and class struggle in the fourteenth century. England's Tudor monarchs already adopted mercantilist, nation-building policies in the sixteenth century; for example, trying to develop England's cloth industry and to protect it from more efficient foreign competitors. Brenner argues that 'French centralization accelerated somewhat later, it was influenced by English development, and was, indeed, in part, a response to direct English politico-military pressure' (1985b:255). English and French development was 'uneven' and 'combined' (1985b:255). Absolutism was the main prop of the old ruling class against threats both from without and from 'below' and relied on the continuation of essentially feudal methods of surplus extraction. Mercantilism suppressed rather than unleashed free markets both at home and abroad. In France, when it became systematic policy under Colbert in the seventeenth century, it involved for example reviving the guilds and raising import duties (Heaton 1948). Mercantilism nevertheless helped to create private accumulations of wealth and involved a process of political accumulation which challenged the competing power of lords within states and the higher power of the church (Brenner 1985b). Thus already some achievements of the bourgeois state were possible. The absolutist state also provided the basis for European expansion and, as will be discussed in the next chapter, a site of class struggle and thence the possibility of social and political transformation at the national level.

Europe had long been linked to other, often more advanced, parts of the world. However, in the fifteenth century it became more outward looking. Partly in response to the obstruction of overland routes after the crusades, first Portugal and then Spain began a series of navigations through which Europeans 'discovered' new worlds and established intercontinental empires. European sophistication should not be exaggerated. When Vasco da Gama first unveiled his gifts to the Samorian of Calicut it provoked open laughter (Rosenberg 1994). Nevertheless, the ability to establish substantial empires confirmed the relative coherence of singular national states and suggests a degree of technological advance, at least in shipbuilding. The Portuguese empire in the East was essentially based on monopolising sea trade and would leave little trace when it collapsed. The still essentially feudal domestic society limited both the imperial operations and any economic transformation it might achieve within Portugal (Rosenberg 1994). The Portuguese were substantially ousted by the Dutch, whose East India Company similarly enjoyed monopoly protection, but its private form 'meant that protection costs were brought within the range of rational calculation instead of being in the unpredictable region of "the acts of God or the king's enemies"' (Steensgaard, cited in Blackburn 1997:187).

In the Americas, European technological superiority was somewhat greater; more decisively in swords and armour than in guns, which remained fairly inefficient (Harman 1999). The New World was relatively quickly, if very painfully, conquered. The Spanish established a huge territorial empire, but their experience similarly shows that plundering wealth need not produce national enrichment. Vast quantities of precious metals flowed back to Spain; between 1521 and 1660, 18,000 tonnes of silver and 200 of gold. About 30–40 per cent of the bullion went directly into the royal coffers and although some paid foreign creditors and funded expensive wars to maintain its European empire, the Castilian state grew rich. However, the silver was mined and had to be bought from New World settlers, who paid for Castilian textiles, oil and wine at inflated monopoly prices. That boosted export production at home, but at the expense of the economy devoted to domestic consumption needs (Anderson 1979a). Arable farming declined, and by the 1570s Spain became a grain-importing country. Meanwhile, wool earned cash, but needed little labour. Peasants were displaced, becoming agricultural workers or unemployed. Others worked for the state, in what Anderson described as a 'premature and bloated tertiary sector' (1979a:73). Bullion poured into Spain and, despite prohibitions, out again, fuelling inflation across Europe. Inflation devalued existing wealth, while higher prices provided another spur to commercial farming. The principal losers from Spanish colonisation were, of course, the Americans and the African slaves. Meanwhile, Polanyi suggests, in Spain commercial sheep farming 'turned gold into sand' (2001:36). The country grew over the course of the sixteenth century at a rate of about a quarter of one per cent per head per year and hardly at all in the seventeenth (Maddison 2003).

Much more lasting success has been attributed to the early French and particularly British imperialisms. Conversely, the scale of the misery and destruction slavery and the slave trade wrought to Africa can hardly be overstated. As valuable cargo, the slaves may have survived the middle passage better than the sailors, but of 21 million captured between 1700 and 1850, 5 million died within a year and only something over 3 million had survived in the Americas by the eighteenth century (Blackburn 1997). The wealth slavery brought to Europe was also vast. For Marx, 'in fact the veiled slavery of the wage-labourers in Europe needed the unqualified slavery of the New World as its pedestal' (1976:925). Williams (1964), Solow and Engerman (1987) and Blackburn (1988, 1997) have more recently reasserted the links between slavery and capitalism. Slave traders made huge profits. In Britain, the Manchester Ship Canal was built with slave money – as was much of the success of cities like Bristol, Liverpool and Glasgow. Colonial markets also provided a significant demand for European manufactures. In Africa, slaves were usually bought from relatively sophisticated traders who could not normally be fobbed off with a few trinkets, but who would buy textiles and, of course, guns. The slave colonies largely grew their own food, but also provided important markets, protected by the Navigation Acts (Blackburn 1988). British exports to America and Africa jumped nearly sevenfold in the first three-quarters of the eighteenth century and from 12 to 43 per cent of the total (Blackburn 1997). Britain's textile industry would also rely on slave-produced cotton.

However, slave wealth did not produce capitalism in Spain or Portugal, which had been leading slaving nations, but whose economies went backwards compared with those of northern Europe. Nor did it produce a comparable industrial revolution in France, despite the French making more profits from slavery than the British and by the 1760s exporting more refined sugar and cotton goods (Blackburn 1988). Even in Britain it was a long time from the establishment of slavery to anything approaching industrial capitalism. Britain's slave colonies were in decline by the end of the eighteenth century. Domestic accumulation may have been more important (Brenner 1977; Crouzet 1990). If slavery contributed to Britain's industrialisation, it did so in the context of an already growing and commercialised economy. In terms both of supply – it made the goods to sell in Africa and America – and of demand, there was a domestic 'mass' market for tobacco and sugar. A dispossessed poor also provided a supply of free settlers and, for a time, even of indentured servants. French colonial exports were also more diverse, including larger quantities of cacao, coffee and indigo as well as sugar. Many of these were then exported within Europe, at least in part because of the relatively small domestic markets (Blackburn 1997:445). Amassing wealth, in the absence of particular institutional frameworks and relations of production, did not lead to capitalism.

As with many of the developments discussed in this chapter, it is impossible to prove any necessary causation or to discern how the world might have turned out differently. Policies of state and empire building had mixed results. The Portuguese and Spanish empires declined. The Dutch republic did not sustain its growth into the eighteenth century. Britain, and to a lesser extent France, established relatively coherent, singular, imperial states and continued to grow slowly and to become more commercialised. However, this should not be exaggerated. In 1800 at most 10 per cent of Europe's population was urban and only 17 cities had 100,000 inhabitants (Hobsbawm 1987; Horlings 2001). Draught animals and firewood predominated as power sources even in Western Europe. France at the time of the revolution had 3 million oxen and 1.8 million horses compared with a human population of 25 million (Braudel 1974). Subsistence agriculture was still common (Crouzet 1990). It had largely disappeared from Britain, already established as the leading power. However, even after the first decades of industrial revolution in 1820, Britain's per capita wealth had still not reached the level the Netherlands had attained in 1700 and then lost – probably somewhat below that of contemporary India (Maddison 2003). Britain's total wealth was about that of modern day Sudan. All this was about to change.

Conclusion

This chapter has introduced a number of elements that have often been seen as essential components of the transition from feudalism to capitalism. The way the features are presented perhaps implies conceptual priorities, but these were not separable processes. Rival accusations of economism and politicism have characterised Marxist debates about the origins of capitalism. However, the separation of politics and economics, which has become normalised under contemporary capitalism, was only beginning to be established over the centuries discussed here.

There was nothing inevitable about Europe's leadership. Indeed, 1000 years earlier Europe had been a relative backwater and this meant that it was able gradually to appropriate technological advances made elsewhere. Its backwardness also meant that it was subject to severe demographic crises. These accelerated processes of commercialisation in what became mutually reinforcing interactions between a monetised rural economy, agricultural innovation, increasing trade, urbanisation and growing political centralisation. The compulsion of markets increased (Wood 2002).

This remained a slow and uncertain process. On the eve of the industrial revolution, Western Europe, particularly Britain, had already established a considerable economic lead over other parts of the world; but no one could have anticipated the changes that were about to happen.

6

THE MAKING OF THE GLOBAL ECONOMY

The previous chapter emphasised a range of explanations – or a range of explanatory elements – for the transformation of Europe, and particularly Britain, up to the dawn of the industrial revolution. It argued that economic development even in the Middle Ages should be conceived 'globally'. Outside influences and international relations within Europe were already significant. This is not a claim about quantity. Even with the discovery of the Americas, the weight of gold and silver brought back to Europe was small, almost trivial by today's standards. But there is an important sense in which there was already a world economy in 1500. Political economy was emphatically global by 1800. Over the next 150 years the intensity of these international relations increased, and this chapter attempts to outline key developments in this process.

It first discusses the two moments of the 'dual revolution', a term used by Hobsbawm to describe what he sees as linked processes of political and economic transformation stemming from France in 1789 and from the British industrial revolution. The revolutions, he suggests, together constitute the most important event in world history, 'at any event since the invention of agriculture and cities' (Hobsbawm 1962:29). Figure 6.1 shows some of the national detail behind the European growth already depicted in Figure 5.1. Before 1820, major European economies changed slowly and unevenly. They then grew rapidly and in closer alignment. However, as in the previous period, although change centred on Europe and depended crucially on changes within European society, this was never simply a European transformation, either in cause or effect.

The chapter then discusses the imperialism which from about 1875 divided the world. It was also a key driver towards what Dowd (2004) has called 'the thirty years' war' – the period between 1914 and 1945. The chapter finally discusses this period of interstate rivalry, bracketed by two world wars, as a sharp retreat from the earlier phase of apparently peacefully increasing prosperity. Necessarily, these momentous events are sketched briefly and schematically, but they show a world radically transformed from the agrarian society of the late eighteenth century into one recognisably global in its scope and in its domination by markets, industry and rival national states.

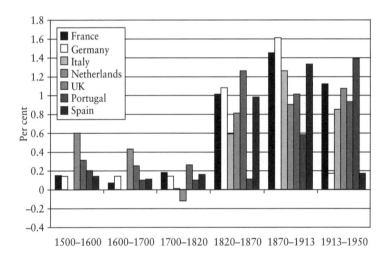

Figure 6.1   Average annual GDP per capita growth rate (per cent), selected European countries
Source: Maddison 2003

Bourgeois Revolutions

The concept of bourgeois revolution was not introduced by Marxists but subsequently became important to their historiography (Nygaard 2006). The great French revolution of 1789 provides the classic example. Mass uprising overthrew absolutism and eradicated the vestiges of feudalism. Representatives of the young capitalist class overcame both more conservative and more radical wings of the revolution to install a bourgeois republic. Earlier revolutions – those in the Netherlands in the late sixteenth century and in Britain in the seventeenth, and the American War of Independence – are then usually read as less pure examples of the same thing. Later revolutions can be understood in a similar framework, although they were more strongly influenced by capitalism's establishment elsewhere and by the rise of working-class movements. This interpretation can be defended, but with some caution.

As discussed in the previous chapter, the slow increase of productive capacities within European feudalism made possible the emergence of capitalist agriculture and of non-agricultural, including urban, forms of wealth. It increased the surpluses which could be traded and contributed to the rise of new classes of richer peasants, merchants and manufacturers. These new classes represented new sources of power within the old system and a potential challenge to it. They were hampered by feudal laws, things like internal tolls and the guild system. Sometimes they found innovative ways round them; for example, the putting-out system avoided the urban guilds. Nevertheless, they faced the fundamental obstacle of the old feudal rulers' opposition to change. Peasant rebellions were repressed and a second serfdom reimposed in Eastern Europe. A revolution in Bohemia was crushed shortly before that in England succeeded. There was no automatic progress. 'Common ruin' and social regression remained entirely possible. However, if there was to be social progress, revolution was necessary. Securing capitalism meant sweeping away the old order, which the French revolution, in particular, accomplished in dramatic style.

More recently both anti-Marxist and Marxist critics have challenged the idea of bourgeois revolution. Many non-Marxists combine a general opposition to sweeping characterisations of historical events with a rereading of the specific revolutions in non-class terms. There were few, if any, overtly bourgeois revolutionaries. Revolutions should instead be understood either as the participants themselves understood them: for example, as religious wars or national revolts, or as essentially accidental – perhaps as wars between court and country provoked by the folly of particular rules. Some Marxists have similarly dismissed the concept. For Wood, bourgeois revolution is a relic of 'mechanical materialism' (2002:62). There is no place for it if capitalism was already established in the English countryside several centuries earlier. As Tawney, who supported the idea, admitted: 'Bourgeois revolution? Of course it was a bourgeois revolution. The trouble is that the bourgeoisie was on both sides' (cited in Callinicos 1989:122). Conversely, if capitalism's origins are agrarian, it cannot have been made by the bourgeoisie in the literal sense. 'Burghers' are by definition urban.

There have been two sorts of Marxist response to the revisionist charges. The first defends claims of the class composition of the revolution. For example, historians of the English revolution, such as Hill (1993) and Manning (1992), acknowledge that classes were not homogeneous, and that the participants did not, of course, identify themselves as capitalist revolutionaries. People articulated social demands in the religious language available. However, the revolution was predominantly composed and led by people of 'the middle sort' (Manning 1994). Both yeomen in the country and lower-ranking London merchants were crucial. The American and French revolutions also had imperfect but recognisable class characters. The Girondists were indeed 'representatives of the propertied bourgeoisie' (Kinder and Hilgemann 1978).

The alternative Marxist response has been to see these revolutions as bourgeois in terms of their achievements (Callinicos 1989). This recognises the timid role the bourgeoisie plays in its revolution (Blackledge 2006a). Capitalists had much to lose and often sided with the old order against more radical revolutionaries. Nevertheless, the outcomes favoured capitalism. In England the revolution destroyed feudal reaction and thus marked the vital first step subordinating merchant capitalism to industrial (Takahashi 1976). The English parliament established its rule over the monarchy and abolished feudal tenure and institutions like the Star Chamber. It introduced mercantilist practices like the Navigation Acts, institutions like the Bank of England and laws of

Habeas Corpus protecting individual liberty and property (Braudel 1985; Callinicos 1989). In France the revolution abolished the guild system and overcame numerous internal divisions within France in terms of language and state bureaucracy. The Code Napoléon guaranteed personal liberty, legal equality and private property. Napoleon's European invasions introduced similar modernisations elsewhere, either by force or by competitive example. France and Europe were opened for business, whatever the participants' motivations. Later transformations saw still less capitalist agency; in Bismarck's Germany and perhaps most strikingly in the Meiji restoration in Japan, old ruling classes reformed themselves to clear the path to capitalist development.

These two approaches are in some tension. The bourgeoisie was seldom revolutionary. Success often meant accommodating with, even dissolving into, the feudal order and the bourgeoisie could thus become targets, not agents, of revolution. Alternatively, if the revolutions were bourgeois only in terms of their achievements, there would seem to be a danger of losing the vital element of human agency and reverting to teleology. Revolution remains only as a ghostly presence, inferred from the later establishment of capitalism. It may nevertheless be possible to defend an interpretation of bourgeois revolution that acknowledges both its class character and its achievement, to see it as an 'intersection of objective historical processes and conscious human agency' (Callinicos 1989:126). Unintentional, structural processes created a class of capitalists, who then tended to support and develop those trends and to oppose alternatives. In the interminable struggles of the early modern era – the wars, rebellions and revolts – capitalists were more or less consciously forced to take sides. In doing so they increased the class colouration of such conflicts. There is what might be described as a process of 'bourgeoisification' of revolution. Revolutions are necessarily impure, in class terms and in the extent of disjuncture they achieve. There are often strong elements of continuity, and social transformation is not accomplished absolutely or at a stroke. The external environment tends to drag back or pull forward processes of change in any one place. Both advance and retreat remain possible.

The achievements of the British revolution were threatened by the Restoration, reaffirmed by the Glorious Revolution, but again partially eroded by the later Georgian monarchy. There were still powerful tendencies towards regress, which might have choked industrial development, perhaps repeating the rise and decline of the Italian states or of the Netherlands. So the revolution might have been necessary, but was not sufficient to guarantee a capitalist future. However, the political changes provided important bases for the nearly threefold economic growth in the eighteenth century. While a relatively modest expansion compared with what would come in the following hundred years, this provided a stimulus and challenge to others. As Callinicos argues, 'each revolution alters the terms for its successors' (1989:141). British success forced monarchs '(or rather their advisors) to attempt programmes of economic, social, administrative and intellectual modernization' (Hobsbawm 1962:22). France, from a lower base, grew at a similar rate (Crouzet 1990). Economic growth within absolutist France then exacerbated social and economic tensions. The monarchy continued to depend on landed nobles even as they promoted economic change that undermined the nobles' position. Successful capitalists bought their way into feudal privileges even as their rise threatened these privileges (Hobsbawm 1962:23). It still took revolution to sweep away that old order. This then had repercussions far beyond France. Under the impact of revolution and revolutionary wars, British capitalism was strengthened economically, but also then emboldened to abolish residual but important feudal legislation in the first half of the nineteenth century (Polanyi 2001). There were still ebbs and flows. Absolutism attempted to reassert itself in France, leading to further revolutions in 1830 and 1848. It held on, for example in Russia. However, as capitalist economy conquered Western Europe it imposed a stark choice on other countries. Feudal rulers became more willing to adopt capitalist ways. In an emerging capitalist world, the achievements of bourgeois revolution became more urgent requirements even as capitalists became more fearful of revolutionary challenges.

Industrial Revolution

If the political side of the dual revolution was centred on France and moved outwards, the industrial revolution radiated from Britain. This was not a process that can be neatly defined or timed. However, over the next century first Britain then other European countries and the United States would become urbanised and industrialised and would increase their wealth as never before. In 1800 most of the world was still rural and agrarian. Much of Europe was still feudal. Even in England, over 70 per cent of the population lived in the countryside (Allen 1998). By 1900, across Western Europe, industry contributed more to national wealth than agriculture. As late as 1850, Paris and London were the only European cities of half a million inhabitants. By 1900 there were 19 (Mitchell 1998). The US expansion was still more remarkable, both in terms of territory and in the growth of cities and industry. The industrial revolution began in Britain, but was quickly assimilated elsewhere.

There was a technical aspect to the transformation. There were a series of innovations; Watt's steam engine was produced in 1775, Crompton's spinning mule was introduced in 1779 and Cartwright's power loom in 1785. However, much of the early advance relied on making effective use of technologies that had been available for some time. The flying shuttle and the coking process in iron production had been invented in the 1730s. Bairoch suggests that 'during the first decades of the industrial revolution, technology was to a much greater extent a factor governed by the economy than one governing the economy' (cited in Braudel 1985:567). Crouzet (1990) sees bottlenecks in production as stimulating the unique creativity. Again, this was precedented, but the way processes of innovation continued to gain in intensity and to expand geographically was new.

The industrial revolution was simultaneously an inherently international and a distinctly British process. British domestic political economy, in particular the relationship between agriculture and industry, distinguished it from earlier prototypes in which capitalism did not last. The enclosures of the late eighteenth and nineteenth centuries transformed the countryside. They contributed to increased agricultural efficiency, so that a shrinking sector (more or less) successfully fed a rapidly rising population (Brenner 1985b). Enclosure also pushed poor peasants off the land, producing a working class. Capitalist farming already existed in terms of the rationale of growing crops for sale. However, 'not until large-scale industry, based on machinery, comes, does there arise a permanent foundation for capitalist agriculture' (Marx, cited in Cooper 1985:147). The seed drill, for example, was invented in 1733, but only became widely used in the nineteenth century (Braudel 1985). With the second agricultural revolution (of 1815–80) 'something like half the farmland and half the farm output – though undoubtedly a good deal less than half the individual farmers – came under the sway of commercialized farming' (Thompson, cited in Cooper 1985:191). It was often a brutal process, but in terms of establishing a national economy there was something of a virtuous cycle, as industrial products were sold at home, increasing agricultural productivity and forcing more people off the land into industry. Britain was from the start less reliant on food imports or on commodity exports than earlier, smaller manufacturing centres like those in Flanders, and it gradually established 'mutually interdependent, mutually self-developing agricultural and industrial sectors at home' (Brenner 1985b:326).

Hobsbawm (1962) does not see this as sufficient, stressing the international dimensions. The British industrial revolution drew on wealth generated by slavery and the slave trade and on Russian, Dutch and Prussian finance (Blanchard 2001). For most of the crucial early years, Britain was at war with France, an expensive business, and it is conceivable that growth might otherwise have been even more rapid. Nevertheless, amongst other things war stimulated important industries like shipbuilding and ironworking. The foundry was 'almost identified with the casting of cannon' (Hobsbawm 1962:96). National debt rose nearly fourfold between 1793 and 1816, and this indebtedness changed British social structure by diverting increased tax revenue from the population to rich 'fundholders' who after the war had spare cash to throw at new projects (Hobsbawm 1962:95). Textile manufacture in particular relied both on imported cotton and on foreign markets. Already in the eighteenth century these grew (from a low base) nearly ten times as fast as home markets. It was cotton, the export industry, which then fuelled demand for steam power and coal. Success in textiles also accumulated capital in quantities necessary for the scale of operations in later industries like railway building. However, cotton consumption rose much more rapidly than total exports in the first half of the nineteenth century (Mitchell 1998). Overall, at this time British exports grew relatively slowly, from £53 million in 1800 to £83 million in 1850, and only then leapt ahead to £354 million in 1900 (Mitchell 1998). In quantitative terms iron, coal and, from 1830, railway building, were primarily national industries, and their growth was mutually reinforcing. The internal transformation was undoubtedly dramatic, and Britain's per capita wealth grew more in the 50 years from 1820 than it had in the previous 220 (Maddison 2003).

Industrial transformation both created the basis for and in turn required further political reform within Britain. In the early nineteenth century there were still substantial obstacles to the effective compulsion of markets – for Wood (2002:6–7), the essence of capitalism. The 1832 Reform Act widened the franchise and established urban capital's representation in the House of Commons, which then passed a series of Bills that began to achieve this compulsion. Polanyi (2001) identifies three crucial reforms: the Poor Law Amendment of 1834, the Bank Act of 1844 and the Anti-Corn Law Bill of 1846. The first repealed Elizabethan Poor Law to establish 'free' labour markets. 'Outdoor relief' had deterred the desperate search for employment needed by capital. The terror of the workhouse guaranteed it. The Bank Act established the gold standard, with the Bank of England as sole issuer of currency, and supply limited to reserves of gold. As Block writes, 'it was an institutional innovation that put the theory of self-regulating markets into practice, and once in place it had the power to make self-regulating markets appear to be natural' (2001:xxx). The Anti-Corn Law Bill established freer trade. Grain imports reduced prices, allowing capitalists to cut wages. Moreover, other countries could sell Britain grain and now afford the latter's manufactured goods (Hobsbawm 1962). However, Polanyi's point was that free markets are unsustainable. The brutality of exploitation meant rich profits, but threatened to undermine its own basis. The horrors of working-class life in mid-nineteenth-century Britain are well documented. Although it was still recruiting from the countryside, this threatened to undermine the quantity and quality of labour. Poverty also limited domestic consumption. For Polanyi this eventually required the counter-movement against the market. The movement for reform was waged by workers themselves, but also supported by more far-sighted capitalists. This mainly consisted of protective legislation and limits to the length of the working day and to women's and children's labour.

Conceived globally, British capital also had the option of what Harvey (1982) calls a 'spatial fix'. With the abolition of the Corn Laws, Britain adopted a more or less consistent free-trade policy. In the 1860s it negotiated openness within Europe, notably in the Cobden Chevalier treaty with France, then in deals which extended free trade to Belgium, the German Zollverein and other countries. Germany's steel producers, for example, now benefited from being able to buy cheaper British pig iron (Kindleberger 1975; Milward and Saul 1977). Trade rose rapidly. Despite fears that this would consign other European countries to the role of agricultural suppliers to Britain (see, for example, List 1997), their industries also grew, often broadly replicating the sequence in Britain. Other countries established textile, coal and steel industries. The railway boom also spread, with railways often being financed by British capital and even built by British firms. British foreign direct investment (FDI) jumped, with the railway builders being followed by hundreds of mining companies and many others. By 1914, British outward FDI stocks amounted to over half its GDP (Dunning 1993).

After 1870 other European countries and the United States grew more quickly than Britain. As they established industries, first in textiles then in other sectors, demand for British products declined (see Tables 6.1 and 6.2). The movement towards freer

Table 6.1 Britain's exports of cotton piece goods (per cent)
1820–1900

	Europe and USA	Underdeveloped countries	Other countries
1820	60.4	31.8	7.8
1840	29.5	66.7	3.8
1860	19.0	73.3	7.7
1880	9.8	82.0	8.2
1900	7.1	86.3	6.6

Source: Hobsbawm 1969

Table 6.2 Britain's exports (per cent) 1854–1913

	Europe and USA	British empire	Latin America	Others
1854	48	35	8	9
1876	51	32	8	9
1900	48	32	8	12
1913	40	37	10	14

Source: Barratt Brown 1974

markets went into reverse. The United States had started to become less open as early as 1861. Germany turned inwards after 1879. It continued to grow, developing larger-scale and more efficient production than Britain in key sectors like steel and its own distinctive industrial revolution based on chemicals. By 1913 average tariffs were 12 per cent in Germany, 18 per cent in France, 20 per cent in Japan and 33 per cent in the United States. Only Britain held out (Kenwood and Lougheed 1992). All of which made markets in poorer countries correspondingly more important. As the explorer Stanley remarked of Africa in 1878, 'there are forty million naked people ... and the cotton spinners of Manchester are waiting to clothe them' (cited in Young 1996:196).

As with trade, the patterns of investment changed. Firms from other countries also invested abroad. Many were small, but amongst what would become more familiar names, Colt, Singer, Coca-Cola,

Gillette, Heinz, Ford and United Fruit were all established multi-nationals before the First World War. So too were German firms like Siemens, BASF, Bayer, Bosch and Hoechst (Dunning 1993; Jones 1993). Other operations became truly multinational. The Papal States railway alone 'was conceded to a Paris banker; he sold stock mostly in France and Italy, the rails came from Newcastle, the locomotives from Brassey's works near Paris, the wheels from Belgium and the carriages were built in Italy' (Milward and Saul 1977:498). Of total British FDI, in 1830 two-thirds was in Europe, in 1870 only 25 per cent and in 1914, 5 per cent. The proportion within the British empire rose from 2 to 46 per cent over the same period (Kenwood and Lougheed 1992).

This situation begins to make sense of the drive to empire. Britain had long relied on imports, particularly of cotton. The main source was the southern United States, but 'free trade' was also imposed on Egypt in 1841, after which that country's cotton exports grew rapidly, reaching nearly 400 million kilograms by 1913 (Robinson 1972; Kenwood and Lougheed 1992). Britain bought a range of food and raw materials from other, mainly poorer countries. Most notoriously, the Opium Wars also opened China to trade, to devastating effect for that country. The effects of openness on others are less clear. Some historians have suggested that deteriorating terms of trade for primary producers were probably less significant than the volatility of primary product prices (Milward and Saul 1977). Initially, non-European countries largely had only Britain as a market, giving it a substantial degree of monopsony power, but growth elsewhere in Europe fed rising export prices (Platt 1972). The empires were not entirely closed, but colonisation partially restored the monopoly/monopsony position. The threat of closure may also have fuelled inter-imperialist competition. Empires were an important source of raw materials and significant outlets for exports and investment.

Imperialism

There was a dramatic revival of imperial expansion in the late nineteenth century. The maps of the world quickly became filled with the colours of a few major powers, though their presence on the ground was uneven. In the eighteenth century, European colonialism, except for Russian control of Siberia and the British East India Company's occupation of Bengal, was largely confined to isolated coastal settlements. From 1875 it leaped ahead. Britain and France led, but the Dutch, Portuguese, Germans, Americans and Japanese all established significant empires. Only South America was substantially free of foreign occupation – but countries like Argentina were seen as part of Britain's sphere of influence or informal empire. Africa was transformed. In 1800, Europeans held a few coastal strips. By 1900, they controlled 93 per cent of the continent (Hunt and Sherman 1981).

Thus patterns of empire changed rapidly. There were significant continuities, sometimes even direct causation between earlier relations and the new imperialism. For example, some African writers understood their continent's disunity and weakness in the face of European invasions as having been a direct result of the damage wrought by the earlier slave trade (Hodgkin 1972). But the sudden change still needs to be explained. Even accepting some primordial lust for power or logic of international rivalry, it would seem necessary to explain how and why it took this new form. In terms of 'how', perhaps most decisively, Europe advanced in heavy iron and steel production and thus in armaments. Previously, Europeans had won naval battles, but except in the Americas had struggled to overcome local populations on land. The new superiority was most devastatingly shown in massacres like that at Omdurman in Sudan in 1898 and Satiru in Nigeria in 1906 (Harman 1999:395). This made territorial empire possible. Previously, methods of production and commercial organisation in places like India and China had been broadly comparable with Europe (Hunt and Sherman 1981). By the middle of the nineteenth century the latter had clear advantages in cost and quality (Fieldhouse 1973).

Hobson's pioneering and influential explanation (Hobson, J. A. 2007) identified an 'economic tap root of imperialism'. He argued that, within Britain, monopoly increased the profit share and concentrated it into a few hands. This led to a vicious cycle.

An increased proportion of profits was saved, limiting domestic investment, contributing to a lack of demand and increased saving. Capital export was the only outlet. This led to pressure for annexations. Hobson acknowledged incidental and accidental processes in the practical development of empire, but he believed that the underlying rationale was an economic one. He opposed imperialism as bad business – bad for democracy, bad for the colonised people and bad for Britain's reputation. Despite being against the national interest, elite groups who benefited were in positions of power over the state and able to win popular support for aims couched in terms of spreading civilisation. It would be better to invest at home, which could be achieved through income redistribution. The poor would save less and spend more of their income than would the rich. Early Marxist theorists, notably Lenin (1965), drew explicitly on Hobson. Luxemburg (1963) also argued that the insufficiency of domestic demand pushed capital abroad. The emphasis in different accounts varied, but empire was widely seen as an extension of capital's economic expansion (Hilferding 1981; Lenin 1965; Bukharin 1972).

An obvious and repeated objection to economic explanations is the paucity of evidence that empire 'paid'. Most obviously, Britain and France, which carved out the biggest empires, fell behind Germany, which joined the imperial scramble only late and to less effect. Smaller Western European nations like Sweden and Switzerland, which had little or no imperial presence, also did well. France, which sent only 11 per cent of its exports to its colonies, did better than Britain, which sent 37 per cent (Milward and Saul 1977). Similarly, after the Second World War the West did better without empire than it had previously done with it. However, this does not exclude economic motives. Firstly, for Western capitalism as a whole the period was very successful. Overall growth rates after the 1870s were higher than in the preceding period. Although Britain and France fell behind Germany, it is impossible to tell how they would have done without their empires. Britain ran trade surpluses with its empire, which went some way towards offsetting its growing deficits with Europe (Milward and Saul 1977). Magdoff (1969) has argued that imperialist gains may be hard to quantify, but may nevertheless be qualitatively vital. If, as with Spain three centuries earlier, it was not the principal imperial power that reaped the greatest rewards, that confounds neither the benefits from imperialism nor the economic motives.

Secondly, a lack of success would not demonstrate the absence of economic motivation. All business enterprises try to make a profit, but many fail. Nor does a business stop trading the moment it stops making a profit (Samuelson et al. 1975; Harman 1999). History is littered with mistakes. As more recent military adventures confirm, the costs of maintaining armies and the level of resistance may prove greater than anticipated.

Thirdly, political economy should be read in class terms rather than (simply) national ones. The particular significance of Hobson's argument is that imperialism was against national, but in particular class, interests. A similar emphasis of course also underpins the Marxist writing of the time. Finance capital – understood as an amalgam of financial and industrial capital – had a particular interest in extending its domestic monopolies (Hilferding 1981; Bukharin 1972). The characterisation of an interlinked banking and industrial capitalism fitted the German evidence best, but powerful British and French companies profited from the imperial project. There was a particularly rapid rise in Britain's imperial investments in the 1880s, during what in Europe was the first Great Depression. Total FDI leapt from £95 million to £393 million between 1883 and 1889. More at this time was in Europe than in the British empire, but capital outflows amounted to 5.75 per cent of GDP in 1890 and 7.38 per cent in 1910, and the proportion within empire increased rapidly (Foreman-Peck 1983). The proportion going from France to its colonies only reached 9 per cent, but total foreign investment tripled between 1881 and 1914 (Kenwood and Lougheed 1992). The Belgian example is perhaps clearest. When governments refused to support him, King Leopold grabbed the Congo as a private individual (Milward and Saul 1977).

If even national gains are questionable, it becomes particularly doubtful that workers in the imperialist countries benefited. Some may have done so. Lenin thought that 'morsels of the loot' found their way to a labour aristocracy (cited in Cliff and Gluckstein 1986). Many workers undoubtedly supported the imperialist projects, but it seems clear that they had little say in the matter. Opposition at home was also repressed, if seldom as brutally as abroad. This was the era of the robber barons in the United States and of anti-socialist laws in Germany. It begins shortly after the massacre of the Paris Commune; even in liberal Britain a bare majority of men gained the vote only in 1884. Conditions for some workers in Britain were beginning to rise, but empire eased a substantial net outflow of capital and declining investment at home.

It is hardly shocking that powerful class interests preferred to have the option of making profits abroad rather than being confined to the domestic economy. That does not mean that the experience of imperialism was reducible to these interests. At the very least, imperialism could not be articulated in terms of naked economic gain and so needed a 'moment' of its own. This could justify, even require, occupation in which economic importance might be slight, even negative. Practice was then never simply an exercise in economic expediency, but a pragmatic amalgam of force, bribes and all sorts of 'underhand means' (Polanyi 2001:14). The political and economic objectives of leading states and the major interests within them were intertwined and sometimes in tension. Many imperialists no doubt genuinely felt themselves more or less 'dragged in'; for fear of rival claims, by settlers, or to settle disputes amongst the fractious natives (Fieldhouse 1973). However, as Hodgkin writes, 'it yet remains true that imperial expansion could not have occurred unless it had been willed by dominant interests within the ruling classes of the imperial powers' (1972:107).

Imperialism brought profound changes to the social structures of the colonised societies, but was also conditioned by them. Imperialism was, of course, seen by its perpetrators (as well as by some subsequent historians, Ferguson 2002) as something benign. Most obviously it spread capitalism and its unique dynamism. In purely economic terms it often brought growth. China, forced into trade openness and buying opium, but not formally occupied, was the most substantial exception. Its income declined in real terms by about 17 per cent between 1820 and 1870 (Maddison 2003). Local societies and cultures could also be ripped up. Imperialism for the most part was extensive and no longer a marginal trading presence, like the Portuguese, Dutch and early British settlements. It varied in intensity, but there were often significant changes in production and therefore in class relations within the colonised societies.

Non-European subjects were seldom simply passive victims (Fieldhouse 1973; Robinson 1972). The imperial system relied on repression, but also persuasion, collaboration and the construction of institutions to perpetuate (capitalist) order (Hodgkin 1972). The colonised societies were themselves, of course, different from each other and internally divided. This could profoundly affect the colonial experience. Individuals and social groups within the colonies may have benefited and more or less consistently collaborated with the imperial projects. This meant imperialism often involved at least tacit bargains. If these were too one sided they would not be effectively kept, either by the cooperating indigenous elites or by the local societies over which they had authority (Robinson 1972:121). Effective collaboration allowed the imperial power to withdraw more overt forms of occupation. If local rulers could be trusted to keep their territories open for business, as was the case in Latin America and China (after the defeat in the Opium Wars) and in the 'white' colonies, formal imperialism might even be unnecessary. Conversely, resistance could require direct rule and a heavier imperial presence.

Bukharin's (1972) classic account of imperialism highlighted the tension between processes of internationalisation and nationalisation of capital. The internationalisation was manifested in increasing foreign investment and cross-border links, both between rich countries and into the periphery. This sort of process led Kautsky (2004) to identify the possibility of 'ultra-imperialism' and of cooperative capitalist carve-up. However, for Bukharin, there was an opposing tendency towards increasing nationalisation, the domination of national economies by major trusts and their dependence on and use of state support to achieve both domestic and international success. This trend predominated as restrictions on trade increased and empires became more important to those who held them. The tendencies towards nationalisation increased the autonomous political logic of interstate competition and provided at least a key driver towards war.

The Thirty Years' War

Dowd (2004) describes the period from 1914 to 1945 as the 'thirty years' war'. While the outcome was perhaps not inevitable, mutually reinforcing pressures of economic and geopolitical competition finally led to war. These were three decades of unprecedented destruction. The First World War, in fact mainly a European conflict, was industrialised war on a new scale causing perhaps 20 million military and civilian deaths. Post-war recovery was brief and hugely uneven, both socially and geographically. It soon gave way to the Great Depression, itself only relieved by the Second World War. The scale of this genuinely global war and the destruction it caused overshadowed even those of the Great War. About 55 million people were killed. This thirty years' war changed international relations profoundly and left the US state and US capital in a uniquely strong position.

The First World War was fought to a standstill in the trenches of the western front and, slightly more fluidly, to the east. It was ended abruptly in the east by the Russian Revolution. Social conflicts were growing in other capitalist societies before the war and after a hiatus with the outbreak of hostilities intensified even before it was over. The Bolshevik revolution provided a huge further stimulus and point of reference for post-war polarisation. In the immediate aftermath of the First World War, at least until 1923, other countries appeared to teeter on the brink of socialist revolution.

Capitalism survived. However, the war ended any semblance of harmonious economic integration. The Western invasion of the Soviet republic, although finally defeated, drove the country further into backwardness and hollowed out the soviets or workers' councils as organs of participatory government. Stalin's consolidation of power and subsequent transformation of Russia's economy and society has been usefully interpreted as a second revolution against the first. Dowd suggests that the brutality of Stalin's regime and his 'realistic paranoia' (2004:102) can be understood in the context of the same processes of capitalist and imperialist competition that shaped this whole period. In the West, after a brief initial post-war boom, economic recovery was fragile and uneven. The German hyperinflation of the early 1920s was the most dramatic of the early upheavals. In Britain a period of comparatively modest inflation was checked in 1920 by deflationary policies. Wages fell and unemployment ran at 10 per cent, sometimes 15 per cent, throughout the supposedly 'roaring twenties'. Elsewhere, particularly in the United States, but also in France and Germany after 1924, there was substantial growth (Kindleberger 1973). However, the post-war economy involved two crucial dislocations.

Firstly, there were systematic inequalities at the international level. The United States emerged from the war as by far the richest country. It was also a massive creditor nation, demanding that France and Britain pay back debts. They in turn insisted on war reparations from Germany, which wrecked that country's economy; it was unable to pay until the United States provided loans – temporarily completing the financial circuit, but increasing the overall debt to the United States. Industrialised Europe's declining share of world trade also undermined its ability to repay. Cut off from European imports during the war, other countries had developed their own industries and these afterwards demanded protection. The pre-war tendencies against free trade increased. Europe's share of world trade fell from 54.4 to 43.1 per cent between 1913 and 1928 (Kenwood and Lougheed 1992). Perhaps most fundamentally, Britain continued its relative industrial decline. Despite this, it went back to the gold standard in 1925 at its pre-war parity of $4.86. Gold could only be kept in the country through high interest rates. The strong pound and high interest rates both suited rich bankers in the City of London, but they meant recessionary conditions, further decline and deepening trade deficits. Capital continued to flow out. France, meanwhile, rejoined gold at about a fifth of its pre-war value in 1928. This made French exports competitive; trade surpluses and its foreign currency reserves rocketed. Investment capital rushed in, effectively withdrawing funds from the rest of the world. In 1927 the United States lowered interest rates, in part to ease the pressure on the pound as Britain's loss of gold threatened to undermine the delicate international balance, but also to stimulate its domestic economy (Kindleberger 1973).

Secondly, there were also significant imbalances within the United States. Overall growth was rapid, but very uneven. Corporate profits rose 62 per cent between 1923 and 1929. Meanwhile, firstly, the still significant rural population did badly. Across the world in the post-war period agricultural prices tended to fall. This was in part because of increased global supply, further increasing the pressures towards protection, and in part because of falling relative demand. As wealth grows people spend relatively less on basic foodstuffs. There was also a decline in sectors like construction once the war-time slowdown was fully made good. Perhaps more fundamentally the good times in the 1920s were (even by capitalist standards) disproportionately good for those at the top of society. In 1929, 40 per cent of families had incomes only three-quarters of that reckoned necessary to supply basic necessities (Dowd 2004). Mass consumption was limited, despite being encouraged through the introduction of hire purchase or instalment credit in 1925, which produced escalating debts. Limited consumption amplified tendencies to overproduction. The rich were more likely to save and to invest. The latter took increasingly speculative forms, with a US stock market bubble also diverting funds from overseas lending, which fell drastically from 1928. The interest rate cuts in 1927 sustained the debt, but fuelled borrowing and the bubble. Share prices doubled in two years to 1929 – then almost halved in two months (Kindleberger 1973).

The economic impacts were rapid. Industrial production crashed. So automobile output, which had been 622,000 in March, fell to 169,500 in November. The Federal Reserve took over bad loans and repeatedly cut the interest rate. The Smoot–Hawley Act raised tariffs. However, the damage was done and the vicious cycle of decline of falling production, layoffs and falling consumption was set in train. The effects quickly spread to the rest of the world economy. Some stock markets were already falling and several major economies already struggling, but now everywhere followed a similar downward course. Around the world stock markets went into decline. Permanent unemployment was supposed to be impossible. Providing wages fell, workers would be hired again and profits restored. Governments should withdraw, to allow markets to function effectively. This all looked increasingly implausible and, what is more, was socially unsustainable. Unemployment rose and wages fell, but rather than restoring profitability this deepened the slump as markets collapsed. The attractive option of selling abroad disappeared as countries raised their tariffs. Trade spiralled downwards (Kindleberger 1973). Even Britain finally gave up the gold standard in 1931 and free trade in 1932.

This all exacerbated the social polarisation and struggles that characterised the whole inter-war period and what Polanyi (2001) characterised as a 'double movement' against the market. Mass socialist and communist parties developed, particularly in continental Europe. In the 1930s, France again seemed on the brink of revolution; Spain went further. The United States, too, became home to militant unionism and the sit-down strike. Germany repudiated its war reparations in 1931, even before the Nazis took power in 1933. Other militaristic and authoritarian governments were established in Hungary, Portugal, Spain and Japan.

Already in the second phase of the New Deal in the United States, Roosevelt's government had begun to adopt increasingly interventionist policies. Liberal orthodoxy was also, of course, rejected in Nazi Germany, Japan and the USSR. All, with hindsight, might be described as practising 'military Keynesianism', and their economies grew quite quickly. Elsewhere, in most places, the depression persisted until rearmament and war finally revived the economy, but – of course – at terrible cost.

There were marked declines in the level of integration measured by ratios of trade and investment to GDP, but the global political economy remained inexorably interconnected, attested by the universal nature of the depression and persistent interstate rivalry.

In many ways, the Second World War repeated the devastation of the previous war, but on a more truly global scale and with more casualties. It further established the United States's lead over its rivals. Its economy ended the war 80 per cent bigger than it began. At its end, a repeat of the inter-war instabilities seemed likely. Few if any expected that the post-war period would establish an unprecedented period of prosperity and economic integration.

Conclusion

There had been many auguries of capitalism during the previous centuries. However, only with the unique conjuncture of political transformations, which broke absolutism on a national basis and established national capitalist economies, was the industrial revolution consolidated. This heralded economic expansion on a scale unprecedented in world history. Its dynamism was also contradictory. Domestic problems and crises could be solved temporarily and in part by pushing beyond national boundaries. This tended to offset and delay the contradictions, which were then played out in the form of national imperialist projects and competition between the imperialist powers. The First World War caused massive destruction, but left the United States as the world's most powerful economy. Competition continued, with the world less open than hitherto; but others proved unable to develop independently, as proved by their failure to escape the effects of the disastrous downturn that began in the United States in 1929. A final, catastrophic, challenge produced the Second World War.

7

BRETTON WOODS AND
THE GOLDEN AGE

The quarter century from immediate post-war reconstruction until the 1970s was one of unique growth and stability. From the immediate post-war turmoil until the 1970s the global economy expanded, with only minor interruptions. The United States and a few other countries went into recession in 1958. However, they quickly recovered. On a world basis, every year between 1947 and 1974 was one of growth. This chapter concentrates on the phenomenal experiences of the Western capitalist world, but the communist (second) and poor (third) worlds also did relatively well, albeit from much lower starting points. Table 7.1 shows that Asia, other than Japan, in aggregate, did even better after 1973. Everywhere else grew faster between 1950 and 1973 than at any other time. Even Africa's economy, which grew more slowly than others, expanded more quickly than anywhere else had ever done before. Capitalist society remained exploitative and unequal, with huge differences between North and South and within countries, not least between men and women and between white and non-white populations, and the period also witnessed dramatic struggles against these inequalities. Nevertheless, in its own terms, the system appeared to be working remarkably well.

The boom needs to be understood (like the depression before it) in terms of the specific conjuncture between domestic and international social relations. This chapter emphasises three elements of these. Firstly, it describes changed social relations between labour, the state and capital within rich countries. Secondly, it briefly considers the cold war between East and West,

Table 7.1 Rate of growth of GDP per capita for selected world regions and countries 1820–2001 (per cent)

	1820–70	1870–1913	1913–50	1950–73	1973–2001
Western Europe	0.98	1.33	0.76	4.05	1.88
Eastern Europe	0.63	1.39	0.60	3.81	0.68
USA	1.34	1.82	1.61	2.45	1.86
Latin America	−0.03	1.82	1.43	2.58	0.91
Japan	0.19	1.48	0.88	8.06	2.14
Rest of Asia	−0.10	0.42	−0.10	2.91	3.55
Africa	0.35	0.57	0.92	2.00	0.19
World	0.54	1.30	0.88	2.92	1.41

Source: Maddison 2003

which produced unprecedented levels of peacetime arms spending. Thirdly, it discusses the increased power of the United States relative to its allies, which created new patterns of accumulation. However, there were tensions in each of these relations, which contributed to the boom unravelling in the 1970s. Discussion of these provides the background to the crisis of the 1970s. The resolution of this crisis had lasting implications, many of which are analysed later in this book.

The Post-War Settlement

The war had brought death and destruction on an unprecedented industrial scale. Something like 55 million had died in the fighting, bombing and mass extermination. At the war's end, amongst the capitalist countries Japan was probably in the worst condition (Takemae 2003) but in Western Europe large swathes of infrastructure were destroyed, there was a housing shortage estimated at 16 million, diseases like tuberculosis became epidemic and millions became refugees. Much of the economy failed. The United States suffered least, but a quarter of a million Americans were dead and demobilising 12 million servicemen raised the prospects of a return to pre-war mass unemployment. Schumpeter commented at the time: 'The all but general opinion seems to be that capitalist methods will be unequal to the task of reconstruction' (cited in Armstrong et al. 1984:23). Capitalism not only survived, but apparently did better than ever before. However, it was a reformed capitalism, unlike that before the war.

Workers' struggles within capitalism, as Luxemburg (1989) described, are ever a labour of Sisyphus, and many of labour's gains were being undermined almost as soon as they were achieved. However, the post-war period introduced significant and widespread changes. In the United States, the radicalism and workers' militancy of the 1930s continued into the war despite an official ban on strikes and opposition from union leaders. A further 4 million joined unions, bringing the total to 14 million. Real earnings increased 19 per cent between 1941 and 1944. These gains were threatened after the war, but effectively defended, through a total of 116 million strike days in 1946 (Armstrong et al. 1984). Confounding expectations, from 1947 economic growth returned, with even demobilisation having little impact on employment levels. The US ruling class avoided open confrontation with organised labour, but channelled militancy into safe economic demands, ceding pay rises in return for commitments to increased productivity and, with Ford setting the pattern, winning for management the unchallenged right to hire and fire. When, in 1950, General Motors cut a deal with the United Auto Workers, it was suggested that 'GM may have paid a billion for peace but it got a bargain' (Bell, cited in Nelson 1996). Such deals allowed a return to the bureaucratic business unionism challenged by the early Congress of Industrial Organizations. Labour leaders could be feted, while the cold war provided a rationale for attacking 'communists' and militants. In 1947, the Taft–Hartley Act banned closed shops and secondary action and gave presidential powers to postpone strikes. Some unions and locals held out longer than others against the anti-communist witch-hunts of McCarthyism, but post-war trade unionism would be of a conservative, cooperative hue. The employers' strategy was successful to the extent that union density, which in Europe would continue to climb until the 1970s, began its downward slide from around mid-century. Labour remained at most a junior partner in any 'tripartite' system or 'post-war consensus'. Many, especially black and southern workers, fared badly. However, millions did win unprecedentedly high pay.

The post-war settlement varied between countries, but in most places involved a class compromise more favourable to labour than previously. Again, this was typically won by a high level of labour radicalism, expressed for example in worker militancy in Japan, the first majority Labour government in Britain and the rise of communism in France and Italy. However, as *The Economist* reported in December 1945, across Europe 'demands for nationalization of banks and large industries ... bore the signatures of Christian Democrats as well as of Socialists and Communists' (cited in Armstrong et al. 1984). Such generalised demands for change produced a widespread recognition amongst the ruling class that social peace had to be bought (Kidron 1970; Went 2000). Local autonomy was much more constrained in the defeated, occupied countries. However, in Germany, amongst other things, workers won various rights, including representation on company boards or 'co-determination'. In Japan, early militancy was repressed and, after some bitter strikes, a cooperative company-based unionism won out. Nevertheless, relatively favourable labour laws endured. Although the immediate threats of radical transformation receded, a class stand-off could continue as long as economic prosperity remained.

The post-war social settlement crucially also saw increased state economic intervention (see Table 7.2). The post-war boom has often been characterised as Keynesian. This may be somewhat misleading, in that where Keynes envisaged specific, counter-cyclical interventions, explicit policy more often attempted to slow than to stimulate growth (Harman 1984; Maddison 1991). Western capitalism did well without much conscious intervention. Maddison (1991) also suggests that Keynes's ideas gained little direct influence on policy outside the UK and Scandinavia. German governments, at least until 1967, remained committed to price stability, competition and work incentives rather than to maintaining demand or full employment. The US Full Employment Act of 1946 expressed a commitment to full resource utilisation, but based on faith in free enterprise – and in practice 'full' employment would be interpreted very loosely.

Table 7.2 State spending of selected countries (percentage of GDP) 1900–70

	France	Germany	UK	USA
1900	15.2	14.2	14.9	7.9
1930	22.1	29.4	24.7	21.3
1950	28.4	30.8	30.4	23.0
1970	38.9	37.6	39.3	32.2

Source: McGrew 1992

Increased state spending and redistribution may have worked more as products of the specific conjuncture of social struggles and pragmatic compromise than of conscious strategy. Forms of state intervention varied widely in quantity and content.

There may however be important respects in which much of this could be regarded as Keynesian, and some forms of spending had what might be considered Keynesian characteristics. Spending on schools and hospitals, for example, was unlikely to be subject to the rapid fluctuations of demand characteristic of the commodity economy and therefore tended to be stabilising. Higher wages and a more equal income distribution also plausibly played a significant role in remedying problems that Keynes had identified in the pre-war economy. Brenner (1998) also suggests that if investors believed that counter-cyclical measures would be applied if necessary, this could have positive effects on capitalist confidence and the desired effect of stimulating activity without actual intervention. However, when the boom ended, more specifically reflationary methods proved unsuccessful, and the consensus broke down as capital tried new strategies.

The ideas of a regulated capitalism and of 'compromise' between capital, labour and the state were developed by accounts that characterised the boom as 'Fordist'. Originating in France in the 1970s, the earliest Regulation School contributions were explicitly Marxist (Aglietta 1987) but Fordism is often something of a Marx–Keynes hybrid – with characteristics of the different parents showing more or less clearly in the different offspring. Broadly comparable ideas were articulated in the United States in terms of Social Structures of Accumulation (for example, Gordon 1978; Kotz et al. 1994). The basic idea of these approaches was that capitalism succeeded because of the way in which it was embedded in particular institutional arrangements.

Fordism is a somewhat slippery concept. It derives in the first place from Henry Ford and the practices of Ford Motor Company, but often too from Gramsci's writings on these from the 1930s. Ford is famous for introducing moving assembly lines into his car factories and mass-producing a standardised product with standardised parts. Ford thereby cut the costs of production. In an era of high inflation, the price of a Model T fell from $950 in 1910 to $360 in 1917 and $290 in 1924 (Rubenstein 1992). In 1914 Ford also introduced the $5 day for (some of) his workers. This succeeded in cutting very rapid rates of labour turnover and high absenteeism, themselves products of the horrible conditions of assembly line work. It also kept out unions like the militant Industrial Workers of the World (IWW), which had begun organising other car plants (Raff 1988). Ford also put a significant spin on this:

> The time will not be far when our very own workers will buy automobiles from us ... I'm not saying they'll sing Caruso or govern the state. No, we can leave such ravings to the European socialists. But they will buy automobiles. (cited in Wolf 1996:72)

The falling prices and rising wages indeed made it possible for workers to buy cars. Of course, Ford's rhetoric notwithstanding, his own employees could not sustain sufficient demand for his rapidly increasing output. Meanwhile, the $5 day succeeded precisely because it was unusual. Workers stayed with Ford because wages were high, roughly double those available elsewhere. This contradiction becomes clear after 1929, by which time wages had risen to $7 a day. Recession meant falling demand, mass lay-offs and, with workers desperate for any job, pay cuts to $4 and then $3 a day (Rubenstein 1992). Models of post-war Fordism seldom discuss Ford's anti-Semitism and fascist sympathies, but do sometimes take something from his 'paternalism'. Unlike earlier pioneers of labour discipline like Fredrick Taylor, Ford was concerned with his workers' general lifestyle and values. His sociology department spied on employees, to keep out drunks, adulterers and reds. Again in the 1930s, at least the last of these proved unsuccessful and after some bloody battles in 1941 Ford Motor Company was finally unionised.

Harvey describes Fordism as becoming 'a total way of life' (1990:135) in the post-war period. However, it seems debatable how much of the original Ford there was in this. The period was characterised by increasingly efficient mass production tied to mass consumption in which workers themselves provided the demand for an increasing range of products. The war may have created a period of what Schumpeter (1954) called 'creative destruction', as furious war-time and subsequent reconstruction activity replaced old with the newest capital. Increasing economies of scale in production now meant cheaper goods, increasing the scope of consumption and allowing further economies of scale. The process was deepened as high wages spurred the search for labour-saving investments, which raised productivity. As with Ford, these mass-produced standardised products increased material welfare, but involved a certain drab conformity and routinisation in production and consumption.

For more overtly Marxist interpretations, specific increases in productivity in consumption industries like cars allowed an increase in real living standards at the same time as a relative fall in variable capital. Therefore rates of profit could be maintained or increased despite rising capital expenditures (Aglietta 1987). The theory of the tendency of the rate of profit to fall (TRPF) (Marx 1981) is controversial even amongst Marxists. While the technical composition of capital tends to rise – the machines get ever more sophisticated – this is offset by various countervailing tendencies. In particular, the whole point of using increasingly sophisticated machines is to raise productivity. This means that real wages can rise while variable capital falls. Similarly, in value terms constant capital can fall even as its physical content increases. The 'law' is therefore better read in terms of the tensions created by the changing composition of capital. In particular, productivity rises occur unevenly. Empirically, in most major economies productivity did rise more quickly than capital was added (see Table 7.3). It also rose particularly quickly in consumer goods sectors like cars (and in agriculture). However, it increased considerably more slowly in construction, provider of the other classic Fordist consumption commodity, standardised housing (Lipietz 1985).

Table 7.3 Annual growth of major economies 1950–73 (per cent)

	France	*Germany*	*Japan*	*UK*	*USA*
GDP per capita	4.0	5.0	8.1	2.4	2.5
Labour productivity					
Primary	5.9	6.3	7.3	4.6	5.4
Secondary	5.2	5.6	9.5	2.9	2.9
Tertiary	3.0	2.8	4.0	2.0	1.4
Non-residential capital per employee	4.8	5.5	7.3	4.6	1.7

Sources: Maddison 1991, 2003

However, theories of Fordism were never simply about an economic law, but, diverging further from the original prototype, also relied on Keynesian-like notions of the importance of state intervention in securing demand. The virtuous cycle of production and consumption was now underwritten by more or less explicit bargains protecting consumption norms. Relatively high wages and more generous social welfare provisions maintained consumption levels, avoiding the cycle of decline of the 1930s. As the term 'regulation' implies, nor was this seen as simply a fortunate economic conjuncture, but one which involved effective political and social institutionalisation.

The approach is attractive, although it is sometimes unclear where it sits on a spectrum between economic theory and sociological description (Kotz 1994). Perhaps more damaging, Fordism only makes sense at the level of the whole economy (Boyer 1990). Yet the initial focus was explicitly on the national

(US) level (Aglietta 1987). The whole economy is necessarily global, and other national economies did well, sometimes better than the United States, with significantly different levels of consumption and structures of regulation and accumulation. What went right, and what then went wrong, would appear to have been systemic.

The Cold War and the Arms Economy

Post-war international relations were substantially changed from the inter-war period. The United States had a particularly good war. Its death toll was slight compared with the other major combatants. It expanded economically and emerged as the over-whelmingly dominant power. Its GDP accounted for about half that of the Western capitalist world. The immediate post-war figures slightly exaggerate the weakness of war-damaged Europe and Japan, but even in 1950 the United States represented about 45 per cent of the Western and 27 per cent of world GDP. The USSR had suffered about 20 million casualties and economically did not regain its 1939 levels until 1949 (Maddison 2003). It nevertheless became the great military rival and the cold war saw uniquely high levels of peacetime arms spending. US military costs, which had not risen above 2 per cent of GDP until 1940, never dropped below 7 per cent during the 1950s and 1960s. The USSR spent at least comparable amounts (Census 1980). Britain and France too devoted high proportions of their income to the military.

It seems reasonable to presume that such high levels of military spending had significant economic implications. Most obviously it was a cost – waste spending ultimately consumed destructively or in obsolescence. However, where Keynes thought it would be better to 'build houses and the like' (1973:129) rather than to fill old bottles with banknotes, some Marxists believed that from the capitalist point of view 'war expenditures accomplish the same purpose as public works, but in a manner that is decidedly more effective and more acceptable' (Vance 1951:12). Arms expenditures had a number of advantages; they did not compete with private capital and did not require higher wages (Cliff 1957). The cold war also provided a compelling competitive logic and political rationale that welfare spending lacked. For Baran and Sweezy (1966) the military budgets overcame tendencies towards 'under-consumption' and meant job security and material well-being for most Americans, who therefore rationally supported them. However, like more explicitly Keynesian theories, this would fail to account for the slide into recession despite continued spending (and increasing wage shares of income).

Later versions of the Permanent Arms Economy by Kidron (1974) and Harman (1984) argued instead that the crucial feature of military spending was its capacity to divert resources from productive investment. Less was available for reinvestments, reducing tendencies to increase spending on constant capital. This offset the tendencies of organic composition of capital to rise and of the rate of profit to fall – which would nonetheless be expected to reassert themselves eventually. The theory depends on a conception of capitalism as a global system (places without high levels of arms spending in fact tended to grow more quickly). However, the counter-tendency can be read as operating against a rather mechanical reading of the law of TRPF. It would seem necessary at least to integrate a discussion of the role of arms spending with other potentially offsetting tendencies, including, for example, the differentiated effects on the value of labour power and constant capital identified by theories of Fordism. Empirically, the economic effects of arms spending remain controversial (Chester 1978; Dunne 1990). Intuitively, a connection between the unprecedented levels of arms spending and the unprecedented boom seems plausible. As discussed below, it also begins to connect the fate of countries which prospered under the cold-war umbrella, but did not spend on arms, with the difficulties that developed both in the United States and wider Western societies. However, it leaves questions of just how the process might have worked at a more concrete level, for example between countries and sectors of the economy. The social settlements and levels of state spending, including military spending, were very different between countries and correlate poorly with overall performance.

The cold war also redivided the world, most obviously between East and West, but also between the rich Western or Northern world and the South. The United States passively supported the process of decolonisation, providing the new states disavowed communism. US economic superiority meant that the United States had no need of formal empire, while the old empires could potentially have been closed to the United States. Many newly independent countries were opened to business, and US military or covert operations to keep them open (while hardly unusual) were something of a last resort. In 1960/1, 42 per cent of US exports and 54 per cent of its foreign investment were directed towards poorer countries, most of the latter in manufacturing, mining and oil (Hummels and Stern 1994). The links with, and exploitation of, the periphery may have been qualitatively vital to the success of the core (Magdoff 1969; Wallerstein 1974). They provided many necessary resources, particularly oil, but also minerals which richer countries lacked. However, quantitatively international trade and investment became increasingly concentrated amongst the rich countries.

International Finance, Investment and Trade

The post-war settlement changed relations between the Western capitalist states. As the war came to an end, the leaders of the United States, the USSR and the UK had divided Europe, sometimes with remarkable cynicism. Germany and Japan remained occupied countries, with serious discussion in the United States of 'pastoralising' the former. However, more outward-looking elements of the US ruling class won out, and major conferences held within, and dominated by, the United States established the bases for a more internationalist post-war order. The IMF and World Bank were established at Bretton Woods in New Hampshire in July 1944, the United Nations at San Francisco in June 1945. Significantly, financial interests in the City of London supported the Bretton Woods deal (Helleiner 1993) and Britain was an important junior partner, albeit now more than ever heavily indebted and subordinate to the United

States (Hudson 2003). Voting at the IMF and World Bank would be by financial contribution, at the time giving the United States alone an effective veto. Bretton Woods also gave its name to the post-war financial system of stable currencies based on pegs to the dollar. The IMF fixed currency values against the US dollar, itself fixed at one thirty-fifth of an ounce of gold. Currency pegs were adjustable, but only with IMF (and therefore US) agreement. With IMF approval, most countries also implemented currency controls to limit financial movements and prevent speculation.

The Bretton Woods financial system appeared to avoid the twin failures of the inter-war years. The gold-dollar standard seemed simultaneously to achieve two crucial functions of money; those of store of value and means of circulation (see Chapter 10). Dollar holdings could be trusted to be 'as good as gold'. At the same time, however, the United States could put more dollars into circulation, providing adequate liquidity as the scale of economic activity increased. A pure gold standard, which stores value effectively, would have been deflationary, as it had been in the inter-war period, unable to provide the bullion to match the increasing scale of international economic activity. Financial stability in turn enabled increasing trade openness. For many commentators, US 'hegemony' thus secured international capitalist prosperity (Kindleberger 1973; Gilpin 2001). The Bretton Woods arrangements coincided with the long boom, which ended shortly after the system was abandoned.

However, the post-war practice diverged from the original plans. Amongst other things, the money available to the IMF and World Bank was insufficient to perform the sort of tasks Keynes, in particular, had envisaged for them at Bretton Woods. Instead, in the context of an emerging cold war, the United States directly financed European recovery through Marshall Aid. The cold war turned the political climate both at home and in Europe, making US internationalism more acceptable. Aid helped create the trade openness, providing the dollars to countries wanting to buy from the United States, but with little to sell. US firms could also offset the post-war trade imbalance by purchasing assets within other countries. Thus US FDI increased as multinationals established a substantial overseas presence. Initially, the largest amounts went to Canada, which accounted for 23.9 per cent of the world's stocks in 1960, while Europe received 22.9 per cent (two-fifths of which went to Britain). Gradually, Europe became more important as an investment location and by 1973 the respective figures were 16.8 and 36.5 per cent. Some of these investments, like that of the car firms in Europe, pre-date this period. There was also substantial reverse investment within the United States and by British and French firms within their respective empires. But US FDI increased, representing 47 per cent of the world total in 1960. It subsequently fell as a proportion of the total as European and Japanese investment increased, but continued to grow in absolute terms (Hummels and Stern 1994; Held et al. 1999) (see Table 7.4).

Table 7.4   FDI stocks in the Golden Age (2005 dollars)

	1960		1975	
	Level ($b)	*Level/GDP (%)*	*Level ($m)*	*Level/GDP (%)*
France	5.0	1.0	12.9	1.2
Germany	1.0	0.1	22.4	1.8
Japan	0.6	0.1	19.3	1.0
UK	15.1	2.2	45.0	4.5
US	38.8	1.3	151.1	2.9
World	82.4	0.7	343.1	1.4

Sources: calculated from Held et al. 1999; Maddison 2003; Heston et al. 2002

As will be discussed in more detail in Chapter 9, for many liberals increasing trade is crucial to prosperity, and therefore to explaining the long boom. In brief, trade allows specialisation, and a more efficient division of labour. This in turn augurs economies of scale, greater efficiency through increased competition in domestic markets and greater consumer choice. Empirically, there is a reasonable correspondence between periods of increasing trade and those of increasing wealth, and certainly the increasing openness of the post-war period contrasts favourably with the miserable descent into protectionism of the 1930s.

The United States was a late convert to trade openness and, in 1947, rejected a proposed International Trade Organisation. Nationally oriented producers were initially reluctant to abandon the isolationist stance of the inter-war period. However, such was its economic lead that US capital had little to fear from international competition and much to gain from increasing markets. International bargaining reduced barriers and technical improvements reduced transport costs. Trade increased at an average of 6 per cent a year from 1950 to 1970 (wto.org 2006) (see Table 7.5).

Table 7.5   Trade/GDP ratio in leading economies 1950–75

	World	France	Germany	Japan	UK	USA
1950	6	7	5	3	10	4
1955	7	9	9	4	10	4
1960	7	9	11	5	10	4
1965	7	9	13	6	11	4
1970	8	10	16	10	11	5
1975	13	18	26	13	15	7

Sources: Maddison 2003; Heston et al. 2002; WTO 2007

Often closely associated with arguments for free trade, the long boom has also often been explained in terms of hegemonic stability. The basic idea is that a leading power bears the costs of providing the 'public good' of openness. It imposes this on what would otherwise have been uncooperative lesser countries. In the nineteenth and early twentieth centuries, Britain provided such leadership and brought free trade and prosperity to the world. With Britain's decline – and US unwillingness to take on the mantle – the world descended into war and depression (Kindleberger 1973). However, after the Second World War the United States finally established its hegemony and global prosperity, though its subsequent relative decline gave cause for concern.

The theory is criticised at several levels. Theoretically, its premises about competitive individualism and the difficulties of state cooperation are questionable (Snidal 1985; Gills 1993). It is historically dubious, particularly in relation to Britain. Politically, it has an unmissably apologetic air. As Higgot (1991) suggests, there is a normative bias in characterising the United States as provider of public goods. Nevertheless, it does appear plausible that the US-imposed order contributed to stability and growth (Lake 2000).

However, the specific role of trade is particularly doubtful. While comparative advantage has a compelling logical consistency it represents at best a static idealisation (Dunkley 2004; Deranyiagala 2005). Empirically, trade rose slowly and from a low base. Particularly for the United States, it represented a small fraction of total output. Of the leading countries, the most open, Britain, did worst. Trade seems to have played a relatively minor part in establishing the long boom, though it was more important for some than others. This became part of the problem.

Contradictions of the Boom

The most obvious relative change in the post-war period was the rise of Japan and Germany. Both became major net exporters. In part, their rise might be seen as an almost natural process of 'catch up'. The United States was furthest ahead and had difficulty sustaining its lead (Brenner 2003). Amongst other things, productivity gains are harder to achieve in services, which increase as countries 'mature', than in industry. Meanwhile, the chasing pack could take advantage of innovations made elsewhere. However, increasing capital intensity is costly and processes of technology transfer are difficult, requiring appropriate institutional supports. Amongst other things, new technologies need both engineers and well-engineered components to work properly. Most follower countries have remained poor. 'Catch up' therefore still has to be explained (Brenner 1998).

Arms spending and the lack of it may also have contributed significantly. Some military spending in the United States had important feedback effects into the civilian economy, notably in what would become leading high-tech sectors like microelectronics. However it seems reasonable to presume that a higher proportion of military investment was unproductive. In the defeated countries, precluded from comparable levels of arms spending, more of their surpluses could be saved and reinvested in productive industry. Japanese non-military R&D expenditures, in particular, outstripped those elsewhere (Archibugi and Michie 1997). The significance of military spending as a drain on the civilian economy would appear to be confirmed by the steeper relative decline of the USSR, which, because its economy was smaller, had to spend a relatively higher proportion on the military to keep pace in the arms race (Castells 1997). Table 7.3 shows the lower rates of capital accumulation and of growth in the United States compared to Japan and Germany. However, it indicates that rates of capital accumulation were almost as high in France and Britain, which also maintained substantial militaries. France also grew quickly, Britain slowest of the leading economies. Intuitively, the idea of military spending as a drain is plausible, but it is not the whole story.

Success has therefore alternatively been attributed to a different and more effective 'model' of capitalism (Hutton 1995; Coates 2000). Rather than relying on a passive comparative advantage, both Japan and Germany adopted 'high-road' development strategies, in particular utilising labour that was initially relatively low wage, but not low skilled. The differences between the Japanese state-led strategies and German 'corporatism' were considerable, but both contrasted with the more laissez faire American model. Capital controls also allowed profits to be kept at home rather than chasing richer financial markets (Brenner 2003). The implementation of successful development strategies depends on mobilising resources and is not necessarily separable from features like arms spending. For example, this may have contributed to higher net savings rates, which in Germany and Japan were 28.7 and 33.3 per cent of GDP respectively in 1965, compared with only 19.6 and 21.1 per cent in the United States and the United Kingdom (Heston et al. 2002). There would also appear to have been specific institutional features of capital accumulation in Japan, Germany and France which were more successful. Amongst these, continental European firms may have benefited from the combination of state support of national champions and the wider market provided by the European Economic Community.

Initially, relatively low wages in Japan and Germany limited the internal market, making exports correspondingly more significant. Both adopted relatively restrictive macroeconomic policies at home, while selling into expanding markets elsewhere in the world. For Germany, trade seems particularly important, with surpluses growing and the share of its manufactured goods which were exported rising from 8.3 to 24.2 per cent between 1950 and 1974. At the end of this period, exports accounted for over 40 per cent of crucial goods like cars and machines (Brenner 1998). However, Japan approached British levels of per capita wealth while still trading less and it was not until the 1980s that its trade surpluses represented anything close to 1 per cent of its GDP (see Figure 7.1). The trade position of both countries improved, even as wages rose. Productivity rises were converted into cheaper exports by the Bretton Woods fixed exchange rate system.

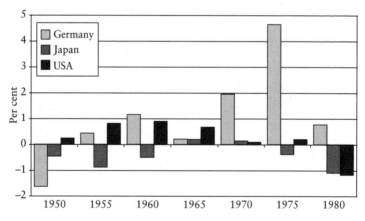

Figure 7.1   Trade balances as a percentage of GDP, 1950–80
Sources: calculated from Maddison 1991, 2003; WTO 2007

Both German and Japanese exports were thus helped by the Bretton Woods system, but in turn helped to undermine that system. The financial mechanism was only gradually adopted in the envisaged form with major currencies only becoming fully convertible in the late 1950s and early 1960s. By then significant tensions were already becoming apparent. As early as 1961, Triffin identified the dilemma that as the quantity of dollars in circulation grew to exceed US gold reserves, their ability to act as a store of value was undermined (Cohn 2005). The US right to issue dollars in excess of its gold reserves gave it privileges of 'seigniorage'. The United States could spend more, in foreign direct investments, in overseas military operations and in foreign aid (also often a vital policy tool) (Hayter 1971; Spero 1982) than earned through any positive trade balance. So long as paper dollars were accepted as international reserves they remained, from the US perspective, like so many uncashed cheques and accordingly represented no drain. As others closed the gap, the US trade surplus shrank. Notably, by the mid 1960s, Germany and Japan established what would become rapidly growing surpluses with the United States (Brenner 1998). With their currencies pegged to the dollar, their exports became cheaper and more attractive. Overall, US trade remained in surplus until 1971, but with its other expenses the balance of payments turned negative in 1960 and rapidly grew. The United States applied some pressure for revaluations, but with only limited success.

The situation was exacerbated by the growth of what were called 'Eurodollar markets'. Encouraged by UK authorities and at least permitted by the United States, American corporations operating in Europe in particular made dollar deposits in London banks. These could earn higher returns and enjoy looser regulation than in the United States. In 1960 there were 3 billion Eurodollars, by 1970, 75 billion (Cerny 1993; O'Brien and Williams 2004). As the quantity of circulating dollars increased beyond US reserves, the tensions grew. There is no predetermined level of acceptable reserves (commercial banks operate with much higher leverage) but trust that paper dollars could be redeemed for gold diminished. Eurodollars could not be cashed in with the Federal Reserve, but they could buy gold on the open market, where they commanded less than a thirty-fifth of an ounce. The market and official price of gold parted company. Something had to give.

Germany had already allowed the DM to float upwards in May 1971, and on 15 August that year Nixon suspended dollar convertibility, also introducing tariffs pending a devaluation. Often read as a response to US decline, this was also 'part of a domestic political game' (Gill and Law 1988:173) and an appeal ahead of the following year's election to nationalist domestic sentiments, threatened by foreign competition. The abandonment of gold has alternatively been interpreted as an effective strategy for the US capital in relation to its competitors (Gowan 1999; Hudson 2003). Other states still held dollars as a reserve currency, giving the United States the same privileges of seigniorage without the burden of supporting it with gold. Nixon also introduced an immediate 10 per cent surcharge on imports pending devaluation, which was agreed in December. The dollar fell 17 per cent against the yen, 12 per cent against the DM. For a couple of years the IMF attempted to revive the Bretton Woods system based on a currency pool or special drawing rights, but by 1973 this was abandoned and an era of floating exchange rates began, in which, nominally at least, markets would decide currency values.

The Crisis and the Unravelling of the Social Consensus

By the late 1960s, social theorists began to imagine that the contradictions of capitalism had been resolved or at least displaced to the political level (Habermas 1976). The political struggles were indeed sharp, but at least in part reflected the economic difficulties. The economic complacency and social consensus was sharply refuted by the crisis of the early 1970s and the prolonged period of slower and interrupted growth that would follow it.

Predictably, the causes of the crisis remain controversial. There are always incidental and accidental elements, and the particular timing and nature of the financial crisis had its own specific momentum. That it should produce a severe and prolonged economic downturn reflected deeper problems. Disequilibria between the major economies produced by the inflexible foreign exchange system were an important proximate cause, but the advent of flexible exchange rates did nothing to alleviate this.

Somewhat similarly, it has been conventional to blame the crisis on the rise in oil prices orchestrated by OPEC. Too much is probably made of this. It cannot explain the earlier slowdown or the onset of recession, which also preceded the price rises. Galbraith (1995) argues, against the perceived wisdom, that the net effect was counter-inflationary, withdrawing money from the system. This, however, may plausibly have then contributed to the subsequent downturn. Oil and food prices, the latter rising steeply even before the oil shock, may also have reflected growing structural imbalances within the system. Food and raw materials prices had fallen steadily between 1951 and 1971 compared with those of manufactured goods (Allen 2005). Now a slight cut in production achieved big price rises, showing how inelastic demand for oil, in particular, had become.

There were also political elements, with oil price rises organised in the aftermath of the Arab countries' defeat in the Yom Kippur war of October 1973. Others have detected US involvement in the OPEC decisions, and certainly its competitors, who were more dependent on oil imports, suffered more (Gowan 1999). Attempts to form cartels among other commodity-exporting countries were notably less successful. North–South relations contributed to the US difficulties in the more obvious form of the enduring expense of the Vietnam War. The long-term drain on resources contributed to the relative lack of dynamism of US capital. In ways that are impossible to quantify, resistance in Vietnam also spurred the social movements within the United States and other rich countries.

Armstrong et al. (1984) attribute the crisis to a profit squeeze and workers' militancy. While the militancy was real, their own figures for the United States suggest that after 1966 it achieved no more than maintaining the 2.2 per cent annual real-wage rises of the previous period. Greater militancy was required simply to sustain what had become the norm.

There would appear to be a more deep-rooted problem of declining productivity. To some extent the virtues of the post-war system appear to have turned into its vices. High levels of state spending helped sustain workers' consumption norms, and improvements in welfare may have contributed to producing labour power of higher value (Harman 1984). However, increasing state spending in many areas may have taken on increasingly unproductive forms from the point of view of capitalist reproduction (Moseley 1999). At least in the short term, the higher taxes needed to pay for it ate into corporate profits. Probably more fundamentally, there were limits to the virtuous cycle of productivity rises and real-wage increases that could be achieved through Fordist expansion. There may have been a technical aspect to this, as processes of cheapening consumption goods through what has been called the 'electro-mechanical technological path' (Atkinson 2006) slowed down once these technologies had become widely diffused. More significantly, there was an economic problem in that the large corporations were now too big to fail; so there was no creative destruction short of major crisis (Harman 2007). In the United States, productivity rises slowed from 3.0 per cent a year between 1960 and 1966 to 1.3 per cent between 1966 and 1973. In other rich countries the change was less and from a higher base, but in the same direction (Armstrong et al. 1984). This meant a declining propensity to invest and an increasing need for each national capital to find markets elsewhere. Thus there was systemic over-production, manifested in intensified international competition (Brenner 1998, 2003).

The crisis, literally a turning point, was sharp, but its resolution involved protracted struggles. Already in the 1960s, governments and employers' associations were attempting to claw back many of the concessions of the immediate post-war period. By the next decade, labour had suffered severe defeats. Eventually, there was also a degree of economic recovery, but no apparent prospect of return to the stability or the level of growth of the long boom.

Conclusion

The Second World War was an unprecedented human catastrophe. It radically changed the global political economy, with mobilisation for war finally producing the creative destruction that overcame the failures of the 'free-market' economy of the Great Depression.

Post-war reconstruction continued to be state led, both within national economies and through US economic and political dominance of the Western capitalist world. There were significant policy shifts as labour forced capital into a more favourable social settlement. This in turn increased working-class consumption and allowed – or forced – capital to expand in depth within rich countries. US capital in particular also increased its geographical scope, within its traditional sphere of influence in the Americas, but also beyond as the share of its investments in Europe and Asia rose (Hummels and Stern 1994). Along with higher arms spending compared with its allies, these capital outflows may have been stabilising for the capitalist system, but also contributed to rates of growth that were lower for the United States than for its competitors. The United States remained overwhelmingly the richest and most powerful country throughout this period, but its relative position declined, and this would undermine key elements of the system.

The financial regime provided stability, but also locked in exchange rates, so that Japanese and German growth produced trade disequilibria. Import competition contributed to declining profitability within the United States, as gains from the Fordist expansions of scope began to be exhausted and the giant firms that made it possible prevented 'normal' processes of restructuring. The apparent stability also masked widening gaps between rich and poor countries. Many former colonies won independence, but remained poor with little sign of 'catch up'. In as far as they were integrated into the global economy it was largely as suppliers of primary products. The problems this implied and with 'development' more generally will be discussed in Chapter 14. The concomitant relative lack of innovation in the supply of key commodities, particularly oil, also contributed to bottlenecks and the crisis of the early 1970s. The social consensus was also an unstable one, predicated on economic expansion, undermined when that expansion faltered, but also then exacerbating the economic tensions. The long boom achieved a remarkable success for a uniquely 'regulated' form of capitalism, but contained internal contradictions and ultimately proved unsustainable.

Part III

Structures, Issues and Agents

8

PRODUCTION

The terms 'global' and 'globalisation' can be used to convey a range of concepts. They can characterise a novel world where places, distances and borders become irrelevant (Scholte 2000). Alternatively, 'global' is used here to mean 'all-encompassing'. In this sense it includes both that which crosses borders and the localised. It allows an evaluation of the specifically border-crossing dimensions relative to the overall accumulation process. Increasing movements contribute to capital's dynamic and differentiated nature, but, it will be argued, there has been much overstatement of contemporary production's mobility. Capital is simultaneously mobilised and immobilised, both by its internal logic and by social and political pressures.

The first section discusses the general nature of capitalist production and its contradictions, including its capacity for movement. It provides a brief historical contextualisation, referring to foreign investment in the periods discussed in the previous chapters. The subsequent sections describe the recent period in more detail, firstly giving an indication of the scale and scope of Foreign Direct Investment (FDI), then showing its contemporary unevenness and finally arguing that FDI tends to follow growth rather than cause it. The evidence does not support characterisations of a runaway world of manufacturing relocation from rich to poorer countries. Most industry remains concentrated in rich ones, while most FDI since the late 1990s, in particular, has been concentrated in service sectors. Nevertheless, international dimensions of production have become increasingly important, introducing new tensions to the overall pattern of accumulation and competition.

Capital's Contradictory Expansion

Globalisation has become fashionable. However, capitalism has always tended both to grow in depth, to increase the scale of production, and to expand geographically. In both respects there are internal contradictions. There are also tensions between the two processes. This section briefly and schematically characterises elements of these interrelations. It draws on, but condenses and inevitably simplifies, lengthy arguments made by Marx (1973a, 1976, 1978a, 1981) and other Marxists (see, for example, Fine and Harris 1979; Harvey 1982; Clarke 1994; Storper and Walker 1989). It notes how the forms and degree of capital's nationalisation and internationalisation varied over time. The following sections will consider contemporary evidence in more detail.

Marx and Engels (1965) described how capitalism expands with a hitherto unimagined dynamism. Relentless accumulation comes with many complications. It creates new polarisations of wealth and poverty. It is often interrupted by profound crises. It can destroy communities and the environment. Nevertheless, capital's accumulation creates unprecedented material abundance.

Expanding across borders merely extends capital's logic of accumulation (Dicken 2003). As Holloway (1995a) insisted, 'capital moves'. It is in its nature to do so. It expands and relocates within nation states. It also moves across borders, and has done so on a significant scale at least since the nineteenth century. It seeks out new sources of labour power and raw materials and new markets for its products. This too undermines previous social relations. However, profits are made in situ rather than in transit, so movement is endemic to capitalism – but as means not end. Capital always relies on at least temporary immobilisation, the exploitation of labour in particular places (Holloway 1994, 1995a).

Capitalism effects two separations, of production from consumption and of economics from politics. (Discussion of a third, no less important separation of people from nature is deferred until Chapter 12.) Both separations contribute to its remarkable dynamism, but also introduce tension and potential dislocations. The separation of production and consumption makes possible the pursuit of limitless accumulation, but also makes crisis a constant possibility. Capitalism achieves a remarkable coordination of complex webs of supply and demand. However, the circuit whereby money is spent on commodities and labour power, which are combined in a production process to produce more commodities, which are sold for more money, is complex and potentially fragile. Even leaving aside problems of raising and repaying credit, at each successive stage there are potential disruptions and loss of value (Bryan 2003). Firstly, the exploitative relationship is contested. If workers win higher wages or shorter hours, or lessen the intensity of production, the share of profit falls. Conversely, low wages, while sought by each individual capitalist can, if generalised create collective problems of under-consumption. Other capitalists also provide demand, but the unplanned nature of production and the need to 'dispose' of ever larger surpluses means that proportionate production of both use and exchange values between sectors of the economy is constantly jeopardised (Marx 1978a; Fine 2003). The continual imperative to invest increases productivity, but this also tends to upset any momentary balance between production and consumption or even between any particular industries (Marx 1981; Clarke 1992). Accumulation also tends to make firms larger, so the system becomes more 'lumpy', further from the liberal ideal of competitive individuals. Adjustments reconnecting production and consumption become potentially more traumatic, and 'consonance may be reached only by passing through the most extreme dissonance' (Marx 1973a:148).

The second separation of economics from politics makes the operation of capital and the market at least relatively autonomous. Economic and political power need not immediately coincide, as they do in other societies. Economics has its own distinct rationale, and capital is not dependent on any particular political power. It has freedom to move across borders, without undermining them, in a way that would have been unthinkable in previous societies (Rosenberg 2006). It is only ever conditionally national (Harris 1981). Again, however, the separation is not absolute. States both rely on effective capital accumulation within their borders and repeatedly intervene to support capital from challenges within or without. Capital also needs particular social conditions, including state support, for its reproduction. This is particularly evident for Polanyi's (2001) 'fictitious' commodities; land, labour and money. States can assist or resist capital's movements, while capital's mobility limits states' autonomy. However, this mobility adds spatial dimensions to the contradictory dynamism of capital accumulation. For example, the benefits of high wages for collective capital can be undermined by the employment of cheap labour elsewhere. Momentary equilibrium between branches of capital can be upset; some industries and firms can and do move more than others; competing producers in different parts of the world can move into what had been a profitable line of business and drag down prices. Conversely, not absolutely tied to territory, capital can seek a 'spatial fix' (Harvey 1982) to its problems of accumulation; low wages overcoming high ones, new markets overcoming the limits of the old.

Earlier chapters argued that capitalism should always be conceived as global in the sense of all-encompassing; it crosses borders and is localised and nationalised. This takes different forms. Chapter 6 described changing dynamics in the nineteenth and early twentieth century as foreign investments and later imperial conquest helped spread the industrial revolution. Figure 8.1 shows the quantitative variation in FDI from the major powers. In relative terms it declined after the First World War, not regaining comparable levels until the late twentieth century. The orientation of investment also changed. Chapter 7 described how the long boom was characterised by accumulation in depth rather than breadth, and showed that FDI similarly became more highly concentrated in rich countries. In 1938, 66 per cent went to poorer countries, by 1960 just 20 per cent (Dunning 1993). In the post-war period relative levels of trade and migration were also lower than previously and many former colonies also won independence. The world appeared less global, and prejudices for conceiving political economy in national terms gained ground.

The separations between production and consumption and between economy and polity are attested by the need, but also the possibility of a Keynesian moment. The state could act as 'collective capital' at the national level, controlling wages and securing levels of spending and consumption. Post-war 'Fordism' produced nationally based concentrations of production and consumption supported by interventionist states. As discussed in Chapter 7, this was an incomplete and ambiguous process. There were also considerable outward investments, particularly by US companies, with important economic consequences. More dollars circulated outside the United States. Trade – and trade imbalances – increased. However, the basic argument for the establishment and deepening of high-waged regions seems clear. Capital can be drawn to particular places by the prospects of lower costs or higher profits, but can then become 'locked in' through virtuous cycles between supply and demand. High wages, for example, provide a market rather than simply being a cost. They simultaneously provide an inducement to invest in labour-saving or productivity-raising technology, which further advantages the developed region against potential rivals. States could add barriers, helping to maintain concentrations of capital (Harvey

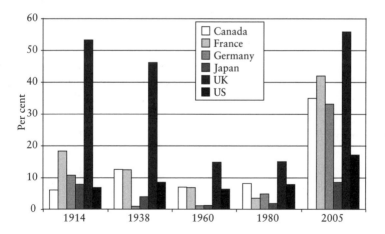

Figure 8.1   Outward stock of FDI as a percentage of GDP

Sources: Held et al. 1999; Dunning 1993; UNCTAD 2006b; Maddison 2003; BLS 2007

2003). Overall, unprecedented economic growth coincided with falling relative levels and more concentrated patterns of FDI.

On the whole, poorer countries also grew quickly during the post-war period. For many this was a time of decolonisation and the development of national economic strategies. Where foreign funding was sought, loans were usually preferred to direct investment, as locals could control how they were spent. However, nation state building and economic development usually mirrored the processes of state-backed capitalist (or state capitalist) development in the 'North'. This in a sense already deepened the global nature of capitalism, for example undermining hitherto non-marketised and subsistence forms of production. There was substantial industrialisation and urbanisation in many countries. Nevertheless, growth rates typically remained lower than in rich countries; so international inequality widened, encouraging the search for strategies and resources with which to 'catch up' more effectively. This provided the background to the high levels of indebtedness, which turned into crisis in the late 1970s; this in turn helped to make many countries more receptive to foreign investment.

The post-war boom was a remarkable period of prolonged prosperity. However, rather than achieving any stable equilibrium, both economic and geographical bases of growth within capitalism are insecure. As classical theories of comparative advantage make so clear (see Chapter 9), self-sufficiency is no necessary virtue. Trade makes sense providing prices are sufficiently different and transport costs sufficiently low. Greater gains can be made through specialisation and trade, which, amongst other things, then allows economies of scale and still greater efficiency. The virtuous cycle can turn into its opposite. Capital relocation breaks the links between high wages, jobs and the final market, so nationally based accumulation can be fragile and contradictory, contested by both labour and at least sections of capital. The inherently global nature of capital means a national 'fix' is inherently temporary. Socially necessary labour time is ultimately determined at a global level, and apparent success in preserving national differences may only mean greater dislocation as capital finally utilises the cheaper alternatives. The economic crisis of the 1970s threw these problems into sharp relief. Processes of internationalisation increased, but to a degree, and with implications that are hotly disputed.

Global Production and MNCs

Figure 8.2 anticipates the arguments below that there has been much exaggeration in claims of transformation. It shows crude aggregates of output in agriculture, industry and services by country wealth in 2004. Most of the world's population lived in poor countries. Most production occurred in rich ones. However, industrial structure changes. Poor countries had proportionately more agriculture, rich ones bigger tertiary or service sectors. The figure also highlights that the vast majority (71 per cent) of the world's industrial output remained in the richest countries, whose population was only 14 per cent of the world total. The share of manufacturing output, relative to population, declined quite sharply with national wealth. Any 'race to the base' of industry remained prospective at best. The richest countries also produced a disproportionate share of the world's agricultural output. Nevertheless, patterns of production did change.

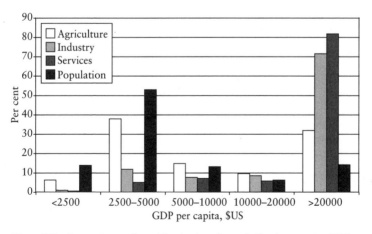

Figure 8.2   Percentages of world output and population by country GDP per capita, 2004

Sources: UNDP 2006; UNCTAD 2006b; World Bank 2006c; Census 2008

Fröbel et al. (1980) characterised a New International Division of Labour (NIDL), the old international division of labour having traded rich-country-manufactured goods for the primary products of the poor. They observed that German garment and textile firms had relocated to various poorer countries. The four 'Asian tigers', South Korea, Taiwan, Singapore and Hong Kong, quickly became the paradigm cases, but other countries in Asia and elsewhere opened to FDI. Often, poorer countries initially established Export Processing Zones (EPZs), where foreign firms were offered special treatment. Later, whole countries might be opened for business on a similar basis. This was unlike the earlier primary-sector investments or the manufacturing operations aimed at local markets. Instead, offshore plants made goods to sell back to their home country or other rich markets. Several subsequent studies observed similar phenomena in a range of industries, with 'global factories' combining different stages of the production process at scattered locations (Held et al. 1999; Perraton 2000). This had strongly gendered implications, with industries in newly industrialising countries (NICs) staffed by women, while the older male-dominated industrial heartlands declined. As the authors of the original NIDL thesis suggested, this would be replicated, as changes in technology and organisation, and falling transport and communications costs, meant that firms could locate anywhere (Fröbel et al. 1980). Some authors went further, to describe an unstoppable structural logic (Strange 1985) as firms became stateless and national economies became indistinguishable (Reich 1991). The distinction between first and third worlds and the international division on which it was based became redundant (Harris 1987).

Some of this theorising involved wild extrapolation. Nevertheless, industrial output in what the UN designated 'developing' countries increased by 75 per cent between 1990 and 2005, jumping from 18.9 to 30.1 per cent of the world total and from 6.2 to 8.5 per cent of global GDP. Three-quarters of this growth occurred in Asia, but there were also significant rises in industrial output of 44 per cent in developing countries in the Americas and of 20 per cent in Africa. Meanwhile, industrial production in developed countries increased by only 1 per cent in real terms. The proportion of output accounted by agriculture declined by 40 per cent in rich countries and, from a much higher relative level, by 30 per cent in poor ones. The service sector increased in both groups of countries (UNCTAD 2007a). Huge new urban proletariats emerged in previously mainly rural and agricultural countries.

FDI levels also increased dramatically. Table 8.1 shows this in absolute and relative terms. Poorer countries' share declined to 1990 (just as talk of globalisation was becoming fashionable) but rose significantly thereafter. By 2005, poorer countries attracted a higher proportion of foreign investment than their share of overall wealth, which was about a quarter (UNCTAD 2007a). Total FDI stocks amounted to 22 per cent of world GDP.

Table 8.1   Total FDI stocks in rich and poor countries (current dollars)

	1980	1985	1990	1995	2000	2005
World ($USb)	561	814	1789	2766	5803	10130
AICs (%)	76	73	79	75	69	70
LDCs (%)	24	27	21	25	31	30

Source: UNCTAD 2006a

By 2006 there were about 78,000 MNCs, accounting for a total of $12 trillion of inward FDI stocks (UNCTAD 2007a). Other huge corporations were uncounted, either because they were private (as opposed to public) companies, or because they were state owned. The true economic weight of MNCs could also be greater than such figures imply because many of them outsourced much of their production to nominally independent suppliers. This varied between industries, but the use of subcontractors by firms like Nike and Gap became well known. Statistics of corporate investment should therefore be read in tandem with those for trade, which also rose quickly. There is, then, evidence of something that might be called economic globalisation. However, in terms of investment flows, a peak in 2003 of $1.4 trillion represented just 3.8 per cent of GDP in 2003 (UNCTAD 2007a). It was also a very uneven process over time and with great variations also between firms, industries and different places.

The Unevenness of Capital's Internationalisation

Firstly, the internationalisation of capital was uneven over time. Figure 8.1 shows this in the long term. More recently, figures for stocks, such as those in Table 8.1, might indicate a steady increase. However, Figure 8.3 shows that changes – or net inflows – were volatile. It highlights, amongst other things, how net disinvestment from poorer countries in 2002 interrupted the upward trajectory.

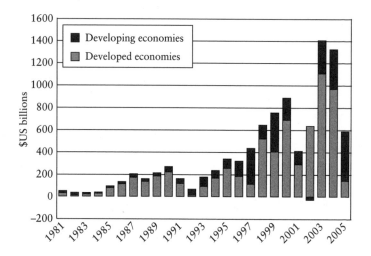

Figure 8.3 Changes in World FDI stocks ($US million)
Source: UNCTAD 2006b

Secondly, the predominantly rich-country origins of FDI have been widely reported. There was some indication of change, especially with the emergence of powerful firms from China and other Asian countries, but the vast majority of FDI in 2006, 86 per cent of stocks and 84 per cent of flows, came from rich countries.

Table 8.2 shows that ten countries accounted for almost three-quarters of the total outward stocks of world FDI in 2005. All of these except Hong Kong were established rich countries (and Hong Kong itself was no longer poor). Similarly, 72 of the top 100 non-financial MNCs came from the G5 richest countries, 24 of them from the United States (UNCTAD 2007a).

Table 8.2   World FDI stocks (per cent) 2005

Outward		*Inward*	
United States	20.2	United States	16.0
United Kingdom	11.6	United Kingdom	8.1
Germany	8.8	France	5.9
France	8.3	Hong Kong, China	5.3
Netherlands	6.0	Germany	5.0
Hong Kong, China	4.5	Belgium	4.9
Switzerland	4.0	Netherlands	4.6
Belgium	3.7	Spain	3.6
Canada	3.7	Canada	3.5
Japan	3.7	China	3.1
Top 10 total	74.4		59.9

Source: UNCTAD 2006b

FDI was also strongly patterned both by destination and industry. Most FDI also went to other rich countries. The top ten recipients accounted for 60 per cent of inward stocks. Again, all except China and Hong Kong were rich (UNCTAD 2006b). Some countries attracted huge investments in both absolute and relative terms, others very little. The ratio of FDI to GDP ranged from 0.21 per cent in Cuba to 7,003 per cent in the British Virgin Islands. Of other countries, 16 had levels less than 5 per cent, 25 had stocks that exceeded their GDP. Most of the latter were small countries, but some, like Belgium, Ireland and Hong Kong were significant economies. These numbers show that FDI and GDP are not strictly comparable categories, the former cumulative, the latter the value added in a single year. Overall, however, stocks of FDI in developed countries averaged 21 per cent of

GDP, marginally below the global average. Levels tended to be high in Europe (averaging 33 per cent of GDP), lower in the United States (14 per cent) and Japan (2 per cent). There was also, of course, great unevenness within countries, notably in China, where initial investments were highly concentrated in the eastern provinces. FDI went overwhelmingly to a restricted number of preferred locations.

The industry variation has been well documented, although it contradicts wilder claims of globalisation and deterritorialisation. Liberal models of the international firm, despite starting from the rather upside-down premise that international expansion is abnormal, capture some of the reasons why one might anticipate a differentiated experience. Vernon (1966) characterised a product cycle, with mature goods being produced in successively less advanced countries, while Dunning's (1993) eclectic paradigm attempted to identify the specific advantages a firm gained from internalising certain operations in particular places rather than relying on the market. Only some firms and industries were primarily motivated by cheap labour. The examples of garments and footwear remain powerful. Many US and European firms slashed local employment as imports escalated (Census 2006; UN 2006; Dicken 2003). The consumer electronics industry also provided many examples of relocation to cheap labour locations, particularly in China. However, relocation seldom simply involved pursuing cheap labour. In an industry like microelectronics, the products were discrete, light and valuable and therefore easily flown between locations, making it possible to split the 'value chain' and locate wherever the mix of skills was most appropriate (Henderson 1989). Agglomeration effects based on highly skilled labour were strong in places like Silicon Valley (Saxenian 1994), but most of the work needed more basic skills. However, even here firms did not always follow the maximum possible division of labour. Often they combined stages of production, for example semiconductor wafer fabrication and photo-mask making, in single locations, often within rich countries (Ó hUllacháin 1997; Dunn 2004a). In general, firms seldom went 'hopping and skipping and jumping' (Glassman, cited in Reich 1991) in search of competitive labour markets. Even where cheap labour was a major motivation for movement, there were then immobilising pressures. Japanese MNCs in China, for example, were reported as investing in areas where there were capable component firms and staying even when wages rose (Thun 2008).

Other resources could be more important. An obvious example is in extractive industries. Oil companies were amongst the most 'globalised' in terms of the proportion of business done abroad, but their foreign operations were necessarily conditioned by the location of appropriate deposits. The construction industry, whose final production was necessarily in situ, also became highly globalised in terms of firm ownership and activity (Dunn 2004c). For other sectors too, proximity to markets appeared to remain primary. Tables 8.1 and 8.2 confirm that most FDI went to rich countries. The largest foreign investments in the automobile industry, for example, were those of Japanese companies into North America and Europe. Automobile-industry investments into China were also predominantly market-seeking: at the time of writing, China had become a major producer, but not exporter, of cars. There can be physical elements to this need to invest near final markets. Some goods are bulky or difficult to transport relative to their production costs. Ready-mixed concrete and perishable goods like food would be examples. However, intangible ties to place through things like face-to-face contact between customers and clients could also be decisive. This seems likely to apply often in the tertiary sector, with many 'business services' concentrated in rich countries. This was perhaps most striking in finance, where the products were immaterial and potentially almost infinitely mobile, but where the activity was concentrated in core 'global cities' such as New York, Tokyo and London (Sassen 1996).

Each industry faced a range of centrifugal and centripetal forces, which played out differently even for particular firms. Of the 100 largest non-financial MNCs in 2005, 58 were from just six sectors, 'motor vehicles (11), petroleum (10), electrical and electronic equipment (10), pharmaceuticals (9), telecommunications (9), and electricity, gas and water services (9)' (UNCTAD 2007a:25). Meanwhile, in the G7 countries between 1970 and

2001 employment fell substantially in textiles and metal products, but hardly declined at all in food, paper products, chemicals or motor vehicles (Pilat et al. 2006). The need for adequate social support, particularly in friendly and stable governments and cooperative or at least controllable industrial relations, also defied images of a 'race to the base'.

When firms did go abroad, they often went to nearby countries and re-clustered in new locations (UNCTAD 2007a:20, Storper and Walker 1989). This is seen in the enduringly regional character of FDI from the largest economies. So, for example, in 2003 over 10 per cent of US FDI stocks were in Canada, a country which had attracted around 1 per cent of Japanese, German and British investments, but 4 per cent of those from France – largely as a result of the latter's historic link to the province of Quebec (UNCTAD 2006b). Similarly, US investments in poorer countries were disproportionately directed towards Latin America, Japanese towards Asia and European towards Africa and Eastern Europe (see Figure 8.4).

The enduring pertinence of geography qualifies notions and measures of corporate globalisation. The Transnationality Index (TNI) has become a standard, weighing firms' foreign sales, assets and employment as a percentage. Thus General Electric, the most multinational firm in terms of total foreign assets, scored 50.1. The majority of its sales, but also of its employees, were in the United States. A high TNI might also be achieved through foreign operations concentrated in a few neighbouring countries. The second ranked MNC, Vodafone, operated in only 19 host countries; and only 29 of the top 100 MNCs had affiliates in 50 or more countries (UNCTAD 2007a). The TNI also neglects other dimensions, including the location of key activities such as research and development, the national composition of senior management and corporate culture, all of which could remain distinctly national (Doremus et al. 1998). Thus even amongst corporate giants, many were hardly global. Many of the other 78,000 MNCs had quite modest foreign operations. Total investments of about $12 trillion implied an average of about $150 million.

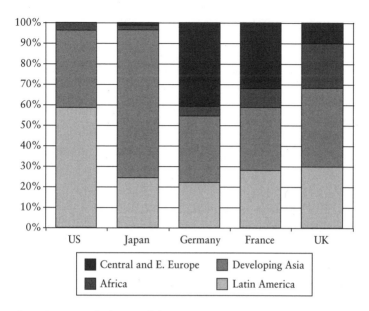

Figure 8.4   Specified regional destinations of G5 developing country
FDI stocks (per cent), 2003
Source: UNCTAD 2006b

Even a strictly economic logic does not mean dispersal.
Instead it anticipates complex and contradictory changes in
capital mobility. For example, innovations in transport remain
in dynamic relationship with those in production 'proper'. As Fine
neatly summarises one influential metaphor, 'to the extent that
space and time are both compressed, absolutely nothing changes'
(Fine 2004). There are few a priori grounds for predicting the
universal prevalence of increased mobility. More concretely,
despite much hyperbole, innovation was discontinuous, uneven
and often highly questionable, any fall in transport times and
costs being dependent upon the medium considered (Dunn
2004b). Moreover, capital is not a 'thing', whose mobility can
be read off from technical improvements. Capital's mobility and
immobility also continued to be profoundly affected by broader
social relations and the actions of nation states. Policy could also
both attract and repel capital.

The Contested Political Economy of FDI

From the 1970s, 'liberal' rich-country governments generally encouraged FDI in the sense of removing formal barriers. They often also intervened more positively than liberal theory would encourage, offering various incentives to attract foreign companies. In the 1980s, the processes of competitive bidding between states to attract Japanese car manufacturers, even within the United States and countries in the EU, proved notoriously expensive. States also championed 'their' capitals' investments overseas. They used various means, including the provision of 'export credit guarantees' and 'tax credits' on foreign operations. It is not obvious that both inward and outward movements could in general simultaneously serve 'national interests'. Nevertheless, deficits on the capital account were seldom regarded with the same aversion as trade deficits, concerns of job losses notwithstanding. In general both home and host states supported capital mobility. Conversely, some industries were protected from foreign takeover, for example by invoking national security, sometimes for rather tenuous reasons (Cohn 2005; Weiss 2006).

The attitudes of poorer-country governments toward foreign investment changed substantially. The share of FDI going to poorer countries dropped with post-war Fordist growth in the North and decolonisation. Then in the early 1970s a wave of nationalisation claimed many of the remaining foreign operations, particularly in extractive industries and utilities (Kobrin 1984). Subsequently, high levels of debt cut access to commercial loans, while rich-country governments and international institutions such as the WTO and the IMF applied pressure to increase openness. The different nature of Western investments, often involving integrated production systems, changed the nature of state–firm relations. Intra-firm supply chains made each specific operation useful only as an input to the particular MNC, also militating against expropriation. Conversely, the importance of each unit to larger networks gave host countries some bargaining power, and FDI usually remained a negotiated process (Dicken 2003). For example, governments won commitments to source local supplies, establish joint ventures with local firms and to export certain proportions of production. The opening to foreign capital remained uneven, and in the early 2000s some countries, notably Venezuela and Bolivia, passed anti-FDI measures and even renationalised major industries. However, the overall trend continued to be one of increasing openness (UNCTAD 2007a).

The role of foreign direct investment thus remained controversial. According to supporters, it provided poorer countries with vital and relatively stable income, unavailable from domestic resources alone (UNCTAD 2007b; Thun 2008). It introduced much-needed technical and management capacities and further increased wealth through multiplier effects. Tax revenues increased accordingly. Technically, cross-border investment in whatever form adds resources and is included in, or 'adds to', a country's GDP. Even the straightforward takeover of existing assets means that the previous owners make money which may be invested or spent within the local economy. Alternatively, foreign multinationals were exploitative. For example, in 2006 they repatriated more than half their income (UNCTAD 2007a). They distorted national economies and societies, muscling out local firms and using transfer pricing to minimise tax payments. The volatility of FDI flows, including the sudden exit in times of crisis (see Figures 8.3 and 8.5), suggested that much FDI was more like short-term share ownership of portfolio investment than is sometimes imagined. The effects were destabilising. Therefore, even in narrowly economic terms, the implications of FDI remained contested (Ram and Zhang 2002).

This is tested by comparing annual growth rates with levels of foreign investment between 1981 and 2005 for 24 major rich and poor country FDI locations. This crude calculation suggests a weak connection between net FDI inflows and economic performance. Because FDI is strictly an element of GDP, the calculation examines the relationship between FDI and GDP net of FDI. In Table 8.3, column 2 confirms that FDI inflows correlated weakly, but positively and statistically significantly, with annual growth rates. Correlation, however, does not demonstrate causation. Strong growth may attract foreign investors rather than being its consequence. Table 8.3 therefore also shows the relationship between GDP growth and FDI flows in the years before (column 1) and after (column 3). In rich countries there was a stronger association between foreign investment in any year and subsequent growth. The coefficients were uniformly positive and on average stronger than those between growth and FDI in the same year. By the second year following FDI the average correlation fell to 0.22. In poorer countries there is little evidence of such a relationship. Indeed, for those countries levels of foreign investment tended, albeit weakly, to correlate more strongly with growth in the previous year than with subsequent growth. Thus FDI may have followed growth rather than being its cause.

The weakness of any association between FDI and growth is not hard to understand. Firstly, very little FDI is genuinely new investment. In 2006, mergers and acquisitions (M&As) accounted for 67.4 per cent of the total. These can make FDI figures swing dramatically, with little obvious change in production. For example, they jumped with cross-shareholding deals such as those between GM and Fiat and the merger of DaimlerChrysler. Production carried on much as before and the firms then separated. Nor is substantive change obvious if, for example, a Spanish telecoms company acquires a British one while maintaining its operations. Similarly, if an Indian steel company moves its headquarters to the Netherlands, or Rupert Murdoch changes his nationality, FDI measures would change, but production might alter little. Reinvested earnings accounted for a further 30 per cent of FDI. This was cross-border investment in only the most formal sense. That leaves about 2.6 per cent as new or 'greenfield' investment (UNCTAD 2007a). Data for FDI should therefore be read as at most something of an upper limit on the cross-border contribution to capital formation. So in 2004, FDI inflows amounted in aggregate to around 4 per cent of global GDP, or 15.4 per cent of gross fixed capital formation (GFCF), but were responsible for only a fraction of this much investment. Figures for the UK and Hong Kong, for example, suggest that FDI levels were 300 and 200 per cent respectively of GFCF. The corresponding levels were 5.5 per cent in the United

Table 8.3 Correlation between GDP growth and FDI in the year before, during and after, 1981–2005

GDP growth v.	1 FDI one year before	2 FDI in the same year	3 FDI in the following year
Australia	0.93	–0.06	–0.14
Canada	0.81	0.73	0.29
France	0.60	0.49	–0.08
Germany	0.35	0.43	0.03
Ireland	0.75	–0.45	0.10
Italy	0.55	0.39	0.17
Japan	0.06	0.24	–0.38
Netherlands	0.63	0.05	–0.37
Spain	0.73	0.35	0.09
Sweden	0.57	–0.04	–0.16
UK	0.53	0.34	0.53
USA	0.49	0.40	0.41
Average	0.58	0.23	0.04
Argentina	–0.28	0.74	0.06
Brazil	–0.12	0.32	0.06
Chile	0.38	0.47	0.53
China	0.25	0.88	0.67
Hong Kong	–0.25	–0.10	–0.25
India	0.79	0.76	0.72
Indonesia	–0.25	0.15	0.28
Korea	0.17	0.22	–0.18
Malaysia	–0.09	0.27	–0.04
Philippines	–0.17	0.38	–0.07
South Africa	0.31	0.47	0.05
Taiwan	0.17	–0.36	0.26
Average	0.08	0.35	0.17

Source: UNCTAD 2006b

States, 0.7 per cent in Japan and, perhaps most notably, 2.3 per cent in China. That country's economic growth remained rapid, apparently irrespective of the volatility of FDI shown in Figure 8.5. In general, domestic resources remained the main basis of economic growth, and the consequences of FDI were typically specific, depending on what and where the investments were made (Nunnenkamp 2004).

Figure 8.5 also confirms the spatial concentration; flows in Asia overwhelmingly went to China (including Hong Kong province). As noted above, overall levels of foreign ownership were on average disproportionately high in poorer countries, representing 37 per cent of GDP in Africa, 28 per cent in Latin America and 23 per cent in Asia in 2005 (UNCTAD 2006b). Notably, it was only the last which closed the gap with rich countries.

From a rich country perspective, increases in outward FDI coincided with declining investment at home and sometimes persistently high levels of unemployment. However, it will by now be clear that the vast stocks of FDI do not imply a rush of manufacturing to LDCs. Only about 30 per cent of all FDI was in manufacturing, down from 41 per cent in 1990, and only 7.9 per cent was in LDC manufacturing (UNCTAD 2007b). Indeed, while total FDI escalated, employment in US manufacturing MNCs fell from 13.2 to 12.2 million between 1995 and 2004 (Census 2008). On a global basis, foreign affiliates contributed perhaps 10 per cent of world GDP in 2006. Employment within them reached 73 million – about 3 per cent of the world's labour force (UNCTAD 2007b).

Smith (2006) has characterised a 'see-saw' movement, as capitalism entrenches inequalities and then undermines them. During the 1990s, developing countries' share of FDI stocks overtook their share of world GDP. The metaphor is tempting, but the evidence of contemporary change suggests that any oscillations remained what physicists would term 'heavily damped'. There was a net outflow from developed countries of over $2 trillion (in current dollars) during the decade. The majority of this came from Britain ($558 billion) and Japan ($495 billion) but with significant investments from Germany ($377 billion) and the United States ($245 billion). These outflows averaged 4.6, 1.2, 2.1 and 0.3 per cent of annual GDP respectively. However, in the first five years of the twenty-first century, investment stabilised, with a slight movement back to developed countries of $33 billion. The impact of FDI may have been greater in certain sectors and thence in local and regional economies. It may also have contributed to the overall pattern of increased output and intensified international competition. However, at least in the US case, it seems clear that outward FDI played at most a very small part in overall deindustrialisation.

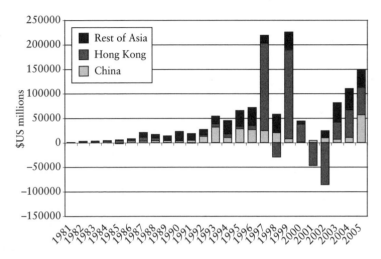

Figure 8.5   Changes in FDI stocks in Asia ($US million)
Source: UNCTAD 2006b

Conclusion

MNCs and FDI had important, but usually specific impacts, whether for good or ill. Capital is never fundamentally national and local firms may behave in similar ways to foreigners, for example in terms of whether profits are invested at home or abroad (Brewer 1990). Indeed, opening the door to capital movements precisely meant letting it out as much as bringing it in. Capital movements increased, but most investments were made on familiar rich-country territory. During the late 1990s there was a significant net shift towards poorer countries, but this was also geographically concentrated. In general FDI contributed little to economic growth.

From the perspective of most rich countries, new outward investment was small in relation to wealth, and any geographical shift contributed at most a small part to their changing industrial structure. Indeed, similar structural shifts from industry to services were discernable in many poor countries. Capital's specifically border-crossing dimensions may be exaggerated. Most investment in most countries continued to be generated by internal processes of saving and exploitation.

9

TRADE

International trade provokes furious debate. On the one hand, it is a rigged game in which 'Free trade is unfair trade' (*New York Times*, 20 July 2003). To support laissez faire is to support US and international capitalism against the world's poor. Alternatively, the association of free trade with wealth and growth remains overwhelming, both in academic and policy circles. Opposition remains 'impassioned but illogical' (Bhagwati 2002:49). Even some left commentators see the critics of free trade as narrow-minded supporters of national business interests (Hensman 2001) or apologists for imperialism (Kitching 2001). This chapter rejects this antinomy. International trade is intrinsically no better or worse than any other set of market transactions. That is to say, it is riddled with inequalities, but seldom the principal cause of them.

The chapter begins with an overview of changing patterns of trade. It then outlines liberal and anti-free-trade perspectives. It then offers a brief statistical refutation of any straightforward connection between trade and wealth or growth and argues that this is predictable, given the limitations of conventional theory. Finally it argues that the sound and fury over trade can obscure other vital and sometimes deeper elements of the global political economy. Questions of 'getting trade policy right' can also impose nationally based perspectives and technical economic criteria on what might better be seen as complex and contested social questions. The polarisation of attitudes towards trade should be seen as a conservative and ideologically loaded historical construction. It sidelines other issues of power and production, as well as issues more resistant to economic quantification, such as gender inequality and environmental destruction.

The Development and Structure of World Trade

World trade rose rapidly in the post-war period, as discussed in Chapter 7, and continued to rise, in spite of the breakdown of Bretton Woods, the apparent decline in US hegemony and several recessionary periods. Overall, the level of merchandise trade rose from $493 billion in 1948 to $11,783 billion in 2006 (in 2006 dollars, WTO 2007). This outstripped economic growth. Therefore the usual measure of trade openness, the trade/GDP ratio, which crashed in the inter-war period, increased. Table 9.1 shows data for the G5 leading countries. By the 1970s, levels of openness already exceeded those of the earlier pre-First World War period of globalisation. Nevertheless, differences between countries persisted. Some of the international variation reflects economic and geographical size. Large economies are likely to produce a wider range of goods, while relatively locally produced commodities might become imports for a sufficiently small country. Luxembourg, for example, has to trade anything made even 100 km away. However, ostensibly similar European countries had dissimilar experiences – even after the EU removed formal policy differences.

Poorer countries also tended to become more open. Many did so particularly rapidly in the 1990s and early 2000s (see Table 9.2). The General Agreement on Tariffs and Trade and, after 1995, the World Trade Organisation encouraged and oversaw processes of opening. Trade was also increased through a series of regional agreements and a plethora of bilateral treaties. Openness was often prescribed by the IMF as part of structural adjustment programmes.

The pattern of trade also changed substantially (see Figure 9.1). In terms of national economies, the greatest change was the relative decline of the United States. In 1948 its exports constituted 22 per cent of the world total. It ran massive surpluses, imports being only 13 per cent of the total. Roughly in balance in the

Table 9.1   Exports as a proportion of GDP for leading economies (per cent)

	1913	1950	1973	1987	2003
France	6.0	5.6	11.2	14.3	22.2
Germany	12.2	4.4	17.2	23.7	31.3
Japan	2.1	2.0	6.8	10.6	11.0
UK	14.7	9.5	11.5	15.3	16.8
USA	4.1	3.3	5.8	6.3	6.6

Sources: Held et al. 1999; WTO 2007

early 1970s and accounting for 12.3 per cent of both exports and imports in 1973, by 2006 its exports had fallen to 9 per cent while its imports had risen to 16 per cent. The UK share of exports fell even more precipitously from 11 to 4 per cent, although declining relative imports meant its deficits rose less dramatically. Conversely, Germany and Japan became major exporters by the 1970s. Subsequently, the rise of several newly industrialising countries (NICs) in East Asia and latterly including China has been most notable. Figure 9.1 shows the exports of the 'Asian 6' (Korea, Taiwan, Singapore, Hong Kong, Thailand and Malaysia) approaching 10 per cent of the world total. By 2006, China alone accounted for 8 per cent of exports and 6.4 per cent of imports. Nevertheless, a very high proportion of world trade remained concentrated within the rich country 'Triad' of Europe, North America and Japan. Europe alone accounted for 42 per cent of world exports and intra-EU trade for fully a quarter of the total (WTO 2007). In terms of content there was a notable shift, with many poorer countries increasing their manufactured exports. Table 9.2 shows the rapid opening to trade and the shift from primary products to manufactured goods exports among 'middle income' countries, but it should be emphasised that these aggregates conceal many exceptions, examples of retreat from openness and of the enduring importance of primary exports.

Figure 9.2 shows the trade position of major countries and regions in different commodity groups in 2005. The most notable structural feature is the US deficits in all commodity classes. These

Table 9.2 Changing trade structure of high-, middle- and low-income countries, 1990 and 2005

	Imports (per cent of GDP)		Exports (per cent of GDP)		Primary exports (per cent of total)		Manufactured exports (per cent of total)	
	1990	2005	1990	2005	1990	2005	1990	2005
High	19	24	18	24*	21	18	77	78
Middle	21	33	22	36	48	33	50	65
Low	16	29	13	25	50*	49*	49*	50*

* Data refer to nearest available year to that specified
Source: UNDP 2007

were slight in food and chemicals, but huge in crude materials and manufactured goods. Europe was in rough overall balance, with deficits in crude materials compensated by surpluses in machinery and chemicals. Within Europe, Germany ran large surpluses, Britain and to a lesser degree France and Italy were net importers. Japan had a large surplus, with reliance on food and raw material imports compensated mainly by machinery exports. The rest of Asia (excluding the Middle East), 85 per cent of whose trade was accounted for by seven countries, similarly relied on materials imports, but achieved a surplus through machinery and other manufactured goods exports. The rest of the world, including

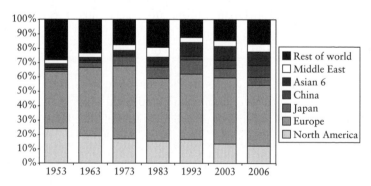

Figure 9.1 The origin of world exports (per cent of total)
Source: WTO 2007

rich countries like Canada and Australia, but also poor ones in Africa, South America and the Middle East, on balance sold more crude materials than they imported machinery.

Service trade rose even more rapidly than merchandise trade, by 2006 accounting for 23 per cent of the value of the latter. These include a variety of activities, some of which stretch the meaning of 'trade' beyond breaking point. For example, 11 per cent of commercial services were actually royalty and licence fee payments. Other major services included travel and transport, financial services, computer and Internet services and architectural engineering and other technical services. Here some of the deficit countries in commodity trade had significant surpluses, notably the United States with a surplus of $81 billion and the United Kingdom with one of $55 billion, offsetting their merchandise deficits by a tenth and a third respectively. Hong Kong, Spain, Switzerland and Luxembourg were also substantial surplus countries. Germany had the largest deficit ($50.3 billion in 2006), equivalent to a quarter of its merchandise surplus. Japan's deficit of $21.5 billion was equivalent to about 30 per cent of its merchandise surplus (WTO 2007). However, large systemic imbalances persisted, and proved unresponsive to adjustments in relative currency values. The following sections of this chapter argue that trade cannot be regarded as straightforwardly good or bad for national economies. However, there were significantly different experiences and important developing international tensions, which will be discussed briefly at the end of this chapter and in the subsequent ones on finance (Chapter 10) and on international competition and cooperation (Chapters 13 and 14).

Problems of Trade Theory

The dualism of trade perspectives finds scant empirical support and rests on fragile theoretical foundations. Ricardo's theory of comparative advantage provides a powerful argument why countries – and by extension the world – get richer through specialisation and trade. It is justly famous for being that rare thing in economic theory: neither trivial nor obvious (Samuelson, cited in

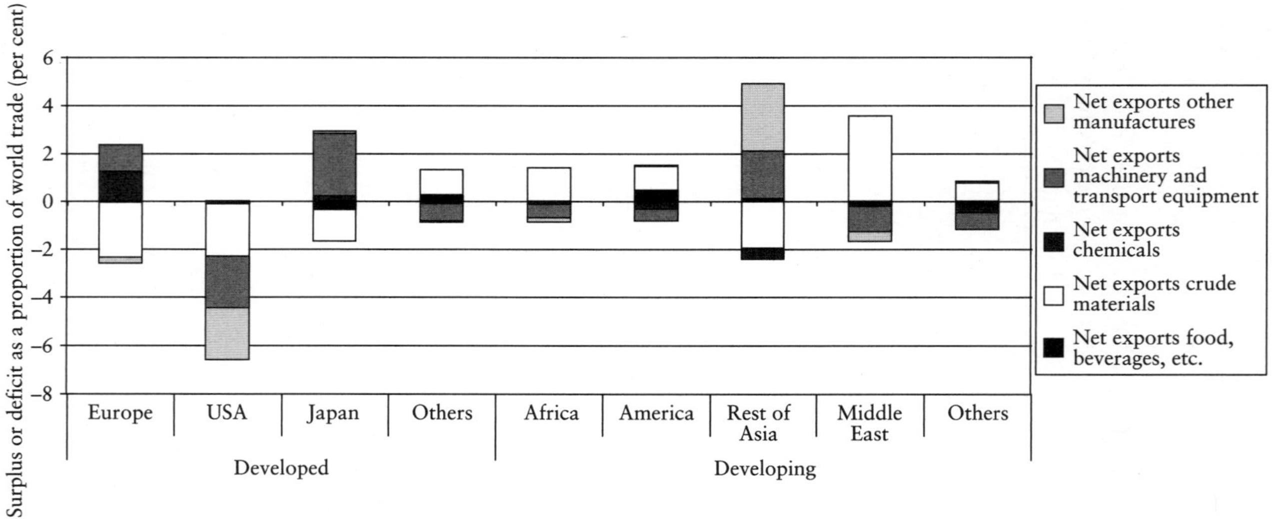
Surplus or deficit as a proportion of world trade (per cent)
6
4
2
0
−2
−4
−6
−8
Europe
USA
Japan
Others
Africa
America
Rest of Asia
Middle East
Others
Developed
Developing
Net exports other manufactures
Net exports machinery and transport equipment
Net exports chemicals
Net exports crude materials
Net exports food, beverages, etc.

Figure 9.2 The structure of world merchandise trade, 2005

Source: UN 2007

Mackintosh et al. 1996). In Ricardo's example, the two countries England and Portugal, despite the latter's absolute superiority in both wine and cloth making, do better by concentrating on that line of business at which they are relatively good. The same amount is produced with less work and the two countries can exchange their wine and cloth to their common gain (Ricardo 1951:135–6). Alternatively, more of the goods could be made with the same amount of labour. The potential benefits are clear. Radical commentators are more likely to acknowledge that openness need not always be good, particularly for poorer countries (see, for example, Birdsall 2006b). However, assumptions that trade and wealth are positively associated persist (Keily 2003). There are even 'tremendous economic gains associated with deeper and more efficient global markets' (Birdsall 2006a:3), though fairer rules might be needed to distribute them more equitably. A focus on the institutional shortcomings of the WTO and its failure to implement free trade consistently thus converges with orthodoxy (Bhagwati 2005).

However, as Krasner memorably objected, '[h]istorical experience suggests that policy makers are dense, or that the assumptions of the conventional argument are wrong. Free trade has hardly been the norm. Stupidity is not a very interesting analytic category' (1976:319). There are two principal liberal responses. The first explains the failures to achieve free trade in terms of successful 'rent seeking'. The argument is worth a brief discussion and has interesting, if seldom mentioned, implications that within many countries, support for free trade may be anti-majoritarian. Comparative advantage depends upon inequality. Its very essence is difference, both between countries and within them, in the ability to produce different commodities. Ricardo does not specify why labour productivity varies; why England and Portugal should respectively be relatively better at making cloth and wine. Later theorists did this, mostly by developing arguments put forward by Heckscher and Ohlin. The H–O theorem suggests that the basis of comparative advantage lies in relative abundance of 'factor endowments'. Originally, and most generally, these are in land, labour and capital, but also by extension in more specific types of these. Land may be suitable for pasture rather than agriculture or for growing grapes or grains. Labour may be more or less skilled. The model suggests that different endowments, a relative abundance in any particular factor, predict the basis of comparative advantage (Krugman and Obstfeld 2003).

The Stolper and Samuelson (S–S) theorem extends the H–O theorem to argue that owners of abundant resources would favour free trade, which increased their markets and scope of operation (Rogowski 1989). Conversely, those displaced by foreign competition were likely to oppose openness. The S–S theorem is already implicit in Ricardo. The Corn Laws protected agriculture from foreign competition, to the detriment of industrial capital and labour. It was on the basis of endowments of capital and labour that England's trade success depended, yet landed interests controlled British politics. Therefore political change was needed to overcome landowners' 'rent-seeking' behaviour, abolish the Corn Laws and secure free trade and the economic success of the country (and of British capitalists like Ricardo).

Rogowski (1989) argues that trade theory can similarly inform a series of subsequent political alliances. In rich countries with a low land/labour ratio, both capital and labour should support free trade against protectionist landed interests, as in the Britain of Ricardo's day. In a poor country with a high land/labour ratio, agriculturalists would want free trade. Both capital and labour would support protection so that they could enjoy abundant locally produced food while escaping competition from foreign manufacturers. Early US and later South American populism serve as examples. Rogowski suggests that in poor countries where labour is plentiful in relation to land, workers will favour free trade and both land and capital will oppose it, leading to either socialism or fascism, depending on who wins. Labour also opposes both land and capital in rich countries with high land/labour ratios. The US New Deal exemplifies labour's success. The free-trade agenda of contemporary Australia would illustrate labour's defeat.

Landed interests gradually lost political power in nineteenth-century Britain. Today, the presumption is that parliamentary democracies serve majority interests. Yet S–S theory suggests that 'in an advanced economy where both land and labour are scarce, expanding trade will benefit only capital' (Rogowski 1989:13–14). Rogowski implies such cases will be rare. However, recalling that comparative advantage depends on 'relative' endowments, and allowing labour of different skills, there would appear to be numerous situations in which at least unskilled workers would suffer (Reich 1991; Wood, A. 1994, 1998). This is one of several potential situations where a national majority might lose out from, and should oppose, free trade.

Of course liberal theory, unconcerned with distribution, highlights only the potential gains. As Rogowski says:

> The gainers from trade can always compensate the losers and have something left over ... however ... it remains unobvious that such compensation will in fact occur. Rather, the natural tendency is for gainers to husband their winnings and to stop their ears to the cries of the afflicted. (1989:17)

He continues that only exceptionally have governments been able to effect an adequate redistribution. Alternatively, of course, domestic redistribution might 'overcompensate' the already rich and powerful. Labour need not reap the rewards from trade in 'labour-rich' commodities despite its apparently strengthened 'market position'. The owners of land, smallholders or multinational agribusiness might experience a national abundance (or scarcity) in different ways. And, of course, it is ownership that matters. In the land-rich US south, free trade found ardent early supporters, just as Stolper–Samuelson would predict. We might hypothesise that the benefits went unappreciated by the plantation slaves.

Globally, the majority, almost by definition, live in labour-rich areas. Theory predicts that they benefit from openness. Kitching (2001) therefore suggests that a truly internationalist perspective must support this. However, labour's gain in the replacement of one high-waged by two low-paid jobs is not self-evident. Moreover, low-wage jobs supplying export markets are doubly vulnerable. They may disappear with comparative advantage if wages rise. Meanwhile, production on a sufficient scale can undermine prices, reduce earnings and increase the downward pressure on wages (Samuelson 2004). Liberal theory treats labour as a resource whose cheapness provides the basis of trade, which then perpetuates low wages.

The second liberal explanation for the historical rarity of free trade is in terms of the need for hegemonic stability and the frequent absence of the superordinate power necessary to achieve this. As mentioned in Chapter 7, there are both theoretical and empirical problems with this. Liberal trade theory predicts mutual benefits, so it is not immediately clear why cooperation should not be the norm. Failures of cooperation at least shift debate to the terrain of interstate competition and the arguments of liberals' mercantilist opponents.

The starting point for a variety of anti-free-trade perspectives is that capitalism is a competitive system. Unlike the bloodless models of neoclassical theory, real competition 'favours the (comparatively) strong over the weak' (Shaikh 2007a:4). It has losers as well as winners. It relies upon, and often accentuates, inequality between countries. It may therefore be in the interests of poorer, weaker states to restrict trade.

Though it is seldom a strategy of complete closure, many mercantilists advocated selective protection, particularly support for infant industries, as a precondition for later openness. Conversely, attempts by already rich countries to prevent such strategic initiatives amounted to 'kicking away the ladder', refusing potential competitors the methods by which they became rich (List 1983; Chang 2002). Having established its economic leadership, Britain adopted free trade. Meanwhile, both intellectually and in policy, the United States and Germany stayed closer to mercantilism, until by the twentieth century both could outcompete Britain. Indeed, the United States, whilst still relatively isolationist, succeeded in becoming the richest country the world had ever known. Its only possible rival was the still more isolated USSR. At the end of the Second World War, the United States cautiously switched to favouring freer trade. However, most poorer countries remained poor, and it was particularly in relation to these that several critics made important innovations.

Prebisch (1950) and Singer (1950) suggested that trade openness systematically disadvantaged poorer countries. Prebisch highlighted that Ricardian theory depends on assumptions of international-market efficiency, counterfactual in general and specifically so in relation to contemporary US domination. Without this, the distribution of gains from trade would be uneven. Industrialised countries could increase their productivity more quickly than primary producers, without their export prices falling accordingly. Thus, where orthodoxy predicts the terms of trade changing in favour of the primary producers, the trend since the 1870s had in fact been in the opposite direction. Productivity gains in rich countries allowed real-wage rises; won during economic upturn and defended during the downturn. So at least some of the gains from increasing productivity stayed within the core as wage rises and were transmitted to the periphery as higher prices (Prebisch 1950). Singer's argument is the broader, emphasising the greater relative importance of trade for poorer countries, the wider social benefits of industrialisation and the difficulties of achieving it. He describes the paradox that in times when primary products' prices rise, underdeveloped countries gain the means of financing their industrialisation, but, doing well from primary exports, lack the incentive to do so. Conversely, when prices fall they see the advantages of industrialisation, but lack the means to achieve it. Moreover, wage rises are likely to retard development, social welfare and the strength of primary producers (Singer 1950:484–5). An additional explanation sees deteriorating terms of trade as a consequence of demand elasticities. As people get richer (as individuals or as a society) relative demand for food declines. Technical advance also substitutes synthetic products for primary ones. So the demand – and hence the prices – for industrial products tends to rise, those of primary producers to fall (Dos Santos 1970; Roxborough 1979). The Prebisch–Singer thesis and similar early dependency scholarship highlighted important problems and structural inequalities, but remained relatively orthodox in its methodology and moderate in its policy prescriptions.

Later, more radical dependency theorists maintained that relations with the core were inherently exploitative and that to break them required revolution. For Frank (1970), the deeper the links between the periphery and the colonial powers the greater the degree of underdevelopment. Conversely, the satellites did best when their ties to the metropolis were weakest – during periods of war and depression. Significantly, each metropolis had several satellites, each satellite only one metropolis. Hence, chains of monopolistic relations affected unequal exchange, transferring value to the metropoles. Similar ideas to those of Frank would also be developed as 'world-systems theory' (WST) (Wallerstein 1974) and in the more technical articulations of unequal exchange. With these, peripheral underdevelopment also became the explanation of core wealth.

Emmanuel (1972) formulated perhaps the clearest version of unequal exchange (but see also Sau 1978). High wages in the North become the crucial independent variable. It is immaterial whether the North exports cotton, fabrics, looms and spindles, machine tools or special steels for making these:

> So long as exchange takes place and so long as the wage levels are unequal, nothing can stop India from pouring out toward Britain or toward other developed countries part of the surplus value extracted from her own workers. (Emmanuel 1972:146)

Emmanuel acknowledges practical difficulties, but in principle the solutions are straightforward. 'The choice is between unequal exchange and autarky' (1972:146).

Despite its many effective criticisms of orthodox trade theory, dependency theory fell out of fashion. This can be read as a symptom of a more general rightward shift in which (neo)liberalism involved a renewed determination amongst leading states and institutions to open markets. However, there are also non-trivial empirical and theoretical problems. The experiences of export-oriented economies in Asia, however interpreted, undermined contentions of an unchanging hierarchy maintained by power relations or that trade links with the North would necessarily exacerbate underdevelopment.

Evaluating Trade

Rodriguez and Rodrik (2000) review an extensive literature and subject the evidence to a range of econometric tests. The conclusion of their argument (whose technical details need not be repeated here) is that any relationship between trade and growth is at best weak, and that 'there has been a tendency in academic and policy discussions to greatly overstate the systematic evidence in favor of trade openness' (2000:54).

A relatively unsophisticated but clear measure can be obtained from data to 2004 available from the UNDP (2006). For the 163 countries for which figures are available, these show a correlation between exports as a percentage of GDP and GDP per capita of 0.36. Because the propensity to trade varies with size, Table 9.3 disaggregates the countries according to population. It shows that the correlation between wealth and trade openness is more than 0.5 only for microstates with populations below one million. This points to the rather predictable conclusion that such countries, with few resources and unable to achieve economies of scale within their borders, tend to be poor when they are also isolated. For larger countries, once again, any relationship between trade openness and wealth is weak.

Table 9.3 The association between trade and wealth

Country population (million)	Correlation between GDP/capita and export/GDP, 2004	Number of countries in sample
<1	0.66	19
1–5	0.36	39
5–10	0.44	31
10–20	0.40	27
20–50	0.21	24
>50	−0.28	23
Total	0.36	163

Source: calculated from UNDP 2006

Comparative advantage is, of course, an argument about change; that specialising and opening to trade facilitates growth. Therefore, Table 9.4 shows changes in trade openness and in GDP per capita between 1990 and 2004, for the somewhat smaller available sample of 151 countries. The overall correlation is even weaker, only 0.23. It is scarcely stronger when broken down by country size. Trade is clearly not a sufficient criterion; during this period Slovenia, Botswana, Belize, Malta and Mauritius all decreased their level of trade openness, but grew more quickly than the average. Ukraine and Angola became much more open yet shrank in terms of GDP per capita. Nevertheless, overall, the relationship did tend to be weakly positive rather than negative.

Table 9.4   The association between economic and trade growth

Country population (million)	Correlation between change in GDP/capita and change in export/GDP 1990–2004	Number of countries in sample
<1	0.31	15
1–5	0.12	35
5–10	0.32	29
10–20	0.31	26
20–50	0.08	23
>50	0.48	23
Total	0.23	151

Source: calculated from UNDP 2006

The overall weakness of the correlation between trade and growth questions a general case for either openness or closure. More specifically, dependency theory hypothesised that rich countries gain and poorer ones lose from free trade. Table 9.5 shows changes in trade openness and income for the countries considered above, categorised by relative wealth. The correlation coefficients again tend to be weakly positive and there is little evidence of any relationship with wealth.

The weakness of any relationship between trade openness and growth should not be surprising. A variety of theoretical and empirical problems are now well known (see, for example, Rodriguez and Rodrik 2000; Rodrik 2001; Samuelson 2004). Assumptions of rational individualism contrast with the way trade is orchestrated by powerful firms and states. Assumptions of static gains fail to capture the dynamic processes, often including the deepening of inequality, encouraged by trade specialisation. Writing of Ricardian theory, Frank claimed to have 'identified over thirty underlying assumptions each of which is historically and empirically unfounded and several of which are mutually contradictory' (1978:94). Although Frank does not elaborate, other authors enumerate substantial lists (see, for example, Dunkley 2004). A few problems of commission and omission perhaps bear repetition.

Table 9.5   The association of the growth in trade and wealth

Country GDP/capita ($US)	Correlation between change in GDP/capita and change in export/GDP 1990–2004	Number of countries in sample
<1500	0.23	23
1500–3000	0.43	27
3000–6000	0.33	24
6000–12000	−0.10	31
12000–24000	0.11	23
>24000	0.35	23

Source: UNDP 2006

Factor endowments are never simply 'given' (Marx 1977:269–70; Frank 1978; Wallerstein 2002). Even land is usually the product of past management, while labour and capital are more obviously social constructions. Moreover, specialisation involves change, meaning that post-specialisation 'endowments' cease to correspond to the initial bases of specialisation. Land might be over-farmed. Ricardo (1951) himself articulated why the rate of profit in agriculture should be expected to decline, as new, poorer land is brought into cultivation. Industrial capital, on the other hand, might be more intensely and productively invested. More industry tends to mean economies of scale, more agriculture, diminishing returns. Inequalities may thus become entrenched. Moreover, if capital can move, the scenario may be repeated in which 'Portugal did export wine, *à la* Ricardo, but English capital came to control the vineyards' (Dunkley 2004:73).

Comparative advantage predicts a one-off gain (Deranyiagala 2005). Even if specialisation brings increased productivity, it provides no explanation for why, having specialised, countries should continue to grow. Of course, with infinite commodities and an infinite number of countries there might always be more appropriate specialisms. But even if adjustment costs are ignored, the marginal improvements seem likely to decline. The differences seem likely to be greater, for example, between cloth and wine or cloth and semiconductors than in subsequent specialisation from red to white wine or from memory to microprocessor production. Estimates of the static gains from trade (or the costs of closure) vary, but are at levels less than 3 per cent of GDP (Deranyiagala and Fine 2001; Dunkley 2004). These may be worth having, but are hardly the basis for fundamental economic transformation. Acknowledging this, mainstream economists switch their argument away from factor endowments to dynamic gains. Implicitly abandoning comparative advantage, the theoretical basis becomes much less certain and the extent of any gains or losses becomes essentially an empirical question (Deranyiagala and Fine 2001).

Indeed, 'factor endowments' and comparative advantage do not predict observed patterns of trade. This rather fundamental empirical problem was first noted in 1953 by Leontieff. The capital-rich United States imported commodities that were more capital-intensive than were its exports. Subsequent studies confirmed that whether in terms of crude aggregates of land, labour and capital or of more disaggregated factors of production, their relationship with observed patterns of trade was at best weak (Krugman and Obstfeld 2003). The recent rise of Chinese exports might suggest some movement in the direction of trade based on endowments, in this case, abundant labour. The weighted average of GDP per capita of US import markets fell quite sharply from

62 to 49 per cent of that of the United States between 1990 and 2005 (calculated from Census 2007; UN 1996, 2006; Heston et al. 2006; Maddison 2003). However, overall the level of intra-industry trade for OECD countries remained very high (OECD 2008). Fewer poor countries relied on exports of land-based primary products, although this remained important for many, particularly in Africa.

In practice little international trade is 'free'. Firstly, much of it (a figure of 40 per cent is often cited) is 'intra-firm', not involving market relations and therefore not really 'trade' at all. Secondly, those markets that do exist need not be 'free'. MNCs have power to change any 'given' endowments. For example Nestlé and Philip Morris, who controlled half the world's coffee market, did not confront small farmers as equals (Wolf 2005). Firms might actively cut low pay rather than simply utilise it, as happened with US automobile manufacturers in Mexico (Middlebrook 1996; Núñez 1999). Thirdly, and perhaps inevitably when conducted between parties in distant places, most trade did not involve instantaneous responses to price fluctuations. Even in a 'liberal' world, much of it remained more or less organised: subject to long-term contracts, international quota agreements, government lobbying, subsidy, insurance, exchange rate manipulation, tied aid and outright bribery. Therefore assumptions of perfect competition, on which mainstream trade theory depends, seem highly suspect.

This also anticipates problems that arise in transforming Ricardo's argument, which is couched in terms of work, into monetary terms. Such a transformation assumes perfect markets, including universal full employment, and achieves the remarkable outcome that gains in productivity will be enjoyed not where they are made, but as cheaper prices where the goods are sold. Shaikh (2007b) suggests that a monetary analysis should also incorporate the role of credit, which, in a world where capital can move, would normally be more expensive in any (momentarily) trade deficit country. This would then attract profit-seeking capital, and this movement would have to be paid for by trade. Thus short-term deficits beget persistent imbalances.

Moreover, if changing supply is allowed to alter prices, this may undermine claims of overall, let alone mutual, gains. The rise of a country as big as China may not only threaten others, but, as its output reduces world prices, also create a phenomenon of 'self-immiseration' (Samuelson 2004). Moreover, because commodities can be made in different ways – by capital- or labour-intensive methods – it is entirely possible for trade to undermine capital investments and for cheap labour to undermine high productivity as the basis of comparative advantage. Conversely, if in certain circumstances trade reduces inequality, for example when wages in a poorer country rise, this tends to undermine its own basis.

Neoclassical arguments, or the use made of them to claim enormous benefits from unrestricted trade, are wrong. The evidence does not support any such assertion. Nor, however, are the arguments for closure convincing.

Inherently unequal terms of trade are hard to demonstrate empirically. It is easier to test the Prebisch and Singer thesis of *change*. Agricultural prices did fall for 20 years after they first wrote. Contemporary evidence is more ambiguous. While the price of some primary products fell dramatically, for the 78 countries for which data were available (from the UNDP 2006) there was virtually no correlation between the change in terms of trade between 1980 and 2004 and the level of primary products in exports. Dependence on a narrow range of primary exports in particular can have devastating consequences. The examples of Zambian copper and Caribbean banana producers need little repetition. However, the problems, although grave, may be time-, place- and commodity-specific. The terms of trade also fell for several countries that 'successfully' shifted out of reliance on primary product exports – for example, Mexico, China, Pakistan and Thailand.

Empirically, the evidence of monopoly power is also hardly conclusive. For some countries, like Mexico, one metropolitan country (the United States), indeed dominated its trade. For others, such as Chile and Argentina, apart from a brief US predominance around mid-century, there were several comparable – and competing – trading partners. In India's trade, the UK's role declined rapidly. Already by 1970, Britain accounted for only 11 per cent of Indian imports and 8 per cent of its exports (calculated from Mitchell 1998, 2003).

Similarly, positing high Northern wages as the cause of unequal exchange is problematic. It was not until the late 1960s that wage rises in advanced capitalist countries exceeded rises in productivity (Armstrong et al. 1984). Therefore, some of the increasing productivity should have been transmitted as lower prices to the South and increasingly favourable terms of trade. When productivity growth again outstripped wage growth from the 1980s onwards, it produced little obvious systematic advantages for poorer countries. Meanwhile, positing trade as being the source of Northern prosperity too (Wallerstein 1974) implied that the original well of Southern riches ran implausibly deep. Individual Northern firms might have been expected to quit an implied cross-class conspiracy to capture the alleged super-profits available in the South. Yet most investment remained concentrated in the North.

The focus on the transfer of value can also produce some rather trans-historical accounts and blur the distinctive features of its exploitative creation under capitalism (Brenner 1977; Skocpol 1977). Kidron suggests that the apparent radicalism of theories of unequal exchange conceals a rather naive nationalism. 'Slap a tax on exports ... Go for autarky and diversification. Use the North's own weapon against it by forcing through high wages in the South' (1974:114). Domestic interests in the South shift the blame to international relations, obscuring national class conflict. Conversely, some locals may be well served by their international connections (Cardoso and Faletto 1979). They also seem likely to resist the wage increases purportedly needed to challenge unequal exchange. In practice, import substitution could be imposed repressively (as in the original Moscow model). Of course, import substitution industrialisation (ISI) had no monopoly on anti-democratic politics, but that might indicate the potentially elitist implications of a narrow economic nationalism and the different class interests within poorer countries.

The potentially inegalitarian implications of classical theory were mentioned above. Such inequalities certainly exist. However, patterns of inequality diverge from theoretical predictions and trade does not appear to have been as important as this suggests. For example, increased tariffs in the United States in the 1930s 'had a minimal adverse impact on efficiency, income [and] employment' (Dunkley 2004:84). Conversely, if labour helped win protection, it was a dubious victory. More recently, trade has been blamed for the negative experiences of many relatively unskilled workers in rich countries. However, others have argued that overseas trade accounted for at most a small share of unemployment and increasing economic polarisation (see, for example, Rowthorn and Ramaswamy 1997; Rupert 2000; Nayyar 2007). Liberalisation went far beyond questions of trade to other dimensions of social power in production and distribution. It worked not only between countries, but within them. Restructuring found advocates at the national level, and almost invariably at least worked through them (Harvey 2005).

The Artificial Opposition Between Free Trade and Protection

The juxtaposition between free trade and protection is misleading. There is little evidence that trade openness is either an unqualified good or an unqualified bad, while in practice openness and closure are unrealised ends of a broader spectrum of approaches. Proponents of free trade, in particular, often suggest that the only alternative is isolationist protectionism. Sometimes the protectionist bogey is pure fiction. Even in theory, free trade and protection are seldom pure opposites. As discussed in Chapter 1, domestically liberals allow the market to be limited in cases of market imperfection and externality, for example to protect consumers and corporate 'intellectual property'. Internationally too, as Reich (1991) has highlighted, even the most unreconstructed neoliberal is unlikely to advocate free trade in everything; in guns and drugs and people. Smith, the great pioneer of free trade, of course went much further, and claiming him for an unconditional liberalism required a substantial posthumous reinterpretation (Magnusson 2004; Reinert and Reinert 2005). Conversely, few theorists have advocated complete autarky; few would deny the fruits of one climate to those in another where those fruits cannot grow, or restrict the use of mineral fuels to those with appropriate deposits. Certainly, Hamilton and List and most twentieth-century advocates of import substitution explicitly rejected isolation. Support for protection was usually both selective and seen as but a necessary stage in development. Few governments, at least since the collapse of the Tokugawa shogunate in Japan in the 1860s, have disavowed trade. Isolation has typically been thrust upon countries by political adversaries rather than chosen as a strategy. One might therefore be suspicious of the polarised debate.

Marx (1976) argued that the liberal stress on markets masked relations of power and exploitation in production. Of course, the contemporary trade regime is pervaded by iniquitous relations. Trade is seldom 'free' in the sense of involving open, let alone 'perfect', market transactions. The inconsistencies in the WTO's advocacy of free trade are well rehearsed (Oxfam 2002; Birdsall 2006a). However, this also suggests that demands for a more consistent liberalism or a 'level playing field' may be unhelpful, given the inherent inequalities amongst competing states and firms (Birdsall 2006b; Nayyar 2007). Nor is their power exercised exclusively, or even primarily, through trade. In general, and with important exceptions, openness or closure did not greatly affect overall economic performance, although of course its market-oriented nature could transform what might have been socially useful activities into the useless or even destructive; trade in arms and opium remain profitable. The sources of growth lay mainly elsewhere, particularly in capital investments (Maddison 1991; Deranyiagala and Fine 2001). Trade may help finance these; but historically most significant investments were nationally derived.

Debates couched in terms of free trade or protection may have conservative implications in setting agendas and demanding allegiance. Several social theorists describe processes by which established orthodoxies and heterodoxies constitute the terrain of debate and together effectively conceal more radical alternatives. The apparent antagonism masks shared assumptions, which go unchallenged (Lukes 1974; Bourdieu 1977; MacLean 2000). Here, both sides typically advocate strategies for successful capitalist growth, the desirability of which is tacitly accepted. They present national 'development' as a technical, unquestioned desideratum. As will be discussed in Chapter 12, narrow economic measures, in particular, may be insufficient (Dunkley 2004; Makuwira 2006). What matters too is the sort of development: its social and political as much as its economic dimensions. For example, a switch from subsistence to cash-crop farming may improve the trade balance but undermine welfare and increase vulnerability to numerous 'market imperfections'. Different economic activities – growing corn or flowers, building yachts or social housing – have varying effects not captured by aggregate measures of national income or the current account. The commodification or state organisation of previously private labours, particularly by women, may add to measures of national wealth, but only by making people work harder. Economic growth can often be environmentally destructive. Growth may thus be in sectional or class rather than general interests, even within a country. Both main perspectives on trade see this as a question of distribution between countries and so naturalise the nation state as the basis for discussions of welfare and common good. Much of the argument thus sits, more or less knowingly, in the state-centric realist tradition; offering advice to rulers, whose interests in poverty and inequality seem likely to be secondary at best. Competition, in politics or economics, is usually simply assumed. Such agenda setting is socially pervasive, but the apparent difficulty in opposing both free trade and protection contrasts with other aspects of the political economy in which, at least since Marx, many people have recognised the achievements of capitalism while challenging its inequities and contradictions. An adequate critique of trade, as of capitalism in general, requires moving beyond a simplistic dualism.

Nevertheless, the evidence in the first section indicated that trade's importance was growing and that the specific contemporary patterns involved significant structural imbalances. In particular, many poorer countries ran significant surpluses, often levered open to pay debt and often associated with wider processes of commodification and domestic restructuring. Conversely, the United States in particular ran large and growing deficits; its ability to sustain these raised questions that go beyond the purview of trade theory. These issues will be discussed in subsequent chapters.

Conclusion

This chapter has described an increase in trade, both in absolute terms and relative to wealth. The structure of trade also changed, so that while rich countries and regions continued to dominate, several (formerly) poorer countries became successful exporters, particularly of manufactured goods. However, the evidence and arguments for general openness are unconvincing. Amongst other things, conventional theories are based on (but then neglect the implications of) inequalities within countries, which may be exacerbated by trade. Neither openness nor closure are unqualified goods. Some countries became significantly more wealthy through strategies that included opening to trade. Others failed, while increasing competition put strains on even some of the more successful, notably in Asia. By the middle of the first decade of the present century, international trade was being sustained by US deficits, whose increase seemed unlikely to continue indefinitely.

Despite powerful theoretical and empirical criticisms, a liberal consensus prevails. Marx once commented:

> If the free-traders cannot understand how one nation can grow rich at the expense of another, we need not wonder, since these same gentlemen also refuse to understand how within one country one class can enrich itself at the expense of another. (1977:268)

Unfortunately, some putatively radical writing seems so preoccupied with international inequalities that it overlooks those within countries. Nationalist strategies downplay domestic class interests, emphasising economic growth over any recalcitrant democracy or workers' movement, and may be impervious to the social costs, for example of tearing up subsistence forms of production or from environmental damage. Protection too has been an ideology of the rich and powerful. Thus opposition to free trade alone does not adequately challenge the roots of global inequalities and poverty. Trade, at least formally, involves market relations; and while it is useful to show that these are not free and equal, the most fundamental exploitation often takes place outside the trading relationship.

Trade policies often matter profoundly, but trade's role is usually contingent. It is, of course, a two-way process; but patterns of trade may reflect structural inequalities more than they cause them. A broader array of forces within the international and domestic political economy needs to be addressed and challenged.

10

MONEY AND FINANCE

This chapter provides a critique of the contemporary global financial regime and of prevailing theories of this. The dominant view depicts finance as something of a law unto itself, detached from place and determining, but itself little influenced by, other areas of political economy and social life. Financial actors are indeed powerful, but their position is often contradictory; it is supported by particular interests within the wider political economy and potentially contested by others.

The chapter first discusses the general character of money and finance, describing their different forms and some of the contradictions these involve. Secondly, it provides some historical context, discussing the gold standard, the Bretton Woods era and the transition to floating foreign-exchange rates. Thirdly, it describes the contemporary period as something which has also 'evolved' since the 1970s through a series of crises and struggles. Finally, it discusses how contemporary finance remains socially and geographically embedded and in a dynamic relationship with the wider political economy.

Money, Finance and the 'Real' Economy

Money itself is of course perfectly real – as anyone who lacks it knows all too well. Indeed, in modern capitalism it becomes both the point of departure and the destination of all economic activity. In Marx's famous formula Money – Commodities – More Money the intermediate stage, which involves producing commodities, useful goods, becomes simply a necessary and often inconvenient means to increase money. Therefore, only under conditions of a monetary economy do the specifically capitalist forms of production and trade make sense (de Brunhoff 1976).

Yet there also remains something unreal about money. Historically, most productive activity in households and other subsistence forms managed without it. In many societies, money impinged only relatively peripherally. Smith could still lampoon a mercantilist prioritisation of a trade surplus, recognising that money is not wealth. Similarly, few would confuse the hyper-inflations, as occurred in Germany in 1923, with a commensurate increase in real wealth. Today, when the volumes exchanged by foreign currency speculators exceed the world's income more than tenfold, money can have a similar fantastic quality. It also becomes difficult to pin down where and even what money is. For orthodox interpretations, too, money at most oils the wheels of the 'real' economy.

However, financial movements, including the speculative, can have profound effects, as highlighted by repeated crises in poorer countries in the 1990s and 2000s. The availability of money and the rates at which it can be borrowed can influence profoundly the ability of firms to invest and of individuals to consume. As will be discussed below, financial and monetary policies are inescapably class policies. Rates of inflation, interest and foreign exchange, for example, all impact people differently according to their social position. However, despite the spectacular volumes of contemporary financial transactions, which for individuals undoubtedly make money, only exploitation ultimately creates extra wealth, so money and finance are themselves generated within and conditioned by the broader political economy.

An emphasis on money, with its fascinating history and sometimes technical complexity, therefore risks masking other more fundamental social relations. Keen to demystify money, Galbraith insists it is 'nothing more or less than ... what is commonly offered or received for the purchase or sale of goods, services or other things' (1995:3–4). However, money can do more than this and other authors usually list three or four functions of money; as medium of exchange, store of value and unit of account as well as means of payment (Samuelson et al. 1975;

Leyshon and Thrift 1997). Unfortunately, describing something in terms of its functions does not identify why particular forms have arisen historically or how they are socially constructed. It can underestimate how money can be contradictory, even deeply dysfunctional. Money can also serve political functions, exorcised from narrowly economic interpretations. Accordingly, this section very briefly discusses the development of two forms, commodity and non-commodity money, and then how money is inherently political, both in the sense of requiring state authority (while simultaneously limiting that authority) and in the different social interests invested in money and finance.

Commodity money, most usually in the form of gold or silver (but other things from copper to tobacco have also been used), is most obviously 'real'. Precious metals are dug out of mines, transported and processed by human labour and have value accordingly. This allows them to act as 'universal equivalents' in exchange for other commodities. However, specie, precious-metal money, is also particularly effective as a store of value. Gold and silver do not rot. Historically, most money has indeed been stored – in the temples of antiquity, the safes of goldsmiths or the vaults of central banks. The value of gold and silver, like other commodities, can however, vary. Improved techniques cheapen production, while the usual pressures of supply and demand apply. New discoveries, like those of silver in the New World after 1493 and of gold in California and Australia in the mid nineteenth century, lowered their price or (which is the same thing) led to general inflation. Price changes between the two finally undermined bimetallism, the simultaneous use of both gold and silver. The gold standard triumphed in the late nineteenth and early twentieth centuries. Though imperfectly observed, it then made currency conversion simple and predictable, producing an international monetary system in many ways more integrated than today's.

However, specie has drawbacks. As a means of payment and medium of exchange gold and silver have the practical advantage that while relatively small amounts contain substantial value, they can also be divided. However, there are limits. Already in eighteenth-century France, gold had become cumbersome, with porters forced to struggle through the streets of Paris under the weight of their sacks (Mandel 1968). It is also inconvenient for small transactions. At current prices a newspaper might cost a twenty-fifth of a gram. Supply of precious metals is also inherently limited, restricting the value that can be stored and circulated, potentially providing insufficient liquidity to the wider economy.

Of course, this pure commodity role has long been compromised in various ways. In particular, money is backed by states. Sovereigns claimed a right to seigniorage – asserting the value of money while debasing the currency, mixing the gold with lead or other base metals. Concomitantly, the currency of certain leading states – the Greek silver drachma, Byzantine gold solidus, golden florins and Venetian ducats, Spanish–Mexican silver pesos (and pieces of eight of them) and pounds sterling – became particularly trusted (Cohen 1998). However, one country's gold is as good as another. Wealth begets power and that of great international banking houses, from the Fuggers and Medicis to the Rothschilds, always compromised notions of absolute state sovereignty. Within states, private individuals and institutions possess money and therefore power (de Brunhoff 1978). Commodity money could also, of course, be clipped or forged by the private sector.

Some of the problems have been resolved by a series of tokens, which have 'stood in' for commodity money. Base metal coins, paper notes (both Chinese inventions) and cheques were the most significant examples, at least until recently. These tokens have little or no intrinsic value, although on occasion the metal content of low denomination coins has exceeded their face value. It is money by 'fiat', money because law or custom deems it to be money. In exchange, and particularly as a unit of account, the concrete equivalent becomes unnecessary (Itoh and Lapavitsas 1999). States and banks can therefore simply increase supply. Token money potentially solves the problem of liquidity. However, this can undermine the role of money as a store of value. Marx wrote:

> The difficulty in grasping this relation is due to the fact that the two
> functions of money – as a standard of value and a medium of circulation –
> are governed not only by conflicting laws, but by laws which appear to be at
> variance with the antithetical features of the two functions. (1970:120–1)

Re-emphasising a certain unreality to money as a 'thing-in-itself',
it is only good as long as it can be redeemed for something else.
Commodity money does this quite reliably. Token money requires
more complex levels of trust. Banknotes are essentially cheques
issued by banks (since the nineteenth century, usually state-backed
central banks), which like other cheques are only good provided
there are sufficient assets to cover them – or as with a circulating
uncrossed cheque, so long as nobody worries whether there are
sufficient assets to cover them. Historically, the functions of
store of value and means of circulation have been combined in
convertible money – English banknotes still 'promise to pay the
bearer on demand'. This has long been pure fiction: Britain came
off the gold standard in 1931 never to return. However, with such
a link there can be more money in circulation than deposited
gold. Providing, of course, the state remains trusted. A rush
to convert banknotes into specie would prove even apparently
sound monies to be unreliable. Conversely, (faith in) the value
even of inconvertible currencies may be more or less successfully
defended. Faith in money, and fear of money, can become vital
means by which virtual finance is able to dominate other aspects
of the economy, but they can also be fragile.

Bank credit works in much the same way as state money. Banks
issue notes or give credit beyond their reserves. Again, this is
standard and good practice, although what level of leverage
is reckoned 'safe' has varied between countries and remains
theoretically indeterminate. A panic of sufficient scale would
undermine sound as well as unsound banks. That banks should
be trusted at all is uncertain and usually requires state support
and regulation. Levels of such backing have varied historically
and many, probably most, banks have collapsed. In the United
States there were 1,748 bank 'suspensions' in the 20 years before
the Federal Reserve Act of 1913. In the next 20 years there were

another 15,502 (Galbraith 1995). This finally prompted tougher regulation, which was only relatively slowly amended by the 1990s. Nevertheless, reserve requirements endure and faith in central banks as lenders of last resort, bailing out failed banking or other financial ventures, continues to underpin the system.

Banks' ability to create credit poses non-trivial questions of what exactly constitutes money. There is a continuum of more or less liquid assets, from cash, through treasury bills and government bonds, to capital equipment and property. There are all sorts of 'near money' – stocks and bonds and various sorts of derivatives, adding further layers to the variety and complexity. Perhaps unsurprisingly, states' ability to control money or even to measure it has always been limited (Galbraith 1995; Panitch and Gindin 2005). This tends to undermine monetarist ambitions of controlling the money supply, and in practice cruder instruments have sufficed for their political project.

Monetary and financial policy serve social and political ends. The current vogue, for example, is for defending the value of money against inflation. However, price rises are not the universal evil this orthodoxy would impute. Hyperinflations are fairly obviously destabilising, but moderate inflation may be positively beneficial, stimulating investment and growth (Mackintosh et al. 1996). Familiar government targets not to exceed limits of, say, 3 per cent are essentially arbitrary austerity measures. Inflation is a social phenomenon, with winners and losers. Most obviously, borrowers and lenders see debts reduced, to the benefit of the former and detriment of the latter, although speculators may also make quick returns (Allen 2005). Intervention to alter interest rates, exchange rates and the supply of money are similarly not technical questions, but tied to political interests: those of labour or capital, but also of export industries against import, of financial capital against industry. Managing money and finance is often presented as a technical matter (too complex to be understood by non-experts). It is 'depoliticised', for example, in the assertion of central bank autonomy. Monetary policy, sometimes drastic policy, then seems to be non-policy (Cerny 1996), while finance takes on the appearance of a transcendent power.

However, nation states (or in the one case of the euro, a supra-state organisation) remain vital in issuing and authorising money. The most global of finance remains denominated in national, territorialised money, overwhelmingly that of a few major currencies. However, the most basic functions of money highlight inherent limits to sovereignty, to state capacity and independence. The idea of 'one nation/one money' is a modern myth seldom realised historically (Cohen 1998). Money had international dimensions for millennia, with complex, overlapping financial systems already linking Europe, the Mediterranean, the Middle East, India and China by the thirteenth century (Germain 1997; Banaji 2007). States recognised and facilitated the exchange of multiple currencies (Galbraith 1995). Significantly, there is then an inherent contradiction between the domestic use of money, in which reserves may be held as a store of value, and the necessary use of these same reserves as a means of payment in international transactions. Modern 'virtual money', which provides liquidity to a new degree, and which is ever more mobile, provokes countries to hold ever greater reserves of what are considered stable and reliable or 'hard' currencies, particularly US dollars. These too can then be thrown onto financial markets, potentially facilitating useful investments or destructive speculation.

From the Gold Standard to Bretton Woods

The interconnection between the rival domestic and international interests became apparent in the establishment and unravelling of the classical gold standard in the late nineteenth and early twentieth centuries. The gold standard restricted domestic investment within the allegedly hegemonic power as gold moved out to cover Britain's trade deficit. Much later, in the 1960s, Mundell and Fleming (independently) posited three wants – the free movement of capital, national policy autonomy and stable exchange rates – of which states can achieve only two (Mundell 1963). Often presented as an 'objective' 'trilemma', the choices are political. The free movement of capital is a pro-finance policy, whereas 'national policy autonomy' can be a euphemism for pro-labour and welfare policies (Bryan and Rafferty 2005). Until the late nineteenth century, labour movements were weak and few workers even had the vote.

War also made policy autonomy a priority, and in 1914 links to gold were quickly cut (in Europe although not in the United States). After 1918, attempts to re-establish the link with gold faced more assertive labour movements. States were forced to accept 'domestic autonomy'. Britain finally abandoned gold as a more or less direct consequence of a strike in the navy (the 'Invergordon Mutiny', Ereira 1981), the United States in 1933, others, including France, slightly later in the decade. The crash also provoked states, notably the United States, into tighter domestic financial legislation, restricting what banks could do, creating 'firewalls' between their borrowing and lending, between different sorts of financial activity (between types of banking and between these and insurance and share dealing), and even restricting banks to single US states. Regulation Q set a maximum interest rate and banned giving interest on chequing accounts.

The post-Second World War Bretton Woods system allowed for compromises with labour, and most countries maintained capital controls and 'policy autonomy'. The United States alone allowed its capital to move freely beyond its borders, with powerful US interests more or less openly avowing a new American imperialism (Panitch and Gindin 2005). Separate national systems developed. For example, German business could raise money through loans from house banks while American firms might offer shares and seek venture capital. Americans did not normally borrow from German banks or Germans invest in American share flotations. However, this hardly represented the suppression of finance advocated by Keynes. Indeed, throughout the 1950s and 1960s the profits of US financial firms would grow more quickly than those of the non-financial firms (Panitch and Gindin 2005). However, Bretton Woods allowed for a period of remarkable currency stability, and the prejudice of seeing unrestricted capital mobility as a 'good' is a recent one.

As discussed in Chapter 7, the Bretton Woods 'gold-exchange standard' involved something of a compromise between the strict gold-standard regime which had collapsed in the inter-war period and that of autonomous currencies. The US dollar alone was linked to gold at $35 an ounce. Other currencies were pegged to the dollar at values which were changeable by negotiation. So the pound, initially valued at more than $4, was devalued to $2.80 by 1949 and eventually to $2.40 in 1967. With other countries keeping foreign reserves in either gold or dollars, the United States had advantages of seigniorage. At one level this simply made sense, as the United States was the largest exporter, foreign investor and aid donor. But unlike the British before the First World War, the United States escaped the financial discipline of gold. As some foreign leaders, notably de Gaulle, complained, it could print dollars to fight wars, buy foreign businesses and get into debt. The outflow of dollars, firstly as Marshall Aid and latterly in payment for its imports, foreign investments, overseas aid and military adventures, also supplied liquidity abroad. Thus, after an initial shortage, dollars became more readily available. Unlike gold, dollar reserves could be reinvested in the United States at interest.

However, the system unravelled. The United States could supply the world with dollars only by running balance-of-payments deficits. Other countries held dollars only so long as they could be redeemed for specie, or because of political expediency. Echoing the contradiction highlighted by Marx a century earlier, Triffin pointed out the conflict between the liquidity and confidence functions (Cohn 2005). Chapter 7 discussed the rising US balance-of-payments deficits and the outflow of gold as other countries began to reduce the productivity gap with the United States. The surplus countries might have revalued their currencies, but had little motivation for doing so: this would have been deflationary domestically and would have threatened the export surpluses they enjoyed. Nixon finally suspended US gold convertibility in 1971. After two years, attempts to maintain a managed international currency system were formally abandoned. Markets would henceforth set exchange rates.

However, the International Financial Institutions (IFIs) created at Bretton Woods, the IMF and the World Bank, survived. The former had overseen changes in currency peg values, but had also been intended to act as a lender of last resort in the event of short-term balance-of-payments problems. The role endures, although in major crises the IMF has seldom had sufficient resources to act alone and has instead provided a conduit for US funds. Lending has also tended to be for longer terms than intended. Controversially, it is 'conditional', paid in 'tranches' according to compliance with liberalising, anti-welfare and anti-labour policies. The World Bank or International Bank for Reconstruction and Development (IBRD) was initially intended to provide reconstruction loans to a war-damaged Europe. Lacking the funds later provided by Marshall Aid, its focus shifted from Europe to poorer countries, typically providing money for particular development projects, such as infrastructure or power generation. However, from the 1980s its lending overlapped that of the IMF. The Bretton Woods institution served the leading states and the leading classes within them well and they endured even when the original monetary arrangements were abandoned.

Nixon's suspension of US-dollar convertibility became the symbolic moment of shift from one financial system to another. The floating-currency regime was a significant departure. For liberals, floating rates proved the failure of planning and would bring stability. Moreover, other governments would now be free of the constraints of US policy. Alternatively, without coordination the world's monies would fluctuate unpredictably, leading to chaos and in particular undermining trade openness. With no objective standard, there was more room for inappropriate and arbitrary government intervention (Gilpin 2001). Confounding more dire predictions, the system proved compatible with increasing international trade and investment. However, there was undoubtedly instability, including severe crises and variations in exchange rates (for example between the United States and Japan) far out of proportion with any change in their underlying economic performance. Moreover, against orthodox predictions of equilibrium, there were long-term and widening trade imbalances, in recent times most notably between China and the United States. Significantly, there were strong continuities with the previous regime, with currency values typically managed rather than left to the market. Weaker states often continued to peg their currencies to those of the powerful. There was however a lengthy and contested process which saw the 're-emergence of global finance' (Helleiner 1994).

The Achievement of the Global Financial Regime after Bretton Woods

In the United States, attempts to overcome the economic downturn through Keynesian methods were abruptly abandoned with the 'Volcker shock' of 1979. The new chairman of the US Federal Reserve orchestrated sharp interest rate rises. Real rates jumped from −2 per cent in 1979 to an average of 7.5 per cent between 1981 and 1985 (Brenner 2003). Occurring immediately after the introduction of the European Monetary System (EMS), high interest rates helped secure the dollar's position as the key international currency as investors earned more through holding it. The dollar, which had fallen from its Bretton Woods value of ¥360, to ¥200 in early 1979, reached a high of ¥277 in 1982. However, the motivations were also, perhaps primarily, domestic. This was the assertion of monetarism, an attack on inflation and on labour and the social spending which had increased over the previous two decades. It represented the triumph of the 'banking complex'. There was also a process of lifting the restrictive legislation within the domestic financial sector introduced in the inter-war period. Regulation Q was abolished in 1980, and there was a loosening of the segmentation between states and sectors, even before their formal abolition in the 1990s. The United States also began what would become, according to Helleiner (1994), a process of competitive deregulation amongst leading states. Others see it instead as a process of 're-regulation' (Moran 1991; Leyshon and Thrift 1997). However characterised, it attempted to 'lock in' the defeats of labour of the 1970s (Helleiner 1994). Capital controls, which the United States reintroduced in 1963, were scrapped in 1974. Britain under Thatcher abolished them in 1979 and deregulated its financial market in the 'Big Bang' of

1986. Japan lifted capital controls in 1980; France had its 'little bang' in 1986. As one country after another abandoned policy autonomy it became harder for others to resist, for fear of being left out as capital sought the most conducive environments. There remained significant differences between countries, but there was a relatively consistent emphasis on anti-labour, low-inflation and pro-finance policies.

The interest rate rises also precipitated the debt crisis in poorer countries. Rates on international loans, which had been about 2 per cent in the early 1970s, rose to about 18 per cent in the early 1980s, and the share of profits from foreign operations for the seven largest US banks rose to 60 per cent (Gill and Law 1988; O'Brien and Williams 2004). Loan repayments increased, while inflation, which had helped to ease real interest rates, now fell. The recessionary conditions Volcker provoked in the North also restricted Southern export markets. Competition between commodity exporters increased, further cutting prices. Even indebted oil exporters suffered as oil prices fell in the 1980s. In August 1982, Mexico defaulted on its debt. This sparked a prolonged crisis, whose resolution, as will be discussed in Chapter 14, also helped open many poorer countries to financialisation.

The floating exchange rate regime also encouraged the development of various financial derivatives. Potential currency fluctuations made it necessary for firms involved in international trade to 'hedge' their exposure to foreign currency. Financial actors would cover this risk for a premium. Exposure to fluctuating commodity prices could be managed in a similar way with futures contracts. However, these instruments created the possibility of trading, not because of any belief in their underlying value or innate properties, but as a speculation. A whole raft of derivatives, financial tools derived from something else, became vast markets of their own. Futures trading in 2006 reached a global total of $1262 trillion (20 times the size of the world's economy). Options trading reached $547 trillion and the total outstanding derivatives at the end of 2006 stood at $415 trillion. An explosion of share markets was also aided by capital-friendly policy. Cuts in corporate and income tax for the wealthy fuelled financial speculation.

In the United States, the rare combination under Reagan of high interest rates and fiscal expansion also drew in foreign capital (Brenner 2003; Allen 2005). Privatisations of formerly state-owned industries added to market capitalisation, while privatised welfare required increased insurance, whose premium payments were also then reinvested on stock markets. Firms borrowed to buy back their own stock and inflate the price (Brenner 2003). Even as Volcker induced sharply recessionary conditions and declining industrial output, the financial market boomed. Even as unemployment, already 7 per cent in 1980, jumped to 9.5 per cent in 1983, the Dow Jones Index rose from 328 to 472 (Census 1990).

Reagan's expansionary domestic policy (based on tax cuts and increased military spending) soon jettisoned monetarism. It increased consumption; but the stronger dollar meant that much of this came from abroad and the current-account deficit widened, reaching the then remarkable $122 billion in 1985. Japan's surplus was $56 billion (IMF 1992). The Plaza and Louvre accords of 1985 and 1987 coordinated central bank interventions to increase the value of the yen, which would rise from 250 to the dollar in 1985 to 82 by 1995 (Federal Reserve 2007).

From the perspective of Japanese capital, revaluation made investments within the United States still more attractive. Investments became cheaper, but also avoided the difficulties of higher import prices and the threat of formal trade barriers. The car firms made major 'greenfield' investments. Sony's takeover of Columbia and Matsushita's of MCA were the most prominent acquisitions. Reduced interest rates and the inflow of Japanese funds further fuelled stock-market speculation, which, having faltered in 1984, surged ahead. The bubble burst in October 1987, when the Dow Jones experienced its biggest ever fall of 23 per cent (Lapavitsas 1988). Markets around the world followed it downwards. However, coordinated state intervention, particularly sustaining low interest rates, meant there was no generalised economic downturn.

In particular, Japanese recovery after 1987 was rapid. Low interest rates fuelled investment and inflation, while new international banking regulations, limiting asset to capital ratios, also prompted Japanese banks to sell assets and issue more shares (Strange 1998). Holders of financial assets became richer, helping to fuel a new speculative bubble. Once this burst the Japanese economy experienced a sharp downturn, but also persistent stagnation which neither low interest rates nor state spending did much to redeem (Murphy 2000). Similarly, the devaluation of the yen in 1995 helped exports, but the domestic economy remained sluggish at best. This also helped produce the Asian crash two years later.

This and other significant financial crises will be discussed in more detail in Chapters 13 and 14. However, a few general points can be made about how these in practice reinforced financialisation. The open financial system is prone to speculation. Many poorer countries attempt to stabilise their currencies, either through pegs or explicit 'dollarisation', using a foreign currency in local markets. Currency pegs can be set against one hard currency or a weighted basket, which attempts to match that of the country's trading partners. Advocated by the IMF, such strategies make trade relations predictable and, amongst other things, also protect foreign investments from devaluation. However, it has been argued that 'government decisions to maintain overvalued exchange rates reflected domestic political constraints rather than the influence of global financial markets' (Crystal, cited in Helleiner 2005:171). As with the earlier gold standard, pegged currencies limit domestic economic autonomy. Poorer countries represent a higher risk, so they have to pay investors higher interest rates to retain parity; the net effect is contractionary. This 'disciplines' labour, but protects the savings of the rich and the price of imports. Pegged currencies, combined with free capital mobility, also remain vulnerable to speculative attack.

Mexico's restructuring after the debt crisis was so thorough that it convinced finance capital, especially portfolio investors, to return en masse. Money could be borrowed in New York for 5 or 6 per cent and earn 12 or 14 per cent in Mexico (Strange 1998). Capital inflows provoked a speculative bubble and fresh collapse in 1994. A similar scenario was played out on an international scale in Asia three years later. An inherent asymmetry means that pegged currencies can become tempting targets for speculators, who know there is little danger of appreciation, but real possibilities of substantial depreciation. States can easily maintain currency values on the 'up' side, by reducing interest rates or simply by issuing local currency to the sellers of hard currency. The states do not seek to go above the pegged values, so the speculators' losses are limited. On the 'down' side, governments try to honour commitments to retain the value; increasing interest rates and buying their own currency as the speculators sell. This is more difficult as hard currency supply is limited. Sufficient speculative attack might be able to precipitate devaluation and break the pegs, irrespective of any underlying economic fundamentals. Speculators' potential gains are very large. The IFIs and the US state also encouraged the process by bailing out failed investments.

The conditionality of such rescues imposed financial discipline on borrowing countries rather than lenders. Particularly in much of the South, restructuring packages opened countries to foreign capital. Debt could also be paid by increasing trade openness, higher export earnings, and restrictive domestic policies to limit imports. However, the orchestration of this restructuring highlights that this is not simply a market-driven process. Rich-country governments in Europe voluntarily signed up to (even if they did not always comply with) similarly restrictive policies in joining the euro. Within poorer countries too, local ruling classes, or at least elements of them, have been relatively happy to accept the conditions of domestic austerity, which could nevertheless be presented as a foreign imposition.

That this is what tended to happen does not imply it was inevitable. Even relatively small states, for example Chile, and (after refusing IMF assistance in the wake of the 1997 crisis) Malaysia, implemented quite effective controls on capital movement. They did not suffer noticeably dire economic consequences, and Malaysia recovered more quickly than other countries from the crash. Poorer-country governments have also sometimes mooted a coordinated response. However, the prospects of a debtors' cartel or of an alternative Asian Monetary Fund in response to the 1997 crisis foundered not simply on US opposition, but due to the different positions of the poorer countries. For example, heavily export-dependent economies need to keep access to foreign markets open, while in doing so they can relatively easily meet debt obligations. Less trade-dependent countries might be more willing to resist, although few have done so for long.

The Social Construction of Global Finance

Several authors have argued that its spread and mobility allows finance to steal a march on less mobile actors, on other forms of capital, on labour and (most inherently tied to place) on nation states (Frieden 1991). Its mobility always gave finance structural power, but this reaches new heights. Numerous technical improvements in telecommunications and computing simplified international financial transactions. Billions of dollars, as easily as one or two, can be moved at the click of a button. The power of all states accordingly declines (Cerny 1993; Gill and Law 1993; Strange 1998). Money can go to wherever there are pro-finance policies. So policy shifts to protecting finance and the burden of paying for it shifts to labour; corporate taxes decline, consumption taxes increase.

Since the 1970s, financial firms have become richer both absolutely and relatively. In the United States, for example, financial-sector profits rose as a proportion of the total from 14 to 39 per cent between 1981 and 2001 (Blackburn 2006). The pre-tax profits of the world's 1000 largest banks totalled $786 billion in 2006. Their assets were worth $74.2 trillion, exceeding the world's GDP by about a quarter. The top 25 of these banks held 42.8 per cent of the assets or $31.8 trillion, equivalent to more than half the world's income (*The Banker*, 1 July 2007). Finance has also been prominent as the strongest example of globalisation. Foreign bank loans grew to about $26 trillion by the end of 2006. About a third of all assets were overseas. Some leading banks had much higher proportions outside their home country or even home region than within their domestic economies. Vast numbers of international bonds and notes – with an outstanding total value of $17.6 trillion as of December 2006 – were also issued (BIS 2007). Hence finance has been the exemplar of the 'end of geography' and 'deterritorialisation' (O'Brien 1992; Scholte 2000). Technological change multiplies the speed and volume of interactions, and as new institutions and instruments proliferate, finance moves beyond its original heartlands to play in global markets 24 hours a day (O'Brien 1992; Walter 1993).

The formidable number of financial instruments and transactions can make finance appear as something asocial, which sweeps away all before it. However, the financial sector is itself constituted by people in particular places involved in complex social relations who have more or less potential to alter the structures of which they are a part. The picture of global finance should be qualified in several respects. Firstly, even in terms of assets, but particularly in terms of the actual work, it remained highly geographically concentrated, mainly within rich countries. Even some rather 'hyperglobalist' accounts acknowledge the role of key 'global cities' such as New York, London and Tokyo. More generally, links within the financial sector and between it and the wider political economy appeared to tie it to place quite strongly. Indeed 'gravity models', predicting transactions between large and proximate countries, worked as well in financial as in commodities trade (Portes et al. 2001), and 'home bias' in portfolio investments, for example, remained undiminished (Kho et al. 2006). The vast quantities of financial 'flows' did not necessarily go anywhere but back and forth between Wall Street offices. Net flows were much smaller and mainly headed towards the United States (Eatwell 1996; IMF 2007b).

Perhaps most particularly, states appeared to be able to constrain finance. It was noted above that with capital controls Malaysia recovered from the 1997 crisis. Taiwan and China largely escaped the crisis, not having allowed free capital movement in the first place. Rich countries had more resources than poor. Simple legislative changes, limiting bank lending, imposing taxes, blacklisting tax havens, could stem financial movements (Strange

1986, 1998). Politically unfavoured countries like Cuba were effectively boycotted. The US state had access to technologies to monitor financial movements at least comparable to those of the financial sectors (Henwood 1998). Moreover, what each crisis made clear was just how much of 'liberalised finance' remained underwritten by the state. The US government repeatedly, either directly or through the IMF, in the LDC debt crisis, the domestic Savings and Loans crisis, the Asian crisis, and sub-prime mortgages in 2008, reimbursed the casino's losers and put the onus of repayment onto other, more vulnerable sections of society. This has also been acknowledged and criticised as 'moral hazard' by more consistent liberals like Friedman. It propagated imprudent behaviour as the inefficient survived.

What liberals are less likely to acknowledge is that global finance works as it does in the interests of powerful states and powerful interests within them. Financial assets moved across borders with state encouragement. US governments led the process of opening and continued to press this – for example, regarding capital mobility as a form of 'trade' to be freed under WTO legislation (Underhill 1993). While major rescues and restructuring are rightly notorious, what often goes unseen is the whole raft of legislation supporting liberalised and globalised finance. This particularly gets missed if politics and the state are equated with parliaments and elected governments, many of which depoliticise the economy (Moran 1991).

> Ultimately, the risks involved in international accumulation are contingent on confidence in the dollar and its material foundations in the strength of the American economy, and in the capacity of the American state to manage the inevitable volatility of financial markets. (Panitch and Gindin 2005:65)

Many poorer countries also remained heavily indebted. Indeed, for what the World Bank (2006a) classifies as 'low-income countries' debts grew from $333 billion in 1990 to $427 billion in 2004, and for 'middle-income countries' from $1004 billion to $2329 billion. The resolution of the 1980s debt crisis eased fears of bank collapse, but increased repayments. This also required greater openness to trade to earn the necessary dollars. Much heralded relief to some of the most heavily indebted very poor countries contributed to a fall in the amount paid as a proportion of national income, for the low-income countries from 3.9 per cent to 3.0 per cent between 1990 and 2005. Because these countries are absolutely poor, this costs creditors little. The Paris Club nevertheless 'ensure[d] that debt restructuring was granted only in cases of imminent default and that the debt treatment provided reflected countries' financial needs and the objective of ensuring debt sustainability' (World Bank 2006b:90). Moreover, for middle-income countries this debt service continued to rise as a proportion of GDP, from 4.5 per cent to 5.5 per cent between 1990 and 2005. However, as most poorer countries became more open, devoting a greater proportion of their output to exports, they earned the foreign currency with which to pay their creditors. The ratio of payments to export earnings for both low- and middle-income countries fell, from 20.3 to 14.3 per cent and from 27.1 to 13.7 per cent respectively between 1990 and 2005 (UNDP 2007). The enduring debt and its exacerbation of poverty and commodification nevertheless remained a source of protest in both North and South.

Increased exports also allowed poorer countries to accumulate foreign-currency reserves with which they could meet future speculation and possible deficits (Strange 1986). In real terms, government reserves rose from $872 billion in 1985 to $4280 billion in 2005. Perhaps more remarkable, developing countries' share of this rose from 41 per cent to 68 per cent. In 1965 it had been just 17 per cent (IMF 1992, 2006), see Figure 10.1. Amongst currency reserves, the dollar was the most important (see Table 10.1). However, unlike gold held in bank vaults, these 'reserves' were churned back into financial markets. In particular, dollars were lent back to the United States, which as the safest market also paid the lowest interest rates. In 2005 the United States earned $11.3 billion more from credits than it paid on debts that were $376.8 billion bigger (calculated from IMF 2006). The United States continued to accrue benefits of seigniorage. It could buy goods without transferring any commodity equivalent value. The foreign borrowing also fuelled lending at home. Moreover, US debt could then be inflated or devalued away (Gilpin 2001) and as the dollar depreciated in the early twenty-first century, losing about a third of its value (Federal Reserve 2007), the value of these reserves was correspondingly diminished. However, in response some developing countries sold dollars for euros, threatening to undermine the United States's advantage.

Table 10.1   Currency composition of official reserves (per cent)

	1995			2006		
	All	Developed	Developing	All	Developed	Developing
All	100.0	100.0	100.0	100.0	100.0	100.0
$US	59.0	52.3	70.3	64.7	71.9	59.7
ECU/euro	24.3	30.2	14.4	25.8	20.4	29.6
Yen	6.8	6.7	7.0	3.2	3.5	2.9

Source: IMF 2007a

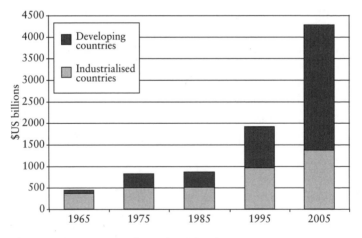

Figure 10.1   Total reserves (2005 $US billion)
Sources: IMF 1992, 2006

Meanwhile, devaluation did little for US trade deficits. Figure 10.2 shows the changing trade position of the United States and Japan as their currency values altered. However, finance continued to flow in to cover the deficit. Unlike the post-war period, when the dollar was backed by most of the world's gold reserves, by 2006 the United States had total reserves of $66 billion, $11 billion of gold – barely enough to cover a fortnight's imports (IMF 2007a). The need for such flows increased. Creditor countries for whom the US market remained crucial had a vested interest in maintaining confidence in the system, but it was unclear how long this could be sustained.

The power of global finance is also rhetorical perhaps as much as it is structural. Financial practices, as Keynes (1973) long ago asserted, depend on faith and expectation. The objective of financial actors, for example, is often to hold assets, not because of their underlying soundness, but because other people thought them sound and wanted them. However, a whole industry, from merchant banks launching share offerings and funding mergers and acquisitions, to share traders, to market researchers and journalists, depends on perpetuating the system and maintaining confidence. Ratings agencies like Moody's and Standard and Poor's grade companies and countries, and this then substantially

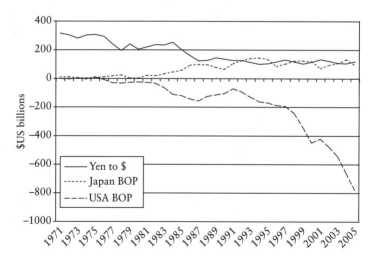

Figure 10.2 Exchange rate fluctuations and the balance of payments of the United States and Japan ($US billion), 1971–2005
Sources: IMF 1992, 2006

influences their economic worth. As long as everything goes upwards everybody can take their cut. The system is biased to produce success and to attract more resources, but ultimately these have to come from willing lenders within the real economy.

Conclusion

There is a reality to global finance, often a harsh reality. However, financial globalisation should be seen firstly as a political achievement. It has been enabled not just by policy choices back in the 1970s, but by the ongoing orientation of major states. Without their financial and legislative support it would collapse. A series of crises has compelled states to employ ever new forms of intervention to sustain it (Moran 1991).

To maintain the value of its assets, financial capital has to assert its power to discipline states and labour. Powerful governments, notably in Europe, have signed up to restrictive policies in the name of financial responsibility. It seems impossible to buck the market. As one British Labour politician is alleged to have said when the National government came off gold in 1931: 'They never told us we could do that' (cited in Kindleberger 1973:47). Yet the evidence simply does not support claims of finance trashing state powers to tax and provide welfare. High levels of state spending including welfare spending were maintained in many countries, without negative consequences for their overall economic performance (Garrett 2000; Glyn 2006).

Finally, the achievements of finance remained contradictory. In particular, it enabled US trade deficits to grow to what would otherwise have been impossible dimensions. It enabled borrowing to sustain consumption without commensurate increases in income. Cuts would have had unknown economic and political consequences. Finance achieved real redistributions within the real economy, but it in turn contributed to growing disequilibria, the effects of which it could not indefinitely escape.

11

THE NEW ECONOMY AND THE TRANSFORMATION OF LABOUR?

This chapter considers claims of a radical transformation sometimes couched in terms of the establishment of a 'new economy'. The industrialised world, including the world of work, changed substantially in the late twentieth century. Novelty and change are endemic to capitalism, but there were also important continuities in terms of relations between production and consumption, economic performance, relations between firms and between capital and labour. Recent transformations, it will be argued, do not require new conceptualisations nor do political strategies have to be re-imagined from scratch. The next section outlines the purported shift from 'Fordism' to 'post-Fordism', or the new economy, identifying central claims of transformation. The following section suggests that these claims tend to overstate the extent and success of economic restructuring. Finally, the chapter considers the implications of structural change for labour and labour organisation.

After Fordism

Characterisations of the post-war boom as 'Fordist' were discussed in Chapter 7. In brief, this involved systems of mass production and consumption underpinned by high levels of state intervention and, albeit to varying degrees and in different ways, the incorporation and accommodation of organised labour. Mass production of standardised goods allowed economies of scale providing cheaper commodities, which further extended the scope of consumption and thus production. Although named after the production methods, pay and 'paternalism' pioneered by Ford, the period was alternatively summarised from a US perspective by the slogan, 'What's good for General Motors is good for America'. Other national capitalisms fitted the model more or less well. This was still capitalism and therefore still a class-divided society; but it was an organised version, in which competition within capital and between capital and labour was moderated. In America there was also, of course, a particularly stark racial division, with the southern states still systematically segregated. Fordism was also strongly gendered, with household 'breadwinners' assumed to be male. The grey conformity implied by standardisation and mass production and the political conservatism of the cold-war era also constituted downsides to Fordism conceived as a 'total way of life' (Harvey 1990). However, capitalism's success meant relatively plentiful well-paid jobs and cheapening real consumption costs. Living standards and profits could both rise. Trade union organisation was typically strong, at least in core 'Fordist' industries, while state-backed welfare systems protected workers and underwrote the consumption norms on which capital's expansion rested. For the longest period in capitalism's history, all apparently went well.

In the late 1960s and early 1970s this was upset. Economic crisis meant an end to anything close to full employment. The apparent class peace was broken. Profit rates fell as increasingly militant workers won wage rises beyond productivity increases, which employers fought to win back. Keynesian methods of economic stimulus and state intervention were challenged, while the virtuous cycle of production and consumption was also broken. The US economy experienced what became chronic trade deficits with Japan, Europe and later East Asia, while American companies like GM could either assemble their cars in other countries or import their parts (Reich 1991).

There has been much discussion whether what Regulation School theorists termed a Fordist mode of accumulation (Aglietta 1987; Lipietz 1987; Boyer 1990) was being, or could be, superseded by a new one of post-Fordism. A substantial literature identified various elements of transformation. Those attributing the shift to geographical change and 'globalisation' were discussed in Chapter 8. This chapter outlines what for many authors was a related but analytically distinct process of social transformation. This involved profound changes in the relations between capital and labour, within production and between production and consumption.

Numerous different terminologies are used to characterise what for many was nothing short of a new information-based industrial revolution. While the long boom still bred optimism, Bell (1974) already heralded the arrival of a post-industrial society. The original industrial revolution had depended on, but then reinforced, increased agricultural output. Thus fewer agricultural workers fed more people. Now the post-industrial revolution depended on fewer industrial workers producing the necessary material goods. Increased productivity raised material wealth until at a certain level of abundance non-material ends became more important. The service sector grew, meeting the demand for increased leisure and learning, the latter reflecting the growing importance of knowledge within the economy and society at large. More critical commentators suggested that increased material abundance and increased leisure were unlikely to be distributed evenly (Gorz 1982). Instead, a society divided between the busy rich and un- or underemployed poor was emerging. This seemed closer to the realities of Western capitalism in the early 1980s. However, with a modicum of economic recovery, theories of the new economy were reinvigorated, reaching a crescendo of hyperbole in the boom of the late 1990s. The tone subsequently softened, but the core ideas remained pervasive, with Castells' (2000) account particularly influential.

The Fordist boom ran out of steam as the productivity gains associated with innovations like automated production lines, continuous-flow technologies and numerically controlled machine tools became widely diffused (Atkinson 2006). Economies of scale reached their maxima. However, transformations in computing and telecommunications (Information and Communication Technologies or ICTs), and perhaps also in biotechnologies, provided the basis for a new period, not simply of economic growth, but of social reorganisation (Castells 2000). Innovations in computing were particularly impressive, with rising microchip capacity and falling prices. Microprocessor technologies were also then embedded in a vast array of other products and processes. Telecommunications were also transformed through satellites and fibre optics, which again drastically cut costs (Held et al. 1999). Their combination brought profound changes, particularly through the Internet. The third prong of the high-tech revolution, in biotechnology (Castells 2000), was slower to yield conspicuous success. However, great hopes were placed in genetic engineering, both in crop production and in medicine, and from the 1990s pharmaceuticals was the fastest growth industry within the OECD (Pilat et al. 2006).

Increasing employment and economic output in service sectors (and a relative decline in manufacturing) continued long-term trends, but for leading countries this accelerated in the 1990s and 2000s (see Table 11.1). In part, industrial decline might be accounted for by displacement to poorer countries. Particularly in the United States and the United Kingdom, there were significant net imports of material goods, both primary and industrial. However, as Chapter 8 suggested, this should not be exaggerated. Most industrial production remained concentrated in rich countries and indeed the service sector also grew in many poorer ones. In China, for example, service sector employment growth between 1978 and 2004 outstripped that in industry by 181 million to 100 million (NBSC 2005). In terms of output, industry's share continued to rise in poorer countries, but primarily at the expense of agriculture (see Table 11.2). More significantly for theories of the new economy, it was increased manufacturing productivity in rich countries that allowed the service sector to grow. From the mid 1980s the manufacturing share of employment fell almost everywhere across the OECD, most steeply in Germany, Britain and Luxemburg, least quickly, but still significantly, in Canada, Ireland, Italy and Spain (Pilat et al. 2006).

The ICT revolution heralded a new era of success, producing a new round of creative destruction (Atkinson 2006). ICTs produced economies of scope (the ability to do different things), which

Table 11.1   The rise of services employment in G5 countries 1994–2004 (per cent)

	Agriculture		Industry		Services	
	1994	*2004*	*1994*	*2004*	*1994*	*2004*
France	3.3	2.5	24.7	21.3	73.1	76.3
Germany	1.2	1.1	32.9	29.1	65.9	69.8
Japan	2.1	1.6	33.9	29.0	64.0	69.4
UK	1.7	1.0	30.6	24.3	67.7	74.7
US	1.9	1.3	26.4	22.0	71.7	76.7

Source: Census 2008

Table 11.2   Share of output by sector in developed and developing countries 1990–2005 (per cent)

	Developed			Developing		
	Agriculture	*Industry*	*Services*	*Agriculture*	*Industry*	*Services*
1990	2.7	31.8	65.4	14.9	35.9	49.2
1995	2.2	29.2	68.6	12.8	35.9	51.3
2000	1.8	26.9	71.3	10.8	36.7	52.5
2005	1.6	24.9	73.5	10.5	37.8	51.7

Source: UNCTAD 2007b

replaced those of scale (the ability simply to do more of the same). They allowed more-efficient communication between and within firms and hence produced a rise in 'total factor productivity' (TFP). For a considerable time this was contentious. In 1987, Solow joked about how 'we see computers everywhere except in the productivity statistics' (cited in Atkinson 2006:63). While computer processing power increased exponentially, productivity growth remained sluggish. The computer industries themselves showed high rates of growth, but these were slow to generalise (Gordon 2000). Castells suggests that the new paradigm did not immediately become established as people 'hardly had time to process technological change and decide on its uses' (2000:86). Earlier inventions like the electric motor had also taken time to become efficient and widely diffused. However, by the mid 1990s a relatively clear association of productivity increases with the application of ICTs did emerge, and this apparently underlay a significant economic boom, particularly in the United States (Atkinson 2006). This was given official sanction by Federal Reserve chairman Greenspan's depiction of a virtuous cycle of expansion in which the expectation of productivity increases through technology breakthroughs fuelled expectations of higher profits, which fuelled higher equity prices, which allowed increased capital investments and thence the application of the high technologies (Brenner 2003). Even when the dot-com bubble burst, the productivity gains endured. Figure 11.1 shows the rather volatile, but nevertheless substantial rises in hourly output in the US economy. The rises in productivity and adoption of ICTs were lower in Europe, but elsewhere similar effects were claimed on both a national and an industry basis (Keane 2007).

However, what was at stake was more than just a change of a few percentage points in the productivity figures and the employment structure. What was being created – and critics were quick to discern elements of technological determinism (Bromley

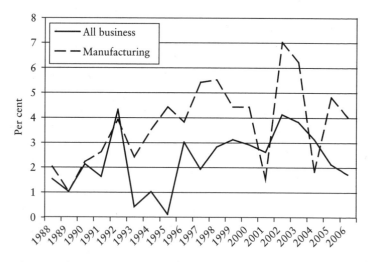

Figure 11.1 Annual percentage changes in productivity in US economy, 1988–2006

Source: Census 2008

1999; Rosenberg 2000) – was a knowledge-based economy that transformed production and its relation with consumption. As increasing productivity satisfied material wants, these lost their primacy, and consumers demanded ever greater variety and quality. Consumers rather than producers now called the shots. Services became more important, but even when consumers bought manufactured goods it was often the immaterial that was valued. This was perhaps most obvious with computer software. The initial creation may take much effort, but the reproduction was cheap. People also bought things like designer clothing for the label or style rather than for the warmth or comfort. Hence too there was an increased corporate concern with protecting intellectual property from potential imitators. DVDs and jeans were easily copied. Intellectual piracy is hardly new, but it was less important with 'old fashioned' consumer durables for which the work of manufacture still contributed most of the value.

This then impacted profoundly on the production process, in which the ability to produce flexibly became crucial. This, fortunately, was facilitated by the application of ICTs. In (what was left of) manufacturing, these allowed the introduction of flexible or lean production systems. Such systems reduced the rigidities and inefficiencies of assembly line methods, for example, the need for specific cover for breaks and absences. They also reduced waste, producing only what was needed rather than stockpiling 'just in case'. Most fundamentally, they produced a greater variety of products. However, some of the greatest gains were in the service sector. For example, computerised inventory transformed wholesale and retail trade, and telecommunications achieved major innovations in banking and other sectors of finance. Thus knowledge became the key commodity, and the key description of social position was location in relation to networks of knowledge creation and distribution (Castells 2000; Touraine 1971).

The ICT revolution then transformed the nature of relations between and within firms. The old leviathans, such as Ford, GM and, perhaps classically, IBM, proved slow to innovate. The route to success lay in 'flexible specialisation' (Piore and Sabel 1984).

Epitomised by small- and medium-sized clothing companies in the 'Third Italy', this involved producing smaller volumes of goods for more specific markets. Being able to adapt rapidly to changing tastes required the use of high technology, but also of relatively skilled and flexible labour. Small firms could respond better than large, with outsourced networks of production allowing enterprises to specialise in their particular area of expertise and product niche. However, larger firms also learned to outsource a higher proportion of their inputs and to concentrate on 'core competencies'. Thus networks replaced hierarchies as the dominant economic form.

Relations within firms became less hierarchical as they became smaller, but also because work and workplace relations were transformed (Lash and Urry 1987, 1994). There were fewer routine jobs, more 'highly-skilled, entrepreneurial, consultant-like employees' (Landry et al. 2005:132, Reich 1991). Other writers used different language, but Piore and Sabel's (1984) 'flexible specialisation' depicted a 'neo-artisanate' which enjoyed new freedom to work when, how and for whom they pleased. Thus some skilled workers gained more control over their own work, enjoying greater satisfaction and good pay. However, they had ever less in common with those at the other end of the spectrum, who were peripheralised and made all the more easily disposable as processes of deskilling and displacement advanced. The unskilled became, as Pollert (1988) objected, the object of flexibility, forced to work when and how managers decreed and for anyone who was willing to employ them and easily disposed of when no longer required. Labour thus became more polarised, with more workers concentrated at the two ends of the skill spectrum least susceptible to union organisation: the highly skilled (and less alienated) and the unskilled (and marginalised) (Hyman 1999). Even in the old 'Fordist' sectors, the introduction of more efficient practices learned from Japanese manufacturers, especially Toyota (Altschuler et al. 1984; Womack et al. 1990), meant more team-working, in which each member needed greater skills to work flexibly and to perform all of the team's various tasks. Each worker became simultaneously a customer and a supplier, for example, bearing individual responsibilities for product quality. Labour markets accordingly also became more differentiated and incomes polarised, accentuating gender and ethnic divisions (MacEwan and Tabb 1989).

This transformed relations between capital and labour. It may have added to the spatial dispersal of jobs wrought by globalisation. However, the 'onshore' social dispersal may be even more profound. Reduced firm size and hierarchy made it harder to organise (Lash and Urry 1994), as did the increased intra-class polarisation, while those industries in which workers had been well organised – like mining and cars – declined (Hyman 1999). In this post-material economy people conduct politics around issues of 'identity' rather than of class and material exploitation (Castells 2000).

Questioning Transformation

There are reasons to question many of these characterisations. Broadly, they posit too stark a dichotomy between the 'Fordist' and 'post-Fordist' periods, misreading both. The former has been discussed in Chapter 7 and only a few key points will be repeated here. The discourses of the new economy and networked capitalism will be dealt with at slightly greater length.

Few firms in the post-war period fitted the model of mass production of single, standardised products. Indeed, Ford had long since abandoned the practice. From the early days of the US automobile industry, GM had offered a 'car for every purse and pocket', producing a greater range of cars than Ford and using more flexible production methods, including a higher proportion of skilled craft-workers. They quickly overtook Ford (Rubenstein 1992). Other industries, for example in electronics, did reproduce production line methods. However, some were less susceptible to – or for one reason or another did not adopt – similar techniques. The other great standardised consumption commodity, housing, was constructed piecemeal, much-anticipated developments in industrial production and prefabrication notwithstanding (Winch 1994). Despite evidence of capital concentration there was also

always a mix of large and small employers, with even Ford's
famously integrated systems in practice relying on substantial
bought inputs. There were also substantial differences between
countries, in levels of consumption, methods of production and
the experience of labour.

For workers, Fordism was also much more ambiguous than
is sometimes assumed. Ford himself was of course vehemently
anti-union, while the production line methods were also typically
reckoned to deaden intellect and class consciousness. An important
point of Gramsci's (1971) famous writings on Fordism was
precisely to contest this. There was, however, certainly nothing
automatic about labour organisation within or between 'Fordist'
operations. Winning solidarity was always a more or less difficult
business, with the need to overcome objective and subjective
heterogeneity (Panitch 2001). In the post-war period, accords
with employers or their organisations and legally recognised rights
and protections did often create a more favourable climate, but
this too could be contradictory. In practice in the United States,
industrial peace was achieved by eliminating radical unionism and
undermining shop-floor militancy (Rupert 1995). The divergence
between the US and European experiences also highlights the
essentially subjective element to labour organisation even in the
Fordist period.

The world undoubtedly looked very different in 2000 to the
way it had in 1975 or 1950. There are innumerable examples that
give credence to narratives of globalisation and of post-Fordism
and the new economy. These included some considerable successes
in restructuring against labour, with the increasing profit and
declining labour shares in income. Capitalism is ever restless.
However, the changes since 1975 are probably better interpreted
as ones of degree rather than as a paradigmatic shift.

Firstly, it is unclear that any change should be characterised
as consumer-led. There are important, if rather long-standing,
sociological debates about the importance of consumption
to identity and economic life (Bourdieu 1984; Veblen 1998).
Equally, firms engage in systematic product differentiation
and marketing. Consumer demands for greater choice in the

satisfaction of post-material wants also sit in some tension with income redistribution within rich countries, notably the United States, which for many during this period of post-materiality increased material deprivation. Even average wages in the United States were lower in 2000 than they had been in 1968 (Brenner 2003). US household spending on some material goods did fall; for example, on food and clothing, by 2.4 and 1.6 per cent of the total respectively between 1990 and 2005. The most significant rises were in personal insurance pensions (2.1 per cent), housing (2.0 per cent), education (0.6 per cent) and health care (0.5 per cent) (Census 2008). These were important service sectors, but perhaps testify less to a shift in lifestyle choice than to the withdrawal of welfare.

Secondly, the conceptual distinction between services and manufacturing and the implications of increasing employment in the former sector are not obvious (Wood, E. M. 1998). Services encompass a heterogeneous range of activities. Some of these are 'in-person services', such as education, health care, leisure and catering. Others involve long-distance more 'high-tech' and typically 'new economy' activities, such as banking and telecommunications. Marxists have usually emphasised the distinction, not between industry and services, but between productive and unproductive labour. Despite much controversy, the most important point is that 'services' can contribute to the production of value. Manufacturing can be unproductive in the sense that its products are wasteful from the point of view of capital accumulation. So labour is productive if it produces workers' consumption commodities (whether bread or circuses) or if it produces means of production (machinery or raw materials that serve as inputs for capital). Transport and research and development, although immaterial, contribute to the productive process in this sense. Conversely labour can be unproductive whether its output is material or immaterial – tanks or TV commercials. There are inevitably grey areas. Design shades into marketing. The arms industry drains the overall productive system, but can generate many useful spin-offs. The same iron can be used to build military or agricultural tools. Moreover, the productive–unproductive distinction only makes sense at the level of the whole system. For each particular capital, advertising may be as effective as innovation; for each national capital, financial seigniorage or tanks can win economic gains. Individual capitals may then experience similar compulsions to competitive accumulation irrespective of the industry–services or productive–unproductive distinction.

Similarly, the role of 'knowledge' and the extent of technological innovation is questionable. 'Information' and knowledge are difficult to evaluate. There might be similar quantities of them in the *Racing Post* and the *Financial Times*, in *Capital* and the Bible, but their respective utility depends on circumstances. The Internet opens access to huge quantities of information, and the speed of access across distance is undoubtedly often welcome, but its economic effects are less clear. The rise of computing power has indeed been remarkable, but it remains possible to be sceptical about its impact compared with previous phases of innovation, particularly those of the late nineteenth century (Gordon 2000). New technologies are, of course, simply tools, and the uses made of them are socially constructed. Economically, their introduction may be costly rather than beneficial. Firms can over-invest, as both Fiat and Nissan, for example, discovered in the 1980s. Baily (2004) gives the more recent case of upgrading bank computers. The overall network required advanced technologies unnecessary for the relatively limited tasks performed by the tellers. He also suggests that such innovations may bring one-off gains rather than progressive increases. The substantial capital outlays lock in particular practices, militating against further innovation.

Empirically, productivity increases did occur in services as well as in manufacturing, particularly in the retail and wholesale trades. Indeed, these two sectors accounted for over half of the acceleration in productivity growth in the United States between 1995 and 1999 (compared with the 1987–95 period). Almost all the rest was achieved by brokers and in semiconductors, computers and telecommunications (Henwood 2003). In many other countries too, services accounted for most of the productivity growth after 1990 (Pilat et al. 2006). Advocates of the new economy then attribute gains made by trading companies to the effective implementation of ICTs by large firms like Wal-Mart. However, others suggest that 'the exit of low-productivity establishments and the entry of high-productivity establishments generated most of the gains in retailing' (Baily 2004:37). Large firms may also have achieved higher profits by driving down supplier prices and by selling through cheaper out-of-town sites. German companies, in contrast with the US retailers and despite using similar ICT systems, had less access to cheap land and did not make similar gains (Baily 2004). One reason for the changing sectoral shares is that historically, productivity increases in services tended to be lower than in manufacturing. Brenner (2003) suggests this was substantially because service sectors were able to increase profitability even when not increasing productivity, because they were effectively shielded from foreign competition. If, or to the extent that, this is the case, it also testifies to the lack of domestic competition and to an enduringly organised capitalism.

Indeed, the extent of change appeared less than revolutionary. If Solow's paradox appeared to be overcome in the 1990s, any association of productivity growth with ICT spending did not prove causation. It may instead have been that successful firms and industries invested heavily but prospectively. By the twenty-first century, the paradox appeared to be reversed. The productivity gains continued even when ICT spending slumped between 2000 and 2003 (Baily 2004). Indeed, having been a major growth industry across the OECD in the 1980s, computer industries shed jobs more quickly than any other manufacturing sector except for textiles and clothing between 1990 and 2003. Radio, TV and communications did little better. Pharmaceuticals aside, the only industries to increase their employment were the medium- and low-tech sectors of plastics, motor vehicles and food, drink and tobacco (Pilat et al. 2006). The international comparisons also appeared salutary. In Europe and Japan, while the implementation of ICTs was slower than in the United States, it did increase. Yet productivity growth continued to fall, even compared with the supposedly disastrous decade of the 1970s. This is shown in Figure 11.2, which also contextualises the US 'success'. Productivity growth was rising only slightly, and from a very low base.

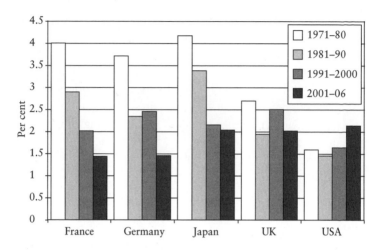

Figure 11.2   Average annual percentage changes in GDP per hour worked,
1970–2006
Source: OECD 2008

The nominal increase in the service sector may also to some
extent reflect outsourcing – another much trumpeted feature
of disorganised capitalism. Even in the 1920s, Ford employed
accountants, sales people and cleaners who may have been
categorised as manufacturing workers. As of 2002, fully 40 per
cent of those still directly employed within manufacturing were
doing 'service-related' jobs. Some of these were susceptible to
outsourcing to more or less independent companies, where they
might become 'business services'. Research and development
laboratories, for example, were sometimes separated organisa-
tionally and so constituted a service. Already by the mid 1990s,
25–30 per cent of the value embodied in manufactured goods
was generated in the service sector (Pilat at al. 2006). As will be
discussed in Chapter 12, the increase in services could also reflect
the increasing commodification of what was previously uncounted
domestic or other non-commodified labour. Cooking food,
cleaning and childcare all became important service sectors. At
least in the United States, the rise of services correlated very closely
with the rise in women's paid employment (Dunn 2007).

Firms did specialise and increase the level of bought inputs. Within these 'networks', however, the rise and independence of small firms may also be overstated. Large and often familiar corporations maintained much of their economic weight. Capitalism's tendency towards concentration and centralisation was always counteracted by a separation of particular trades and specific tasks as distinct industries. Marx (1976) described this in terms of an increasing 'roundaboutness in production'. Moreover, relations between suppliers and major corporations can take many forms, with independence often more formal than real (Gereffi et al. 2005). In the extreme, but not unusually in sectors like construction, it could involve individual workers being categorised as businesses as a tax dodge (Harvey 2001). On the other hand, subcontractors need not be small independents, but can be giant firms in their own right. So in the automobile industry, for example, assemblers bought in more than formerly, but many of the suppliers were themselves often huge corporations. Some small firms have of course succeeded. A reasonable measure of success would appear still to be their transformation into large firms. This applies to the most famous of the 'Third Italy' clothing manufacturers, Benetton, and of course to the high-tech start-ups like Microsoft, Intel and HP. In the United States, usually presumed to epitomise the transformation, average workplace size changed little, with the proportion working for firms of more than 500 rising from 46 to 49 per cent between 1990 and 2004 (Census 2008). Large firms also had power over smaller suppliers to extract lower prices, which in turn could undermine the latter's profits and their capacity to invest and innovate.

The degree of flexibility in most production processes remained similarly limited. Clothing companies could change the colour of their jumpers, car companies offer a combination of different engines and exterior sheet metal, computers contain a (one suspects deliberately) bewildering array of different specific components. However, in each case the range was limited and only the very rich commissioned bespoke production, even of their clothes. Even they bought cars and computers 'off the peg'. Moreover, each of these remained discrete production processes, each factory (or network) dedicated to producing within its own narrow industry. This is particularly stark in a high-tech sector like semiconductors, with vast capital outlays necessary to build wafer fabrication plants dedicated to producing specific microchips. Car plants typically produced only one or two basic 'platforms'. Even in the service sector, firms and departments often remained highly specialised, and the work was routine.

Flexibility, while often posited as a universal good, also had different meanings for different people. Labour market flexibility can be a euphemism for casualisation (Pollert 1988). Flexible work could reflect multi-skilling or an increase in management prerogative. 'Team working' and 'just in time' have been characterised as 'management by stress', requiring more physical and mental effort, rather than as harbingers of less-alienated working conditions (Parker and Slaughter 1988). The 'rigidities' they seek to overcome could be rare moments of reprieve on the production line as workers waited for parts to arrive (Babson 1999; Smith 2000). Braverman's (1974) classic study of the transformation of white-collar labour perhaps understated the diversity and contested nature of change, but amply demonstrated that service sector work need be no more rewarding than manufacturing. However, the social content of new forms of organisation could vary with context. So ideas of work teams, developed in Japan in the aftermath of crushing defeats for labour, might be translated differently into situations where labour was stronger. Team meetings might offer opportunities to voice disquiet, inter-team competition might mean sabotaging the opposition rather than improving one's own team's performance, and the whole process often required more supervision not, as intended, less (Clarke 1997; Delbridge and Lowe 1997; Rinehart et al. 1997).

The next section will discuss questions of whether labour's retreat was a necessary consequence of structural change. However, the fact of retreat may also qualify characterisations of capital's transformation (Walker 1999). TFP can be a euphemism for exploitation, achieved not because of inherent efficiencies, but by making people work harder. Increased profits may be achieved at the expense of wages rather than through innovation. That profits were increasingly churned back into the financial markets, often buying back corporate shares rather than reinvested, would appear to confirm this (Brenner 2003). Innovation did not appear very attractive and the tendency in rich countries continued to be for levels of gross fixed capital formation (GFCF) to fall. Some profits went abroad, but for non-financial corporations financial assets rose from 37 per cent to 49 per cent of the total between 1990 and 2005 (Census 2008). Meanwhile, a consumption-led economy was being sustained, not by heightened levels of wealth, but by increased lending, including to many already basically insolvent (Henwood 2003).

Restructuring and Labour's Agency

The strongest versions of the new-economy thesis insisted that with a post-material economy there was an accompanying shift by which subjective identities replaced objective economic situation as the basis of social action. Not only should left politics not be all about class, but it should not be about class at all. In a somewhat unconvincing twist to the anti-determinist narrative, structural change determines that the labour movement is finished (Castells 2000). The qualifications in the previous section on restructuring suggest that the implications for labour and workers' organisation are unlikely to be as catastrophic as this suggests. Rejecting the post-Marxist excess does nevertheless require an acknowledgement that labour's strengths and weaknesses were always subjective as well as objective.

Structural change matters to labour, but its implications are usually ambiguous rather than straightforwardly negative. For example, the relationship between workplace size and labour organisation is weak (Ackers et al. 1996). Moreover, while in 'industrialised' countries there are few if any factories the size of those in the US car industry of the 1920s, there was little evidence of an overall decline in workplace size. There was certainly no return to the genuinely small-scale or familial units that might plausibly preclude trade unionism. Of course as some large workplaces disappeared others emerged, with no automatic process of unionisation. So, for example, union organisation in the United States held up better in the car assemblers, even as their size fell, than in the parts sectors, where firm size grew. Similarly, unlike their counterparts in older industries, new concentrations of labour in central processing and call centres often went unorganised.

There also seems little reason to imagine that complex networks within and between firms undermined labour. Indeed, such structures and practices, like 'just in time' production, appeared vulnerable to disruption. There are some examples of labour utilising this potential and of managers valuing relations with unions to moderate it (Thelen and Kume 1999; Herod 2000).

Arguments about changes in the labour process and its effects on consciousness and organisation are hard to evaluate. The impacts of technology and the labour process remain controversial (Braverman 1974; Burawoy 1985). There is little predictive success in ascribing labour outcomes according to occupation or workplace conditions (Tilly 1978). Orthodox economics, while sometimes acknowledging the conceptual difficulties (Samuelson et al. 1975), in practice typically adopts the simple but tautological expedient of reading skill polarisation backwards from pay differentials. Increasing pay differentials then reflect increasing skill differentials, which then provide grounds for anticipating difficulties for labour in organising. This, of course, presupposes exactly what the argument purports to show. The line of causation might often run in the opposite direction, with failures of organisation allowing an increased pay dispersal, irrespective of any relation to skill. The evidence is also ambiguous. In the United States there was pay polarisation, but this included sectors like construction in which there was relatively clear evidence that technological change concentrated skill requirements towards the centre (Thieblot 2002). US average graduate wages also fell (Wood, A. 1998). In continental Europe, comparing the lowest decile and the mean, the pay gap tended to decrease (Glyn 2006).

The circularity of liberal arguments around skill may have particularly unfortunate implications in relation to women and ethnic minority workers, whose pay is usually systematically lower than that of white men. However, in at least some cases, but notably including the United States, these tended to narrow, albeit slowly and unevenly (Census 2008). Perhaps more importantly, notions of 'peripheral' status can become the starting point of an unfortunate argument that attributes to differences in skill or objective measures of 'human capital' what may instead be the product of more subjective discrimination and the failures of organisation by labour (Pollert 1988). In the past, many traditionally 'male' jobs were low paid and casualised until they successfully organised. US data for pay differentials between union and non-union labour suggest that advantages from unionisation persist and that when those at the bottom, particularly women and Hispanic workers, do organise they have most to gain (Census 2003). Unsurprisingly then, women and ethnic minority workers do not apparently feel themselves particularly alienated from organised labour, with some studies reporting significantly more positive attitudes towards unions than amongst white men (Bronfenbrenner 2003). This is not to downplay what are often important differences between workers, including substantial enduring disadvantages and discrimination based on ethnicity and gender. However, it directs attention to the way these are complex social constructions, rather than naturalising them or seeing them as determined by the structure of capital. Once absolutist descriptions are rejected, peripheral status is socially inscribed and contestable.

Amongst other things, this may redirect attention to labour organisations' many failings. Trade unions, for example, have both opposed discrimination and, in building on existing sectional strengths and particularistic practices, too often reinforced it. Conversely, changes in the broader political economy or social environment have also meant that forms of oppression, which may in 'normal' times be the basis of exclusion, can become the basis for mobilisation and organisation (Harrod 1987). It is plausible that structural change undermined particular established institutional practices. New structures might be possible, but are not called forth automatically. Finding appropriate organ-isational forms presents difficult practical questions, with solidarity requiring both unity around common positions and the overcoming of differences. However, there seems little reason to believe that workers should cede as secondary concerns questions of exploitation and economic well-being.

Conclusion

The world is ever characterised by continuity and change. Evaluating the two is difficult, and there may be an inbuilt tendency to experience and emphasise the latter more strongly. The claims of a new economy draw on real evidence. In particular, there has been a long-term sectoral change. Productivity rises allowed more people to work outside material production; first outside agriculture and then over the last hundred years also outside industry. The late twentieth century provided some remarkable technological innovations in ICTs and their application in both manufacturing and service sectors. However, there is little evidence that this produced a new phase of accelerated growth or transformation on anything like the scale of the long post-1945 boom. Changes in the relations between and within firms and between production and consumption were in many respects rather modest.

Capital, supported by the state, rolled back many of labour's previous gains. It achieved substantial economic and political successes, for example in cutting wage shares of national income and levels of union membership. However, it is unclear that capital achieved a reliable or sustainable new mode of accumulation or that its structures precluded effective labour organising.

12

THE POLITICAL ECONOMY OF
THE 'NON-ECONOMIC'

This chapter's title refers to a potentially vast range of issues that tends to be excluded by mainstream economics' emphasis on markets and distribution. It is only possible to consider a few; the use and abuse of the natural environment, non-marketised forms of work, the organisation of the labour process under capitalism, and the generation and maintenance of consumption norms, each of which in different ways defies neat monetary measures and models of supply and demand. There is much else that could properly be discussed here. The chapter says very little about subsistence agriculture, still the most common form of work. Numerous other issues are no less intrinsically important, but are perhaps a step further from the immediate questions of political economy considered here (as well as further beyond my competence). The discussion is therefore illustrative rather than comprehensive. However, it uses these examples to develop an argument that there are important tensions between use value and exchange value (necessarily invisible to mainstream economics, for which the two are inseparable) which contribute significantly to the contradictory dynamics of contemporary capitalism.

The chapter begins with a brief discussion of 'embedding' and Polanyi's (2001) ideas that land, labour and money were 'fictitious commodities' maintained only by state intervention. It then considers the appropriation of nature, domestic labour and the reproduction of labour power, work and the production process and finally (completing the production cycle) the disposal of commodities in their sale and their dumping back into the environment.

Fictitious Commodities and the 'Embedded' Nature of Capitalism

Marxist and other radical perspectives emphasise that the market is not self-sustaining, but necessarily 'embedded' in wider social practices. By the same token, most human action is not that of rational calculating egotists, but imbued with all sorts of more or less cooperative social and habitual practices. In particular, Polanyi (2001) insisted that money, land and labour were 'fictitious commodities', because they were not produced by capital. As discussed in Chapter 10, money is produced and reproduced by nation states. There have been some suggestions that this association with the malign hand of government is not a necessary one (Endres 2007; Bryan and Rafferty 2006). Nevertheless, the ongoing intervention of states and the supra-state European Central Bank confirms that for the time being money remains something 'managed', albeit not necessarily very successfully. Money as a social phenomenon depends on institutional support, but is clearly intrinsic to, rather than outside, 'the economy' and is not discussed further here.

Land is discussed as one element of the environment which capital appropriates, but does not itself reproduce. Labour power is sold as a commodity only because workers have been rendered 'doubly free', in Marx's famous expression – free from the means of supporting themselves and free to work for any employer. As will be discussed, its reproduction also continues to depend on non-capitalistically organised work, particularly domestic labour. Also, unlike other commodities, even once the sale is made, labour is not passive and its use value remains a matter of contest.

Polanyi's is an anti-Marxist argument for the primacy of politics over economics. Capitalism only works because it is politically and socially supported. As seen in Chapter 5, the nation state system undoubtedly emerged before anything resembling modern industrial capitalism. Capitalism also drew on and transformed pre-existing inequalities, including patriarchal family relations. A long-standing sociological tradition has similarly insisted that particular ideas were necessary for capitalism's establishment and success (Weber 1930). Ideas and institutions do indeed matter (Cox 1981). For example, it is a truism that capitalism only survives as long as people are prepared to tolerate it. Socialist revolutions would involve transformations in consciousness enabling trans-formations in material conditions. It is a two-way process. But in 'normal' times there may be stronger influences in one direction than another. The state may be more disciplined by capital than capable of disciplining it. Other institutions may have even less power to enjoy a life of their own. In terms of ideas, Harvey writes that 'the odd thing about postmodern cultural production is how much sheer profit-seeking is determinant in the first instance' (1990:336). However, although capital's requirements may shape its exterior more strongly than it is in turn shaped there is an important sense in which it depends on, even as it undermines, its own most fundamental material basis.

The Expropriation of Nature

Some green critics charge Marxism, along with mainstream economics, with systematically neglecting the environment. They suggest that, in common with mainstream economy, Marxism prioritises growth and ignores the consequences. At worst, it explicitly pits humanity against nature (see, for example, Deléage 1994; O'Connor 1994b). Yet again, it seems appropriate to distinguish the policies of avowedly Marxist states, caught in a competitive need to accumulate (in particular militarily) and which were therefore largely guilty as charged, from the original Marxist tradition. Marxism as historical *materialism* indeed begins with the relations between human beings and their environment. People and human history are not separate from, but are parts of, nature and natural history. Therefore as Engels says, 'let us not ... flatter ourselves overmuch on account of our human victories over nature. For each such victory nature takes its revenge on us' (cited in McGarr 2000:111). However, Marx described how 'every self-estrangement of man from himself and nature is manifested in the relationship he sets up between other men and himself and nature' (1975:331). Breaking the essential metabolism (*Stoffwechsel*) between people and their environment, capitalism depletes one area even as it deposits in another. The most obvious example to Marx of this rupture was in the separation of town and country, with human excrement consequently becoming a pollutant rather than a fertiliser (Foster 2000).

This environmental destruction of course undermines capital's ability to derive value from nature. Contrary to much assertion, Marx did not see labour as the source of all wealth. In the *Critique of the Gotha Programme*, he is withering in opposition to just this claim. 'Nature is just as much the source of use values (and surely they are what make up material wealth!) as labour' (1974:341). However, because capitalism can seize nature's use values for free, they have no monetary or exchange value. So the centrality of money, as the medium that socialises otherwise separate social labours under capitalism, at the same time separates people from nature. As the young Marx had written more than 30 years earlier, 'money [becomes] the universal and self-constituted value of all things. It has therefore deprived the entire world – both the world of man and of nature – of its specific value' (1975:239).

There is then a certain inverted logic to liberal schemes to protect the environment by commodifying it. As mentioned in Chapter 3, the suggested solution to the existence of 'public goods' is to privatise them. By making private capital responsible, an 'appropriate' cost might be paid for damage caused or reward received for environment redeemed. This is the rationale behind carbon-trading schemes and 'polluter pays' principles. Of course this repeats capitalism's subordination of use value to exchange value; the original source of many of the problems. The relentless drive to accumulate ever more exchange value continually calls forth new use values to be taken from and dumped back into the environment. The contradiction between use value and exchange value perhaps becomes clearest in the boost to GDP provided by limited environmental destruction and its partial repair (Kovel 2002). That the world would be better off with an undamaged environment and with less effort expended hardly needs arguing.

Moreover, as Polanyi (2001) made so clear in relation to land, the establishment and maintenance of these fictitious commodities is only sustained by state intervention. The importance of the state might point towards reform strategies that limit the market. But while valuable reforms have been won, they are always achieved in tension with the underlying economy and are threatened by it. Policies of rational planning exist uneasily alongside an intrinsically short-termist system and an unorganised economy. The increasingly global nature of environmental degradation, particularly global warming, further highlights the limits of national strategies. The need for action can be almost universally acknowledged, yet in a world of inter-firm and interstate competition the costs and disadvantages to any first mover make the prospects for effective remedies remote.

Domestic Labour and the Reproduction of Labour Power

The circuit, or rather the ever expanding spiral, of capital accumulation draws on the external environment, depleting and degrading it. It also draws on other non-commodified work. Historically, capitalism developed in dynamic relation with other modes of production. It recruited labour, traded and exploited slaves, bought and looted products, sold commodities and extended its investments. It perpetually relies on domestic labour. Since the 1970s, feminist and Marxist accounts have recognised that domestic labour provides a vital use value to capitalism. Women (in particular, but not exclusively) perform unpaid labour, often necessary for the effective reproduction of labour power and often in addition to paid employment. Much homeworking produces commodities, for example fruit and vegetables and clothes. Even where it does not, its qualitative importance is not in doubt. It not only has a directly economic role in reproducing workers, but also, for example, in sustaining the nuclear family, gender norms and socialising labour (Anderson 2000). However, housework is not bought and sold, and therefore, like nature, is usually denied any exchange value. This produces a rather simplistic dualism between use and exchange value and tends to dismiss what is an important component of total social labour.

Marx described how labour power is not produced spontaneously. Workers must first be rendered doubly free. However, unlike Polanyi (2001), for whom labour was a fictitious commodity because it was not produced by capital, Marx maintained that labour power in a mature capitalist system was bought and sold at its value, which was determined, like that of any other commodity, by the amount of work needed for its reproduction (Marx 1976:274). He distinguished labour power, the ability to work, from the work itself; the market equality from the processes of exploitation at work. The value of labour power is then usually taken as equivalent to the value of the commodities that the worker buys with his or her wages (Marx 1978a:454, 1981:121). Unfortunately, this simple equation mirrors and reproduces the contradictions of neoclassical accounts. Mainstream economists have long enjoyed Pigou's anachronistic anomaly that GDP falls when a man marries his housekeeper (Wheelock 1996). In assuming the household as the unit of analysis, domestic work is not paid and so is uncounted. The Marxist consensus similarly maintains that domestic labour does not produce value (Himmelweit and Mohun 1977). It produces use values, but not exchange values. Along with subsistence and sometimes also state labour, it is thus disqualified from contributing to value on the rather neoclassical grounds that its output is not produced for exchange and is not immediately measured or measurable (Masterson 1998). Yet, for Marxists, labour power is sold as a commodity.

Marx's labour theory of value extends the classical concept of Smith and Ricardo. However, for Smith (1997), the value of a product equalled the labour time in production only in primitive societies, in which there were no surpluses or profits. Once profit is added, and assumed natural, Smith instead understood value in terms of 'labour commanded' – how much labour could be bought with the commodities sold rather than how much was expended in production. Ricardo (1951) reverted to and stuck with production, but in a way criticised by many Marxists for denying the specific character of value creation under capitalism. Marx's notion, they suggest, is more specific (Weeks 1981; Pilling 1986). The association of the value of labour power with the price of its consumption goods avoids the (Ricardian) assumption of the inherent commensurability of different (capitalist and non-capitalist) work. However, it does so only by regression to Smith, in that it defines value according to the 'labour commanded', the consumption goods labour buys, instead of the total amount of work required for its reproduction.

In a completely static and self-contained system these would be the same. Yet when a man marries his housekeeper there is no substantive change in work or output, only a formal one, the signing of a marriage certificate. Even in the early twentieth century it was a circumstance sufficiently rare to be reckoned a mere theoretical quirk. However, it indicates a problem that is significant not only conceptually, but historically. The urban industrial proletariat was recruited from the countryside. Much of its sustenance may have come from non-commodified subsistence production. Accumulation by dispossession (Harvey 2005) in many parts of the world continues to supply labour power on a similar basis. Even where capitalism is firmly established, the work involved in reproducing labour power comes not only from commodity production, but also from domestic labour and various forms of state labour – for example, in health and education. The latter have been acknowledged by official data and as value-producing by at least some Marxists. The expansion of post-war welfare states involved a quantitative increase, but also a decommodification of welfare that was nevertheless associated with increasing the value of labour power (Harman 1984). Even mainstream national accounting systems now attempt to measure and include subsistence labour.

Domestic work appears to remain beyond the pale. However, unpaid domestic labour can provide similar use values to paid, can add socially useful labour to that embodied in consumption commodities, and, one might think, must logically be able to add to the value of the labour power (Masterson 1998). There remain significant conceptual as well as empirical difficulties in terms of exactly what should be counted and how (Cloud and Garrett 1996; Beneria 1999). Work in the home is unlike wage labour, not facing the same competitive pressures of capital accumulation to produce at 'socially necessary' rates (Seccombe 1974). The boundary between work and leisure is less sharp. Considered in isolation it would be hard to identify the presence of any value. However, domestic labour does not exist alone, and its product, labour power, is traded in a competitive capitalist system. This makes it possible, at least conceptually, to discern the value of spent labour power, albeit always after the event, the quantitative dimensions revealed only retrospectively, when the labour is thrown onto the market (Seccombe 1974, 1975). If workers with similar attributes sell their labour power in the market, it is irrelevant to capital how this was produced. It is immaterial whether the worker was reproduced purely through commodity production and consumption or to a greater or lesser extent through domestic labour. Therefore, despite the theoretical and practical problems, it is even less satisfactory simply to define away significant differences, for example, between countries, and huge changes over time in the levels and forms of work.

To do so would attribute different values of labour power to workers with equal use values. If no money was spent buying commodities in their reproduction, the labour power of the worker arriving from the countryside or fleeing communism would have no value. The worker, whose childhood involved food cooked at home and education by the state, would have less valuable labour power than her contemporary whose meals were bought and who was sent to the shoddiest of private schools. However, this is not an individual, but a social phenomenon. Levels of paid employment in general and of women's employment in particular grew dramatically in many countries. In the United States the female 'participation rate' rose from 20 to 60 per cent over the course of the twentieth century (Census 2008). Even within the G7, levels of women's employment continued to vary considerably, from 62.1 per cent in Canada to 38.1 per cent in Italy (ILO 2008). For the conventional account, more paid employment, higher family income and greater consumer spending imply an increase in wealth and in the value of labour power being reproduced. However, evidence suggests otherwise. Additional paid work impacts on unpaid labour, the diminution of which causes a real economic depletion (Hoskyns and Rai 2007). The relationship, of course, is complex. Himmelweit (2002) suggests that each extra 100 minutes of paid work reduces the time spent on domestic work only by 28 minutes. Women (and to a lesser extent men) continue to do all sorts of housework as paid employment increases. Women's 'double burden' becomes heavier, and capitalism apparently gets something for nothing. However, this precipitates new struggles and contradictions. One aspect may be seen in declining birth rates and 'demographic crisis'. It seems plausible to associate these with diminishing time spent in domestic labour and to understand them not simply as a matter of changing 'lifestyles' and personal choice, but at the product of contested social relations. Capital accumulation demands more time spent in paid employment. One way that women (and their families) can resist is by doing less work at home (Folbre 1982). The birth rate in the United States correlates strongly (and negatively) over time both with the increase in women's paid employment (0.89) and with the real level of family income (0.95) (calculated from Census 2006). The decline in the intergenerational reproduction is perhaps offset somewhat by individually more valuable (because better educated and healthier) workers. However, despite families' buying and consuming more commodities, it would appear that less value than before is going into labour power's reproduction. The source of this 'missing' value is surely connected to decreasing domestic labour.

If both paid and unpaid work contribute to labour power, that might indicate that its price is always less than its value. The latter would be equivalent to that of the commodities consumed plus the domestic labour. There is no longer equivalent exchange in labour markets; the extraction of labour in the home makes possible a super-exploitation (Humphries 1977). Yet domestic workers also consume commodities, and Seccombe (1975) suggests that the value of the housewife's labour power is simply compensated by the value of the commodities, bought with the man's wage, which she receives. However, this neat solution involves a substantial and rather implausible assumption. There is no 'internal market' to establish an equivalent exchange within the family (Folbre 1982). Moreover, single workers and households with two full-time paid workers are increasingly socially normal and presumably perform uncompensated housework. If we relax Seccombe's assumption, it implies that the home can be a site of exploitation (as well as oppression). This may upset doctrinaire models of 'class'. However, empirically this is hardly shocking. Intergenerational reproduction confirms that domestic labour can add to the value of labour power. Workers can, however moderately, accumulate. In the commodity economy they can save by working overtime. They can retrain in their own time. A limited upward mobility may be 'functional' for capital, but can also be understood in value terms. Conversely, capital can cut wages to levels below the value of the labour power, forcing workers and their families to contribute more to their own survival. However, while it is certainly imprecise and may blur inequalities within the household, in another sense Seccombe's assumption may be a reasonable approximation. Domestic relations lack capitalism's systematic competitive dynamic and it is hard to accumulate its products. Workers seldom become rich. It is particularly hard to imagine them doing so through exploitation of domestic labour alone. However, and perhaps more significantly, like a whole range of processes in which the commodity economy interacts with unpaid work, this should be open to empirical investigation.

The Production Process

Production is of course universally recognised as an essential part of the economy. However, mainstream accounts continue to focus on distribution and largely regard the production process as a 'black box'. The inputs and outputs can be priced and therefore constitute legitimate material for economic discussion, but what happens at work tends to be concealed. In particular, exploitation, the way in which the prices of inputs are transformed into higher-priced outputs, and the 'estrangement of labour' are things the mainstream leaves conveniently obscured (Marx 1975:325). Yet the silences are deeply perverse. As Simon (1991) wrote, if a visitor from another planet saw market and non-market transactions in different colours, say red and green, the thin red strands would link the solid green masses. Large corporations employ thousands, even hundreds of thousands of people. Few of them spend their time trading and even those who do, trade on the firm's not their own account (Simon 1991). Even many formally market relations are perfused with relations of power. Individual consumers and small firms do not confront giant corporations on the basis of equality, and businesses often sign long-term contracts specifying much more than just the price (Gereffi et al. 2005). Institutional economists have long stressed this predominance of bureaucracy and command relations over price mechanisms, and the tensions, amongst other things, between owners and managers (Berle and Means 1991). Relations between capital and labour within firms are also bureaucratically organised. Many firms have attempted to introduce competition and market mechanisms, especially through piece rates. The threat of dismissal and the possibility of resignation condition the command relations. In general, however, the market stops once work starts. The price of labour power is settled before (if paid after) the work is performed. The use value of labour is then settled by non-market means.

It is, of course, labour's unique use value that makes it the source of profit. Increasing the intensity and duration of work squeezes more surplus value. Conceivably one might increase national wealth simply by imposing longer hours. Amsden's (1989) work on South Korea was particularly useful and unusual in stressing the brutally long working days associated with that country's supposed economic 'miracle'. Yet although data exist on the duration of work, they seldom figure even in more critical evaluations of relative economic well-being.

Marx and Engels (1974) reckoned collective social labour to be the key feature distinguishing people from other animals. Yet under capitalism work becomes a drudge, to be shunned like the plague. In Marx's early writings (1975) he described a fourfold process of alienation. Firstly, workers are alienated from the products of their labour. They produce for capitalists not for themselves: they are exploited. Secondly, as will be elaborated below, workers are also alienated from the labour process. What they had themselves controlled comes instead under the control of capital. Production is performed in order to make money. Even if its ultimate end is to satisfy social need, even if a particular product is socially useful, production is motivated simply by profit. So as Marx would later write, 'th[e] "productive" worker cares as much about the crappy shit he makes as does the capitalist' (1973a:273). Thirdly, Marx also argues that people become alienated from each other, confronting each other as superiors, subordinates and competitors (Cox 1998). Finally, people are alienated from their species being. Workers quite reasonably hate work, their specifically human activity, and feel at home only in their animal enjoyments 'eating, drinking and procreating' (Marx 1975:327).

Marx (1976) later historicised and qualified some of this account. In previous societies the division between work and leisure had been blurred. Under capitalism it became stark. Marx also distinguished what he calls the formal and real subsumption of labour under capital. The rather esoteric language merely conveys how initially, although capital exploited labour, early forms like the putting-out system left the workers (men more than women and their children) in control of the production process, which would be organised on a family basis. With the achievement of the factory system and modern industry, capital was able to take away this control. The division of labour, so celebrated by Smith, was not merely about 'efficiency', but also about deskilling labour, as owners and their managers learned to control the labour process. After Marx's time, Taylorism or scientific management developed this further by precisely measuring the time allotted to particular tasks. Fordism then not only relied on a very high division of labour, but physically organised the time and space of production. Braverman's (1974) *Monopoly Capitalism* described how in the twentieth century these processes were extended to white-collar work, which had previously remained relatively skilled.

Alienation can appear to be a relentless process and as something finished and insurmountable. Like Weber's iron cage of instrumental rationality, it appears to offer little prospect of escape (Taylor 2002). Alternatively, alienation can be seen as a process, always incomplete and contested, even under capitalism. There is a vast literature of industrial sociology and industrial relations on the complexities of work organisation and the power and conflict within firms, and many criticisms have been made, for example of Braverman's account (Wood 1982; Jones 1982; Watson 1995). Two elements of this seem pertinent here. Firstly, even in narrowly capitalist terms, the system is ever changeable. So there is not an inexorable process of increasing scale and division of labour. New wants are always being called forth and new trades created. However real the subsumption of labour, it is not absolute, in that capital continues to need specific use values, not only generic 'hands'. So, for example, even the giant Fordist car factories also needed skilled engineers – whose sectional strength was an important basis of militancy in the union revival of the 1930s. Moreover, the rigidities of production-line methods can also create inefficiencies, which things like 'team working' and 'flexible specialisation' have sought to overcome. While in many ways these new systems are management strategies for squeezing more work out of employees (Parker and Slaughter 1988; Smith 2000), they may also require higher skills and imply reduced divisions of labour.

The second element is more active. The workplace is a directly social arena of organisation, cooperation and conflict. It is unlike the fetishised world of the market, where the value of everything, including labour power, is reduced to the question, 'How much?' The use value of work is not so reducible. It remains a complex thing, socially constructed according both to the social relations in the wider society and the specific organisation and struggles at work. Labour's subordination is always relative. There are incessant struggles, both over exchange value – questions of pay – and over use value, the conditions of work and the refusal of labour to behave like a thing, even after labour power is sold. Of course, generations of Marxists have been disappointed that these have seldom generalised into anything resembling a systematic challenge to capitalism. Conflicts can be contradictory, with both workers and capitalists prepared to accept a trade-off. The whole point of Ford's famous $5 day was to buy off resistance to the conditions of work. Conversely, winning high worker commitment can increase productivity and efficiency. The classic example is from South Africa: in 1990, 'Numsa members at the Mercedes Benz factory in East London buil[t] a special bullet-proof luxury car as a gift to Mandela. Each employee worked a few hours unpaid overtime and the car roll[ed] off the line in four days (it normally takes 38), with only 9 faults (the average is 68)' (www.cosatu.org.za/shop/ss0406-26.html, accessed 2008). Capital cannot routinely evince such commitment, but tries to increase motivation in various ways. To this end, there were some interesting experiments at Volvo about redesigning production systems with much-reduced divisions of labour and (relatively) autonomous work groups. However, the pressures to maximise exchange value have tended to minimise worker control, and these systems were abandoned even before the company was bought by Ford in 1999. For capital, the competitive search for ever more profit undermines any temporary accord, but also risks precipitating fresh struggles. The production process involves conflict as well as cooperation, but often in more directly social ways than in the fetishised monetary economy beyond production. Despite the decline of unions in recent years, millions of workers continue to join them as they do no other voluntary associations, and their collective experiences at work may reasonably be interpreted as a significant reason why fetishised and individual-ised market relations continue to be challenged.

Turning Products into Money

If the labour process is alienated, it is in a market dominated by money that commodity fetishism finds its apogee. This most proper setting of capitalist rationality reveals deep social and ecological irrationalities.

Being unplanned, it is always uncertain whether markets can dispose of the 'crappy shit' capital produces. No amount of market research can guarantee that the ever changing and expanding supply of exchange value can find an appropriate use. The supposedly instantaneous adjustment of supply to demand contrasts with the planned and usually long-term nature of the production process. For example, it takes about four years for a new car to progress from the drawing board to the showroom. A new power plant takes considerably longer. By the time the products become available, the demand which called them forth may well have evaporated. Furthermore, rather than simply adjusting around an equilibrium, output continually rises and therefore so too must consumption. The competitive imperatives to accumulate mean that capital has to dispose of an ever increasing surplus. Its success depends on its finding adequate markets and expanding, both in breadth, geographically, and in depth, increasing levels of capital and personal consumption. There must therefore be continual processes of adjustment, including the manufacturing of new wants – a process which again goes beyond what is normally considered the appropriate scope of economic analysis.

A historically and enduringly important way to dispose of the surplus has been through colonising new markets. In Luxemburg's (1963) classic account, this need to sell excess products was the prime motive of the imperial project. That this was really necessary for capitalism or a sufficient explanation for imperialism is certainly questionable. But metropolitan businesses have reaped healthy returns from products sold into poorer country markets. Nestlé's sales of formula milk have also been much criticised as an example of neo-colonialism, and tobacco sales to China follow the path pioneered by opium in the nineteenth century. This 'exterior' has been important in recent depictions of 'accumulation by dispossession', perhaps more for supplying cheap resources, including labour, but also for providing effective demand (Harvey 2003, 2005). The two are complementary. If farmers are persuaded to grow cash crops rather than food, they also have to become consumers. Increased exports allow poorer countries to import more (as well as pay off debts). As discussed above in relation to domestic labour, these sorts of processes are not confined to developing countries. Demand can be affected by the destruction of alternatives. So if public transport systems are destroyed, private ones become necessary. Probably the most egregious examples occurred in the United States between the 1920s and the 1940s with GM and other firms buying and destroying electric rail systems. But road building – matched by the concomitant relative dereliction of public transport systems – continues to stimulate the market for cars (Wolf 1996).

As the post-war period proved, capitalism can grow 'intensively' on the basis of expanding national markets. Capital itself can provide the necessary demand. However, this will only suffice in exceptional conditions in which use and exchange values at least approximately correspond. If a bottle manufacturer's new investments allow the doubling of output, this requires – but hardly ensures – that the brewer will make similar investments, that these will increase capacity, and that new markets will then be found to the same extent. However, contrary to the expectations of a long line of 'under-consumptionist' Marxism (Luxemburg 1963; Lenin 1965; Baran and Sweezy 1966), personal consumption also grew enormously in the advanced capitalist countries over the last century. At the beginning and end of the period, conspicuous spending by the rich predominated. In the years between, workers' consumption increased enormously.

Marx refuted Ricardian notions of an iron law of wages by which competition would reduce them to a subsistence minimum (Rosdolsky 1980). Not only was the value of labour power socially determined, but it could exist in multiples of simple abstract labour power. If more time was spent reproducing better educated workers, for example, the value of their labour power, like that of any other commodity, would rise accordingly. Once workers live above a bare subsistence minimum, capitalists can sell to them, sustaining their markets (and neoclassical notions of choice). A vast sociological literature, much of it hugely pessimistic, has discussed how this is done and its consequences in terms of workers' behaviour and consciousness. Some patterns of consumption and the corporate success that depends upon them are fairly obviously socially and environmentally destructive. Overeating, drinking and smoking increase the markets for their respective products, but not the value of labour power, and they increase individual utility only in a rather narrow, short-term sense.

Sustained by consumer confidence and levels of indebtedness, consumer markets can prove fragile either in general, as experiences in Japan in the 1990s confirmed, or for specific commodities. Even in the (improbable) event that wages and output increase proportionally in value terms, they are unlikely to do so in terms of use value. As people become twice as rich they do not buy twice as many potatoes. The output of any one firm or sector is hardly designed to maximise the inputs of labour power to another.

This contradiction between the use value and exchange value of labour power may become particularly significant in an international economy. As discussed in the previous section, it has been conventional amongst Marxists to make a simple equation of labour power's value with the average wage. Higher wages imply more valuable labour power and rich-country workers may be better educated and healthier and therefore more productive. But both the effective level of wages and what is bought with them are socially constructed and contested. Even increased spending on health and education can simply line the pockets of capitalists in what have become important private-sector service industries. Increased consumption of designer jeans, junk food or gin seems unlikely to change the use value of labour in a positive direction. However, consumption norms remain highly differentiated between and within countries, both quantitatively and qualitatively. Workers receive different effective wages and spend them differently. It is at least conceivable that labour power and thence commodities of similar use values can be produced by the application of labour power of (apparently) different values. However, the socially necessary labour time ultimately asserts itself at the global level, and nationally established social relations are undermined.

The production of ever more commodities again implies environmental destruction. Individual consumers are chided to work harder to recycle, even as they are cajoled into buying and therefore necessarily disposing of more. If commodities are abandoned in the shortest order, more can be sold in their place. An old practice of built-in obsolescence reached particularly obscene levels with the development of 'terminator genes', which stop crops reproducing, so forcing farmers back to the corporations to buy new seeds (McGarr 2000). Other products are piled into landfill or incinerated. Moreover, as a former US secretary of the Treasury remarked, 'the economic logic behind dumping a load of toxic waste in the lowest-wage country is impeccable' (Summers, cited in Kovel 2002:76).

Conclusion

Discussions of global political economy typically focus on a range of narrowly defined economic issues like those discussed in the previous chapters on production, trade and finance or on cooperation and competition between states, which will be discussed in the next three chapters. However, these depend on, but also continually undermine, a broader range of ecological and social relations.

Even within a thoroughly commodified capitalist system not everything is or can be assigned a price. This includes many things that have more or less direct economic significance. The use values not directly under capital's command follow logics not reducible to the maximisation of exchange value and often in contradiction with it.

13

COMPETITION AND COOPERATION
BETWEEN RICH-COUNTRY ECONOMIES

Chapter 8 argued that accumulation should be conceived primarily at the global level. This chapter situates interstate competition and cooperation within that process. It begins with a general discussion and comparison of the major economies since the 1970s. It then concentrates on the 'Triad' of Japan, Europe and the United States before ending with a brief reflection on the overall trajectory. The next chapter discusses North–South relations and poorer-country political economies.

The period from the 1970s was characterised by labour retreat, but without any commensurate capitalist success. However, there was no new Great Depression or descent into inter-imperialist war. States successfully cooperated, both in pursuing anti-labour policies and in averting the worst of economic disaster. However, they proved incapable of coordinating sustained accumulation remotely comparable to that of the long boom. Growth was weak, with contradictions and competitive pressures repeatedly threatening to undermine it.

The Post-Bretton Woods Regime

The abandonment of the Bretton Woods fixed exchange rate regime and the economic crisis of the 1970s sent a severe shock through the capitalist system. However, there was no return to the 1930s, either in terms of the severity of the downturn or in the intensification of interstate rivalry and national economic closure. For some, this is attributable to the maintenance of US hegemony (Russett 1985). The new financial regime has been characterised as Bretton Woods II (Hudson 2003); it continues to allow the United States privileges of seigniorage. The cold war kept the Western alliance dependent on US leadership. Once it was over, the United States had an unprecedented military superiority. This may have moderated competition amongst the major powers, although American wars, even against apparently weaker enemies, proved less than entirely effective. An international 'regime' unlike that of the inter-war period also persisted (Keohane 2005). Liberal ideas and institutions prevailed. To the Bretton Woods institutions was added the WTO and a series of ad hoc negotiations and informal groupings between leading countries. The outcomes were predictably broadly favourable to the US state and major interests amongst US capital. However, at times it appeared that Japanese and European interests might seriously challenge them. Many US authors in the 1970s and 1980s were particularly concerned about the Japanese 'threat'. Such concerns now look exaggerated, but Japanese trade surpluses and concomitant dollar holdings did, amongst other things, give it leverage in negotiations, with the result that US dominance was not as absolute as in the immediate post-war period (Murphy 2000).

Marx saw capitalists as hostile brothers. The same applies to leading states in the world economy. They have rallied against the threat of major crisis in any one part of the system, recognising their own vulnerability. However, they have simultaneously engaged in various competitive practices, selectively liberalising or sometimes resisting liberalisation. They continued to intervene within their economies – for example, directing investment, providing infrastructure, funding R&D and developing sets of institutions to help 'their' capital – as well as sometimes adopting openly protectionist policies, at least with respect to key industries (Lairson and Skidmore 2003; Weiss 2006). There remained strong continuities with the earlier period. Perhaps most significantly, despite the state's well advertised 'retreat', levels of intervention fell at most modestly across the OECD.

Figure 13.1 shows the overall performance of the global economy from 1951 to 2005. The decline seems clear. However, amongst the leading states the picture was very mixed. Figure

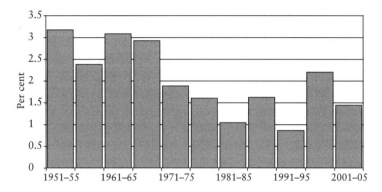

Figure 13.1 World GDP per capita percentage growth, 1951–2005
Sources: Maddison 2003; UNDP 2007

13.2 shows the experiences of the G5. The trend lines should not be taken too seriously; the experiences were anything but linear and there are many reasons to doubt whether these paths will continue. However, they have been added to emphasise the remarkable decline of Japan's growth and the real, if less spectacular deterioration in Germany and France. The United States and the United Kingdom, by contrast, did markedly less well during the long boom, but subsequently maintained their modest growth. The following sections discuss this change in more detail.

Japan: from Economic Miracle to Prolonged Downturn

The Japanese economy achieved remarkable success in the post-war period. In the 1950s and 1960s it grew at 5.7 and 9.4 per cent respectively, per capita, per year. Even in the recessionary 1970s it grew at 3.2 per cent, more quickly than the United States during the boom. It continued to grow at 3.4 per cent in the 1980s, but after the bursting of a speculative bubble in 1990 there was a prolonged downturn. It grew at only 1 per cent per capita per year in the 1990s and no faster in the early 2000s (Maddison 2003).

Elements of Japan's early growth have already been discussed. It was made possible both by the country's position within the

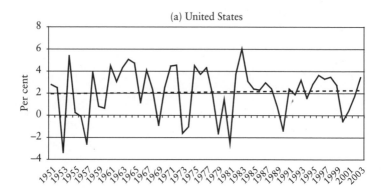

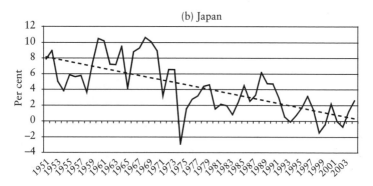

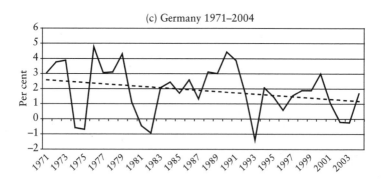

Figure 13.2 G5 annual per capita percentage growth, 1951–2004

Source: Heston et al. 2006

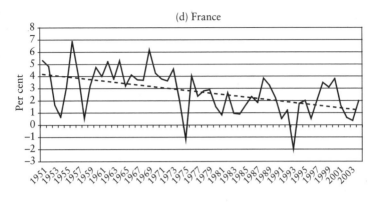

(d) France

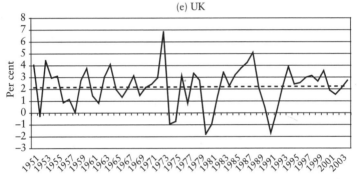

(e) UK

global economy and its specific domestic relations. Occupied until 1952, its post-war economy received an important stimulus from supplying the US military in Korea (Allen 2005). Debarred from military spending at more than 1 per cent of GDP, it also sustained very high levels of productive civilian investment. In addition it developed important export-led industries and by the 1970s ran significant surpluses, particularly to the United States.

Domestically, Japan's political economy was characterised, firstly, by a unique industrial-relations regime. The early post-war years witnessed very high levels of rank-and-file worker militancy. However, the onset of the cold war and the increasing assertiveness of labour organisation reversed US policy to one of repression in 1947. There were still significant sectional strengths amongst particular groups of workers and bitter strikes (for example, in the automobile industry at Toyota in 1950 and Nissan in 1953), but these too were defeated and militants victimised. The settlement still involved carrot as well as stick, and although a cooperative company-based unionism became the norm, it was one within which workers – at least 'core' male workers – gained secure jobs and progressive pay increases. It was in this environment that Toyota pioneered its ideas of 'team working' and 'just in time' delivery systems which came to characterise the automobile and machine tool industries in particular. Wages in the early years were low relative to the skill of Japanese workers. A relatively limited welfare state and limited access to credit also fuelled high rates of savings, which were then channelled into investment (Brenner 2003).

Secondly, and again initially under the supervision of the US occupying forces, Japan developed a distinct model of intra-firm relations. Pre-war conglomerates called *zaibatsu* were disbanded, but these effectively regrouped as *keiretsu*, close-knit networks of firms straddling a range of different sectors. Large corporations were able to achieve economies of scale and, with cheap finance from 'patient' house banks, could make long-term decisions about investment priorities (Boltho and Corbett 2000). There were then typically tiers of subcontractors. This allowed the guarantees of 'lifetime' employment to the core workers alongside greater flexibility amongst the more 'peripheral'. However, the smaller firms and their workers were not simply casualised, and within the broader *keiretsu* there were substantial elements of long-term relations, including technology-sharing processes. Nevertheless, productivity and productivity growth in the smaller firms was lower than in the lead companies. Smaller and independent firms had less easy access to credit. However, this was not an absolute oligopoly, and independent firms did develop, Sony being the most remarkable. Nevertheless, the overall structure of broadly parallel conglomerates both provided and limited competition.

Thirdly, on top of this structure sat the Japanese state. Levels of government spending as a proportion of GDP were lower than in the West, but Japan's 'developmental state', was highly interventionist, particularly through the auspices of the Ministry of International Trade and Investment, the Ministry of Finance and the Bank of Japan. Amongst other things these organised the creation of the *keiretsu*, controlled foreign exchange and technology imports and provided financial support. There was a progressive, strategic industrial 'upgrading'. Japan changed emphasis from textiles to steel, electrical power, shipbuilding, petrochemicals, automobiles, plastics, and industrial and electrical machinery and later from these to high-tech sectors. The Bank of Japan guaranteed cheap loans to the designated industries, while the market for their finished goods was strictly protected (Halevi and Lucarelli 2002; Lairson and Skidmore 2003). At the top of this structure was what came to be called the 'iron triangle' of bureaucratic, business and political elites.

It is common to see Japan's development as having been export-led. However, during the boom, exports were a relatively small component of GDP, typically around 9 or 10 per cent during the 1960s. This was low compared with the 1930s and compared to other rich countries, apart from the United States (Halevi and Lucarelli 2002; Heston et al. 2002). Japan also protected its agricultural sector, banning rice imports, and the home market for many manufactured goods. However, the combination of relatively low wages, and therefore limited domestic demand, and public investment oriented towards capital, providing transport and research and development, for example, rather than housing and welfare, 'skewed' development towards the capital goods sector, and this increased the importance of the exports (Halevi and Lucarelli 2002). By 1984 these reached around 15 per cent of GDP (Heston et al. 2002) as Japan achieved pre-eminence in several key industries and technologies.

Japan had suffered badly in the crises of the 1970s, but appeared to deal with this remarkably successfully. Almost entirely dependent on fuel imports, it now faced rising oil prices that cost about 5 per cent of GDP. The revaluation of the yen lessened this blow, but conversely, exports suffered from both higher currency values and from declining markets caused by the Western recession. In response, Japanese capital accepted reduced profits in an attempt to maintain export volumes and market shares, while attacking labour, speeding up work and cutting real pay. In the process it further undermined the local market and increased its structural dependence on exports. Higher yen values also made foreign investment cheaper. Outward FDI began to grow. Domestic investment as a percentage of GDP, while still high by Western standards, dropped from an average of 37.1 in the first half of the 1970s to 31.8 in the second, then to 29.9 in the first five years of the 1980s (Heston et al. 2002). Nevertheless, Japan continued to run trade surpluses and to grow significantly.

Japanese exports were boosted further by the Reagan boom of the early 1980s, which both revalued the dollar and provided a huge stimulus to demand. However, in response to its growing deficits, the United States organised the Plaza Accord and renewed yen revaluations. For the Japanese this was better than formal trade barriers. It was also supported by Japanese financial capital which gained from a stronger currency (Lairson and Skidmore 2003). Nevertheless, as the yen rose, exports suffered, falling to just 9.3 per cent of GDP by 1994 (Heston et al. 2002). Conversely, FDI increased, much of it to the United States, with outflows peaking at $48 billion or 1.6 per cent of GDP in 1990 (UNCTAD 2007b). The internationally coordinated response to the 1987 stock market crash meant that the Japanese also now lowered interest rates, which fuelled the bubble there. Stock market and real estate prices leapt ahead and firms invested heavily. Bank lending soared 25 per cent a year between 1985 and 1989 on the expectation that the assets against which they lent would continue to appreciate (Lairson and Skidmore 2003). By one account, in the late 1980s the Imperial Palace Grounds were more valuable than Canada (Murphy 2000). The Japanese bubble finally burst. The Nikkei lost nearly half its value. Real estate values dropped by between a third and a half (Allen 2005). Capital investment now fell sharply, beginning a long decline, see Figure 13.3.

The country struggled to overcome the subsequent recession. Above all, systemic overcapacity endured (Boltho and Corbett 2000). Banks remained saddled with bad debt and were therefore reluctant to offer new loans. Low, even effectively negative, interest

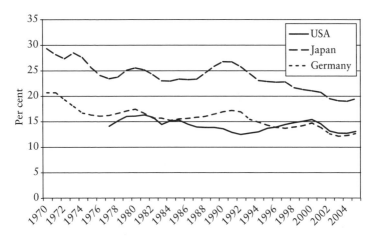

Figure 13.3   G3 gross fixed capital formation, net of housing, as a percentage of GDP, 1970–2005
Source: OECD 2008

rates fail to stimulate investment if firms have overcapacity. Similarly, unconfident consumers may save rather than spend (Murphy 2000). Instead, easy money could be borrowed and invested abroad (Allen 2005). The outflow of Japanese capital increased. FDI rose from $226 billion in 1995 to $450 billion by 2005, amounting to 9.8 per cent of GDP (UNCTAD 2007b). The effects of FDI outflows should not be exaggerated. On an annual basis this amounted to less than 1 per cent. However, with less competitive, domestically-oriented industries staying onshore, this may have further exacerbated relative decline. The sluggishness was nevertheless common across sectors, in large and small businesses. The corporate and state structures appeared to prevent crises from playing their 'normal' roles of eliminating inefficient capital (Boltho and Corbett 2000; Kincaid 2001). The *keiretsu* might be too big to fail, but in certain sectors they were too small to be internationally competitive (Chon 1997).

Much of the investment established manufacturing capacity in cheaper-waged locations in East Asia, and these regional networks initially required capital exports from Japan. However, from a national point of view these countries' exports could become competitors. The reversal of Plaza in 1995 attempted to help Japan's trade. As the yen fell, exports to the United States and Europe increased. However, the upturn was cut short when Japanese exports to the countries hit by the Asian crisis fell by 27 per cent in 1998 (Boltho and Corbett 2000). Between 1995 and 2006, although exports continued to increase in absolute terms, Japan's share of the world's total fell from 9.1 to 5.8 per cent (Comtrade 2007). By the 2000s, it had lost much of its technical leadership in industries like computers and telecoms and had a lower share of high-tech goods amongst its exports than either the United States or the United Kingdom (Murphy 2000; Pilat et al. 2006). Trade surpluses were caused as much by falling imports as by the strength of the export sector (Pilat et al. 2006; Halevi and Lucarelli 2002). However, their persistence increased the upward pressure on the yen, undermining one possible route out of the stagnation.

Government stimulus, including 'concreting the archipelago' (McCormack 2002), helped to keep the economy going, but at sluggish rates. Deficits reached a cumulative 177.3 per cent of GDP in 2005 (OECD 2008). Domestic saving remained high, but this fuelled the growing budget deficits and foreign investment, particularly to the United States. Rather than spending, consumers saved for fear of future economic contraction, particularly worried about demographic shifts. Japan, more reluctant to admit immigrants than most other rich countries and with a very low birth rate, suffered particularly from having an ageing population. The anticipation of this encouraged firms to reduce investments and individuals to increase savings. In 2000, unemployment rose above US levels for the first time since the war (Boltho and Corbett 2000). Figure 13.3 indicates some convergence, but investment within Japan remained significantly higher than in the United States and Germany. However, it was sustained in large part by exports and government deficits, both of which faced economic and political limits (Halevi and Lucarelli 2002).

Japan was that amalgam of market and non-market relations that Friedman (1962) saw as the worst of all worlds. State officials may even have valued technical prowess and industrial strength above economic gain (Murphy 2000). Its remarkable success confounds a free-market fundamentalism. Japan, for all its recent problems remained by any measure one of the richest countries in the world, in 2005 eighth on the United Nation's Human Development Index, behind only Canada amongst the G7 (UNDP 2007). However, the structures that brought such stability became part of the problem in the economic downturn. There were many vested interests in preserving sections of capital that had become relatively inefficient, and that a more cut-throat competition might have creatively destroyed (sending the economy into an even deeper economic recession, at least temporarily). Indeed, Japanese corporations responded to the crisis with a tight wage policy, exacerbating the weakness of domestic demand. Hopes of recovery continued to rest on revival elsewhere.

Europe

The major economies in Europe did better than Japan, but experienced some similar problems of stagnation. Again this was in marked contrast to the post-war boom, when Europe grew quickly. Both the earlier success and the subsequent difficulties were particularly marked in the core countries of continental Europe: Germany and France.

The European Union (EU) and its predecessors enabled large corporations, notably initially in steel, to gain economies of scale in an extended market while still being supported by their respective states. Crucially, the initial project was encouraged by the United States. A successful united capitalist Europe provided a bulwark against communism and an important market for US capital. With the deepening of the free-trade area, other industries could similarly achieve economies of scale within the larger market. The European economies of course also enjoyed the currency stability provided by the Bretton Woods system. Trade within Europe was a major part in the overall increase of the post-war period.

This intra-European trade involved competition. Each country had the possibility of selling into the others' markets if domestic consumption faltered. This was particularly important for the lead economy, Germany, whose 'social market' model meant consistently restrictive monetary policies at home, but allowed expansion through export surpluses to its neighbours. German growth then provided a stimulus for others, but there was an asymmetry to the relationship, and trade competition still had the potential to spiral inwards as countries adopted deflationary policies in response to deficits. However, trade remained a relatively small part of GDP for the larger economies, and it was still possible for European countries to adopt distinct 'models', with French 'dirigisme', in particular, involving an overtly state-led political economy. However, the tendency across Europe was for state spending to increase, and this provided an element of ongoing 'Keynesian' stimulus. The European Economic Community (EEC) also had redistributive effects, especially through regional aid, which helped to level and sustain the boom. In this situation the uneven 'stop–go' policies largely succeeded in generalising expansion rather than contraction (Halevi and Kriesler 2004). The German recession of 1965/6 threatened to undermine the pattern, but unity was only seriously threatened with the end of currency stability in 1971.

With the end of Bretton Woods, the DM almost doubled against the dollar between 1971 and 1979. Orthodox trade theory suggests that devaluation (after a short dip) improves the trade balance (following a 'J-curve'), while revaluation similarly worsens it. However, other European countries were by this time strongly locked into a system of dependence on German goods, particularly capital goods like machine tools. Therefore, the 'dip' was substantial and prolonged. Other European countries paid Germany more, while Germany could pay less for its imports, notably of oil. Italy, on the other hand, allowed its currency to fall. As orthodoxy would suggest, this helped its exports, and its economy grew strongly (Halevi and Kriesler 2004). France, on the other hand, fell between the two. After the wage settlement conceded to end the general strike of 1968 it had little choice but to adopt a relatively expansionary domestic policy. This also accorded with ambitions of parity with Germany and the defence of a strong franc. Although the franc did fall against the DM, it rose by more against the lira. Overall growth remained strong, but imports rushed in while export industries, which in many sectors competed directly with Italy, suffered severely.

For European capital, the costs of hedging against currency fluctuations were also high. The European Monetary System (EMS), formally adopted by ten European currencies in 1979, attempted to limit this. The system involved member countries keeping currency values within 2.25 per cent bands either side of their weighted average. Central banks intervened if they approached these limits. This succeeded in reducing volatility, precluding the Italian strategy of competitive devaluation. However, Germany's predominance meant that because the EMS moved according to the weighted average, others effectively followed changes in the DM. This fell against the rising dollar under Volcker, then rose with the Plaza Accord. The appreciation hurt German exports to the United States, but with all of the EMS currencies effectively revalued in tandem, German firms did not suffer in relation to its major trading partners. The rise hit other Europeans harder. By 1989, Germany had the largest current-account surplus in its history, equivalent to 4 per cent of its GDP, most of this with other countries in Europe. Italy in particular now ran deficits. To sustain these, interest rates had to be high, slowing growth. Worse, countries such as Italy (and Spain) with higher than average inflation experienced real revaluation if their nominal exchange rates were held constant (Halevi and Kriesler 2004). Currency harmonisation and an increasingly liberal attitude to capital movements helped to undermine national policy autonomy.

It was just at the time that European stability was unravelling that the UK (along with Ireland and Denmark) finally joined the EEC in 1973. France dropped opposition to British membership, with Britain now seen as a potentially useful counterweight to Germany. However, the instability of the pound further complicated the currency equation. Britain joined the EMS only in 1990, but as usual defended a strong pound. Amongst other things sound money was important to financial interests in the City of London and to maintaining the momentum of the 'financial services revolution' begun with the 'Big Bang' of 1986. By 1992 both the pound and the lira had come under speculative attack. The inherent dangers of currency pegs were mentioned in Chapter 10. If par values held, speculators could simply redeem their marks or dollars for pounds or lira at par. If the currencies fell, they could redeem them for more than they had paid. Even what became very high interest rates in Britain now had the opposite effect to that intended. Sustainable neither economically nor politically, speculators recognised them as desperation and a good reason for selling rather than buying pounds. The pound and lira were forced out of the EMS, falling by 15 and 16 per cent respectively, while Soros alone may have made $1 billion (O'Brien and Williams 2004:234). Speculators then turned to other currencies. The collapse of the EMS threatened renewed currency competition and trade wars, again with particular pressure on France. However, France in turn could threaten Germany with devaluation, and thus the EMS crisis became a significant motivation for accelerating the adoption of a fixed single currency. Originally proposed at the Maastricht meeting of the EU of 1991, the political difficulties and the recessionary conditions a single currency seemed likely to provoke may even have contributed to the EMS crisis. This crisis then increased the perceived imperative to avoid speculative risk and, ironically, hastened the adoption of the euro.

This achieved currency stability, but at the cost of economic stagnation. A single currency requires coordinated monetary policy. The policy adopted was basically that which had worked so well for Germany. However, it had worked for Germany largely because it was exceptional. Other countries had more expansionary policies. Once every country followed the German model of restrictive macroeconomic policies, there was little exterior into which to sell. Rich European countries did 70 per cent of their trade with other rich European countries (UN 2006). However, although they had a common currency and monetary policy determined by a European Central Bank, and were obliged to follow strict 'convergence criteria', the different countries retained their own structures, tax policies and growth rates. There was some redistribution within the EU, but nothing comparable to that within single countries. So those doing well could tax less but spend more than those doing badly, and differences would tend to be amplified. The preferred way of reducing this was to adopt broadly recessionary policies all round. The efficiency gains from economic union also depended on both capital and labour being able and willing to move across borders in response to economic differentials (Lairson and Skidmore 2003). Labour, in particular, was less willing or able to migrate than this presupposed, and substantial differences in unemployment persisted.

Of course, the stagnation in Europe's heartlands was not simply a 'mistake'. The tight monetary policies were part of a 'neoliberal' strategy against labour. They significantly moderated union strength, whether measured in terms of union density, strike activity or the wage share. The policies strengthened financial capital, protecting its assets against inflation, while allowing it to make quicker gains in speculation or by moving abroad. For manufacturing, the picture was more ambiguous, with intensified competition threatening to root out overcapacity. However, there was the option of relocation. This varied greatly: for example, total net outflows from Italy during the 1990s amounted to less than 1 per cent of GDP. French and German capital moved abroad on a more significant scale during that decade, although there was subsequently some retrenchment. Most investment was still in other rich countries, either elsewhere in Europe or the United States, but German firms in particular did invest significantly in the Czech Republic, Hungary and Poland (UNCTAD 2006a). Figure 13.3 shows fixed capital formation even lower than in the United States, but German trade surpluses continued to put upward pressure on the euro.

This exacerbated Europe's lack of competitiveness. As in Japan, the problem was not low productivity, which on an hourly basis roughly equalled that of the United States. However, most Europeans worked shorter hours than Americans and Japanese, and as the euro rose against the dollar, earned more in real terms (OECD 2008). Europe's labour force participation rate was also lower, particularly amongst women. Labour had not suffered the defeats of the United States, and although the euro imposed austerity, even this should not be exaggerated. Major states, particularly France and Germany, frequently ignored financial 'discipline' when it was politically expedient to do so, much to the irritation of poorer states obliged to comply. In France in particular, anti-labour reform repeatedly met opposition.

Meanwhile, Britain stayed out of the euro, while following broadly similar restrictive practices with the expressed intention of eventually joining. It experienced a degree of economic success compared with the euro area average. What was left standing of British manufacturing after the destruction of the Thatcher years was relatively efficient and it had some export success, particularly in high-tech goods, notably pharmaceuticals. However, on balance Britain remained a big net importer, and much of its success was in the traditional financial sector, from which the gains were uneven and the multiplier effects rather limited. Income polarisation was slightly less than in the United States, but greater than in continental Europe and much higher than in Japan (UNDP 2007). Also, like the United States, its boom was sustained, amongst other things, by debt, itself fuelled by house price inflation, while net savings remained very low (Boltho 2003).

In Western Europe, sentiment against the EU's anti-labour consequences were demonstrated in the votes against the proposed new constitution in France and the Netherlands in 2005, despite its overwhelming support by all sections of the ruling class and major parties. While in principle this should have scuppered the constitution, European leaders prepared to ratify it with moderate amendments. Any political fix, however, seemed unlikely to ease the economic tensions.

The United States and the World

The stories of the United States and of world economies are so intimately connected that neither can be told without the other. Accordingly, key developments within the United States have already been discussed elsewhere in this book and in this chapter. The United States declined from its position of post-war pre-eminence, but in 2005 its GDP still represented 28.1 per cent of the world total (UNCTAD 2007a). Figure 13.2 suggests that its economic performance was volatile, but over the longer term rather consistent. However, while its growth rate may have been more consistent, in many respects US capitalism changed more radically than others.

The first and probably most fundamental transformation was in terms of class and redistribution. This process was begun prior to the Volcker shock and the explicit anti-union policies under Reagan. However, his defeat of the air traffic controllers' union PATCO, in which the entire 11,000 membership was sacked, became symbolic and was used against other workers to win concessions on wages and work rules. Concession bargaining and 'give backs' became common. Real wages fell, recovering only partially during the 1990s boom (Brenner 2003). Population also rose more quickly than in either Japan or Europe, while the United States was also younger, with fewer people over 65 (Boltho 2003). The United States was more successful than its competitors in maintaining the labour force participation rate and the amount of work done by those in employment. Notably during the boom of the late 1990s, average hours in the United States increased broadly in line with the growth in output (Census 2008; OECD 2008). The intensity of work is very hard to measure, but much effort was spent trying to increase this too.

Reagan also introduced – and introduced a tradition of – massive tax cuts for the rich. These did not simply transfer wealth, but underpinned an economic reorganisation. Workers' consumption was limited while the ways of making profits multiplied. For example, reducing tax on capital gains more radically than dividends encouraged firms (and their managers with stock options) to borrow in order to buy back their own shares to boost the price, rather than invest in new capacity (Brenner 2003). Cuts in corporate tax meant post-tax profits could jump significantly, but led to a decline, not just in social welfare, but in 'pro-capital' state investment, for example, in infrastructure and training. Consumer spending would be sustained by debt, bringing more opportunities for financial-sector operators and producing concomitant falls in aggregate saving. Welfare was also reduced and commodified. Although there was less state industry to privatise than in Britain or France, for example, the United States implemented a more thoroughgoing deregulation, or re-regulation, in favour of capital.

The United States achieved a more substantial restructuring than most other countries, and the retreat from manufacturing was steeper. Already by 1990, it accounted for only 18.3 per cent of US GDP, and by 2005 this had fallen to 12.2 per cent. The elimination of the inefficient helped increase average productivity and reduce overcapacity, but there was also significant innovation, particularly in semiconductors, computers and telecommunications (Henwood 2003; UNCTAD 2007a). Industrial output grew significantly even as it shrank as a share of total GDP.

However, this declining manufacturing share also had significant economic consequences. Manufacturing productivity rises had progressively less impact on the rest of the economy as it fell as a share of the total. Fuelled amongst other things by the changes in the tax regime, a higher proportion of investment went to ultimately unproductive sectors of the economy, notably in finance. Moreover, reducing overcapacity in the United States did little to redress what was a global problem.

The US international position also changed quite sharply. It had been a major net exporter throughout the 1950s and 1960s. Even though its current account dipped into the red a few times in the 1970s, it still had a positive balance as late as 1981. The Reagan boom changed that dramatically. Plaza produced devaluation and ten years in which the United States gained in competitiveness. Although it never quite regained a current-account surplus, manufacturing productivity grew both absolutely and relatively. Wage stagnation and a falling dollar meant labour costs much lower than in Japan and Germany (Brenner 2003). By 1995 the United States had entered its 'new economy' boom, while Germany and Japan continued to struggle. The reversal of Plaza allowed the dollar to rise and the United States to import more cheaply. American deficits soon increased, beginning a trajectory which this time continued even once the dollar fell after 2001. As sectors of manufacturing diminished within the United States, it became more reliant on imports. In this context, a falling dollar did not necessarily redress the trade deficit, even in the medium term. Inputs still had to be bought, only at greater cost.

Meanwhile a reluctance to invest meant everywhere an excess of savings over investment and the creation and speculation of more financial instruments. This was unproductive investment, although the brokers and bankers take and spend their salaries, which in the short term can provide a real boost to the economy (Harman 2008). Bubbles can boost the confidence of firms to invest and consumers to spend. But this always proved temporary and the bubbles burst on a regular basis, requiring bail-outs by the US state on each occasion (Henwood 1998). The costs were pushed onto labour, while interest rate cuts attempted to fuel a new boom to pay for each previous one. However there is a limit to this process, and to the resources even of the US state.

In particular, the United States became more dependent on debt, in two different, but related senses. Debt sustained domestic spending, at levels that would otherwise have been impossible, given the falling wage share. The United States also depended on debt to sustain its international position. Capital inflows from Japan and latterly poorer countries including China were huge. This money could then be churned in the domestic market. However, the Federal Reserve then faced a 'double bind' (Brenner 2003), needing to cut interest rates to provide domestic liquidity and to raise them to continue to attract foreign funds. This dilemma became acute with the sub-prime crisis in 2007. As the dollar fell, other countries saw their foreign exchange reserves depleted, and some, notably in the Middle East, discussed moving away from denominating international transactions in dollars.

Other countries shared a vested interest in preserving the US market. Growth since the 1990s was largely dependent on the stimulus it provided, while a collapse of the dollar would wipe out assiduously acquired reserves. However, others' interests in US success were conditional. In the past, dollar holdings were used to gain leverage against the United States – a power of which Chinese creditors were well aware. The open system the United States created in its own interests now limited its scope for unilateral action. Of course, it retained overwhelming military superiority, which also militated against too direct a challenge. It intervened to protect oil interests in the Middle East, but also to issue a political message about its power. Its war may not have been a great success, but it was certainly a disaster for Iraq. Increased military spending may also have provided an economic stimulus, but it accumulated more debts. Neither politically nor economically did the prospects appear attractive.

Convergence or Contradictory Dynamism

The differences in performance between the major economies cannot be attributed to the different economic models, the Anglo-American proving its worth against more staid Japanese and continental European versions. This neglects the previous history and the fact that deteriorating performance came precisely as Europe and Japan became more liberal. Interstate relations are not necessarily a zero-sum game. Capital does accumulate, and in most places the problem was low growth rather than recession. However, in a competitive global economy success and failure are interrelated. Powerful states quite reasonably sought solutions that would displace their problems. Moreover, competition extends beyond the established rich countries. Firstly, it does so in the sense that Asia, particularly China, achieved much more impressive growth. Oriented in significant part towards existing rich-country markets, this exacerbated overproduction and thence interstate competition. Secondly, it does so in the sense that firms too sought solutions beyond borders, in terms of both production and consumption. An open and competitive system made it almost impossible for major economies to expand separately, but it had also become difficult for them to expand together.

Conclusion

The 1970s marked a watershed. To this, labour's defeat was crucial, and wage shares subsequently declined across rich countries. Liberalisation was in large part an attempt to 'lock in' these defeats. However, this left an enduring problem for capital –

that production tended to outstrip demand. Each national capital could potentially sell into other markets and rationally declined to consider global overcapacity its problem.

The experience was uneven, both geographically and temporally, and in terms of both labour's decline and capital's strategies. This left significant spaces for both relative capital success and labour resistance. Persistent more or less successful cooperation between major states averted economic disasters, without producing any coherent systematic reflation. At the national level there was little indication of the sort of social change that might force substantial redistribution. Labour not only confronted capital's need to defend its already low profits, but also the structures of trade and capital openness forged over the previous generation.

Labour's retreat was most severe in the United States, where capital also accomplished its most radical restructuring and strongest growth. The United States's unique position as controller of the key currency also gave it significant advantages as it borrowed from around the world. However, this also meant that the greatest imbalances hinged on the United States. Debts grew, both within the United States and between it and its trading partners. These multiplied, and there were powerful vested interests against calling them in too quickly. Nevertheless, even minor and hesitant adjustments had the potential to cause significant disequilibria to the wider system.

Capitalist growth is by its nature uneven. States act to overcome some of the contradictions that causes, both coordinating policies and freeing capital mobility. At the same time much of what they do deepens the unevenness, adopting strategies to strengthen capital within their borders. The success of intensive accumulation during the long boom was replaced by a period of declining accumulation at home and an intensified search for alternative productive investments. However, much of this took the form of a competitive struggle for markets, against the limits of which capital in the rich countries continued to struggle.

14

PROBLEMS OF DEVELOPMENT AND DEPENDENCY: THE STATE, CAPITAL AND CLASS IN POOR COUNTRIES

This chapter considers the political economy of poorer countries. It begins with a general discussion of poverty and inequality. It then discusses attempts to theorise systematic inequality, emphasising the need to develop an analysis that integrates inter- and intranational relations. This is then discussed in terms of the divergent experiences in the latter part of the twentieth century between many countries in Africa and Latin America on the one hand and in Asia on the other. The chapter finally attempts to situate both within the overall trajectory of global accumulation.

Development and the Persistence of International Inequalities

The global economy is massively unequal, with hundreds of millions of people living and dying in dire poverty. There is much controversy about whether this is getting better or worse and about how the evidence should be interpreted (Wade 2005). It is fairly clear that the spread of global capitalism increased the gaps between rich and poor. Figure 14.1 shows probably the most optimistic estimate for the shares of world income in the major poor country regions of Latin America, Asia (excluding Japan) and Africa from 1820 to 2001. There was steady decline up to 1950, a slight rise in the post-war period and a more substantial one (concentrated in Asia) after 1973. Nevertheless, the three continents contributed only 42.5 per cent of the world's wealth in 2001 compared with 63.1 per cent in 1820. Moreover, because population grew more quickly in poorer countries, on a per head basis the relative decline in wealth was considerably steeper. Figure 14.2 shows changes in GDP per capita. It confirms the recent improvement in Asia, and Africa's apparently relentless decline.

These figures, on a purchasing power parity (PPP) basis, attempt to account for different costs of living; they probably provide a more accurate guide to real wealth and poverty than measures in strict dollar terms. However, countries must pay creditors in real, not PPP, dollars, and many people who rely on bought, particularly imported, goods will not experience the imputed cheaper lifestyles. In strict dollar terms, poorer countries are about three times poorer than PPP values suggest. For China and India, this would have increased the figures by factors of 4 and 4.7 respectively even before a radical downwards revision in the PPP estimates in early 2008 (Elekdag and Lall 2008). In dollar terms, developing countries accounted for 22 per cent of world income in 2005. Asia's recent improvement appears to be relatively modest, while Africa's share and its per capita income fell by a half in the quarter century to 2005 (UNDP 2007).

Even as inequalities between countries showed some sign of decline after the 1970s (World Bank 2006c), those within them

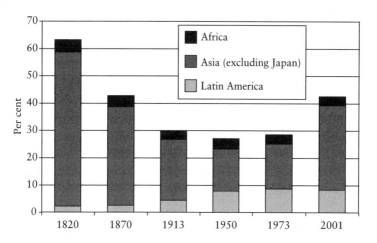

Figure 14.1 Percentage shares of world GDP, 1820–2001
Source: Maddison 2003

increased substantially. Figure 14.3 shows one attempt to quantify both intra- and international inequality, graded on a logarithmic scale between 0 and 1. The long-term upward trajectory is clear.

Conversely, the PPP figures do suggest that in absolute terms even the worst-performing continents got richer, although of

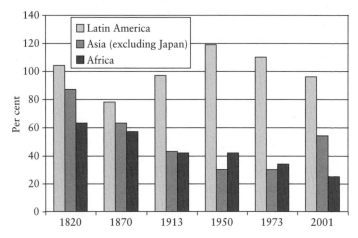

Figure 14.2 GDP per capita as a percentage of the world average
Source: Maddison 2003

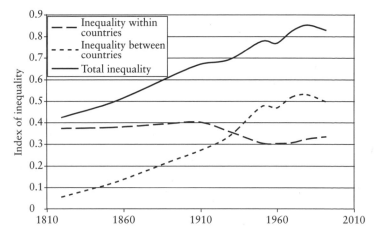

Figure 14.3 Inequality between and within countries
Source: Bourguignon and Morrison 2002

course there was great variation within them. Most measures suggest that the proportion, if perhaps not the number, of people living in absolute poverty fell. This lends some support to liberal models that see development as a progressive process. Most famously, Rostow (1960) posited five stages of growth, from the traditional through transitional, take-off and maturity before arriving at high mass consumption. Even more critical authors have suggested that integration into the global economy can bring privileges or advantages of backwardness (Trotsky 1977; Gerschenkron 1962). For example, it allows the introduction of techniques developed elsewhere and the development of production beyond the limits of local markets. Some Marxists continued to emphasise the progressive character of capitalism and imperialism (Warren 1980; Desai 2004). Latterly, authors from a variety of theoretical backgrounds embraced notions of globalisation: a decentred expansion implying 'the end of the third world' (Harris 1987). Several developmental success stories undermine visions of dependency as something everywhere inexorable. Capitalism's relentless expansion is compatible with economic growth, albeit uneven growth, patterned by both accumulation and resistance.

However, critical commentators emphasise the vast scale of persistent poverty and economic disadvantage. Political and military power also remained disproportionately concentrated in rich countries, particularly the United States, while the structures of global trade, investment and finance still disadvantaged and dispossessed poorer countries. By 2004, the greatest development success story, China, still had a per capita income only 15 per cent that of the United States. The poorest countries in Africa had incomes only a tenth of China (UNDP 2006). Perhaps more fundamentally, narrow economic measures miss the destruction of 'non-economic' but often vital areas, for example of subsistence and domestic work and of the environment (Shiva 1989; Makuwira 2006).

Dependency or Combined and Uneven Development?

In the post-war period, great hopes of 'catching-up' were frustrated, and nominal independence did not end exploitative links between countries, nor within them. International inequalities much greater than those that had existed prior to imperialist intervention suggest that it remained appropriate to depict a process of the 'development of underdevelopment' (Frank 1970). A diverse dependency tradition insisted that small and poor countries' relations with Europe, the United States and Japan were systematically unequal.

Dependency arguments in relation to trade were mentioned in Chapter 9. In particular, an international division of labour typically confined the periphery to the role of primary product exporters, for whom the terms of trade deteriorated. Primary product markets were also highly volatile, and the cyclicity reduced either the means or the incentives to industrialise (Prebisch 1950; Singer 1950). Theories of unequal exchange formalised the trade relationship as determined by the different wages and capital compositions between North and South (Emmanuel 1972; Sau 1978). Broader descriptions incorporated the role of rich-country multinationals in undermining the economic position and political autonomy of poorer countries, while the chains of monopoly power reached deep within peripheral societies (Frank 1970). Financial regimes like the gold standard or pegs to the dollar undermined poorer-country governments' scope for policy autonomy (Prebisch 1950, 1971).

Wallerstein's (1974) 'world-systems theory' (WST) is the best-known attempt to systematise these ideas. Importantly, he insists that the world economy should be understood as a whole and historically, over a long time-span. The current world system is one in which the development of coherent, strong states in Northern and Western Europe enabled them to colonise, and then to dominate through more informal means, societies elsewhere in the world. There developed an international division of labour, based on the core performing key, high value-added manufacturing, with the periphery supplying primary products. A semi-periphery acted as a sort of labour aristocracy, performing basic, labour-intensive manufacturing, but also playing an important political role in preventing the system becoming too polarised. It allowed some flexibility. New core states could emerge from the semi-periphery, others sink into it.

There have also been some important criticisms of this approach. It has been accused of mirroring the categories of mainstream social science, both in politics and economics (Skocpol 1977; Leys 1996). A state-centric account tends to obscure social, especially class, differentiation. Dependency theorists are of course perfectly well aware that systematic inequality also characterises relations within poorer countries, but the explanations are typically 'outside-in' (Campling 2004), with the South being passive victims of Northern exploitation (Cardoso and Faletto 1979). Similarly, a rather undifferentiated North appears to be the beneficiary. The emphasis on exchange relations can underestimate the importance of exploitation in production (Brenner 1977).

Such qualifications do not lessen such analyses' important insights or the importance of identifying the uncomfortable fact that rather than poorer countries 'catching up', patterns of international inequality tended to widen. However, they might be complemented or reinterpreted through an older Marxist framework of combined and uneven development (Trotsky 1977). This concept is also controversial. A literal interpretation insists that the unevenness and combination to which it refers are temporal (Davidson 2006a). Trotsky argued that rather than having to go through successive stages, the Russian revolution could combine its bourgeois and proletarian tasks (Trotsky 1969). However, this at least implies a spatial element (Barker 2006). In aggregate terms the Russian economy was poor compared with Western Europe; it was dominated by a backward agrarian sector in which even the formal trappings of serfdom had been abolished only a few decades earlier. But it also had elements of the most advanced economy, possible because of the way it was inserted into the wider global system. Foreign (particularly French) capital invested in Russia. The state was also able to mobilise resources in key sectors, in particular its munitions works, which became the world's largest factories. Thus combined and uneven development shares with WST a methodological priority of the totality. Russian political economy could only be understood through its connections with global capitalism. Combined and uneven development also admits a vital role for politics and the state. However, the impact of the international is more conditional than in WST, necessarily mediated by class relations within the developing country.

These sorts of ideas were utilised in some of the more insightful accounts of restructuring the contemporary economy (Smith 1984, 2006; Storper and Walker 1989). They also informed some of the more creative Marxist thinking about general processes of historical change (Rosenberg 2006). However, combined and uneven development provides at best a framework for analysis, not a formula for development. Trotsky's account of Russia, and later and less successfully that of China, was based on a careful empirical evaluation. Later attempts to extrapolate, particularly in terms of political conclusions that anticipated repeating the experience of the Russian revolution, proved less successful. The sections that follow, on the persistent problems of development in Latin America and Africa, and on the Asian 'miracle', attempt a schematic overview.

Debt, Dependency and Class Struggle in Latin America and Africa

As mentioned in Chapter 7, during the post-war boom poorer countries did relatively well. Between 1950 and 1973 Asia grew at 2.9 per cent per capita per year, Latin America at 2.6 per cent and Africa at 2.0 per cent (Maddison 2003). The American and African figures were nevertheless below the world average and they fell further behind leading countries. This fuelled both dependency theories and state-based development strategies. Africa represents the strongest case for Frank's (1970) claim of an inverse relationship between development and links with the imperial powers. Here European exploitation dated back to slavery, while almost the whole continent remained colonised until after the Second World War (Campling 2004).

By contrast most South and Central American countries were formally independent throughout the twentieth century.

Nevertheless, many of their economic links with the most advanced countries exemplified international asymmetries, while the United States was more prepared to intervene directly to protect its interests within its own hemisphere than elsewhere (Pearce 1982). Latin America also confirmed the dependency claims that domestic class structures were not simply 'backward'. They had precisely been shaped by European intervention producing the latifundia landowners who benefited from agricultural exports. The continent also produced practical attempts to implement import substitution industrialisation (ISI). This was essentially a strategy for national capitalism in countries where the capitalist class was weak. It often enlisted a broader populist support, but could be strongly anti-majoritarian and anti-democratic, and dependent on the military. It required diverting resources from land to capital, often at the expense of an already desperately poor peasantry. However, in strictly national economic terms, ISI was not the unmitigated failure later imputed to it by liberal lore (Harvey 2005).

In the 1970s, many Latin American countries grew quickly, amongst other things benefiting from cheap loans which became available as oil-exporting countries recycled their 'petrodollars'. OPEC members' surpluses were deposited in Western banks and in turn offered to developing countries, which needed them to pay for imports of oil and grain, whose prices also increased at this time. Supply was high, so the price of the loans was low, even effectively negative after inflation. For the borrowers, these commercial loans also had the advantage of avoiding issues of foreign ownership associated with direct investment and the conditionality often attached to borrowing from governments or international institutions. Between 1972 and 1981, the debts escalated sixfold, to $500 billion, much of this in Latin America (Cohn 2005). However, debt repayments could be met, as economies grew quickly.

As discussed in Chapter 10, the Volcker shock reversed this by dramatically lifting interest rates. By 1982, Mexico could no longer pay and defaulted on its debts of around $180 billion (in 2006 dollars). Others appeared likely to follow. The scale of this default threatened to bring down the international banking system. Leading US banks had loan exposure to the 17 highly indebted countries almost twice their capital and reserves (Cohn 2005). There were a series of efforts by the United States and various international institutions to reschedule the loans. These did shift some resources from the poorer countries back to the United States and contributed to sharp falls in living standards within the debtor countries, but without resolving the crisis. This was only finally achieved by the 'Brady Plan' of 1989–94, involving a degree of debt write-off as the US government persuaded lenders to agree to debt relief and rescheduling in return for bonds backed by the US and Japanese governments and the IMF and the WB. The prospects of bank failure were finally allayed (Strange 1998).

Table 14.1   Growth and debt repayment in Latin America (per cent)

	Growth per capita per year		Debt service as a proportion of GDP		Debt service as a proportion of exports and foreign income	
	1975–90	1990–2005	1990	2005	1990	2005
Argentina	–0.6	1.1	4.8	5.8	37.0	20.7
Brazil	0.4	1.1	1.8	7.9	22.2	44.8
Mexico	–0.1	1.5	4.3	5.7	20.7	17.2
All Latin America and Caribbean	0.2	1.2	4.0	6.6	23.7	22.9

Source: UNDP 2007

Less-developed countries were returned to IMF dependence, but with more stringent conditions. Debtor countries were opened for privatisations, foreign takeovers and portfolio investments. Increased trade openness in particular meant that in many cases export earnings could pay the debts even as these increased. Predictably this did little for domestic development and growth remained very slow; see Table 14.1. Nor did adopting the proposed austerity and monetary policies prevent each of the major Latin American countries from being subject to major speculative attacks. Amongst numerous others, the crises in Mexico in 1994, Brazil in 1998 and Argentina in 2001 produced severe economic downturns. In Argentina, 23 per cent of the population lived on less than two dollars a day, in Mexico 20 per cent and in Brazil 21 per cent (UNDP 2006).

However, the problems of dependency, indebtedness, persistent poverty and inequality were much greater in Africa even than in Latin America. In strict (2005) dollar terms, Africa's GDP fell from $1216 billion in 1980 to $760 billion in 1990 before rising to $948 billion in 2005. This represented a fall in per capita wealth from $2538 to $1192 and $1029 (UNDP 2007). In PPP terms there was a slight rise in average income, but the picture was nevertheless grim. Against the upward trend elsewhere in the world, life expectancy in sub-Saharan Africa barely changed from the early 1970s to the 2000s (UN 2006). In part, this was caused by the HIV pandemic, with infection rates averaging 6 per cent across sub-Saharan Africa and reaching 20 per cent in several countries. Poverty, of course, conditioned HIV prevalence and mortality rates.

Africa more than anywhere remained dependent on exports, particularly of primary products. In sub-Saharan Africa, the average export/GDP ratio in 2004 was 33, compared with only 20 amongst high-income OECD countries. Moreover, unlike in other developing countries, dependence on primary-product exports remained strong, with the share of these in the total falling only from 73 to 70 per cent between 1990 and 2004. For most countries, primary products accounted for well over half their exports, and for many the problems associated with this were exacerbated by dependence on a small number of products. For 25 of 35 African countries for which data were available, the terms of trade deteriorated between 1980 and 2004 (UNDP 2006). There are important reasons why dependency on exports of resources might prove a 'curse' (Bush 2004). However, the international asymmetries should also be understood in the domestic conjuncture in which 'rentier elites' were able to enrich (and arm) themselves from oil and mining operations (Bush 2004). Raising revenues from raw material sales circumvents the need to win acceptance for general policies of taxation. The appropriation of foreign aid, most scandalously the outright embezzlement by

Mobutu in Zaire, may give credence to the liberal agenda which blames local rulers for persistent poverty. However, this is clearly an insufficient explanation, and the nature of the social relations within African economies are shaped by their relations with the wider global political economy. For example, Zaire's ruler received aid as a loyal supporter of the West during the cold war. One study showed that in general US aid was disproportionately directed towards corrupt governments (Alesina and Weder 2002).

Africa was never such a sound investment prospect for Western banks as Latin America, and only a few countries such as Morocco and Nigeria incurred comparable levels of commercial debt. This made Africa more dependent on official lending. There were some well-publicised schemes for reducing this through the heavily indebted poor countries (HIPC) initiative, but this too remained conditional on opening Africa to international capital. To some extent this succeeded. Investment levels are very low in terms of the world total, but high as a proportion of African wealth. However, Africa confirms the general finding in Chapter 8 that capital follows growth rather than causing it, and while there was a close spatial correspondence between GDP and levels of FDI, investment fell even as its foreign proportion increased. Bond (2004) describes a crash in gross fixed capital formation from 25 per cent of GDP in 1980 to only 15–18 per cent in the subsequent two decades, although it did then rise slightly to 19.2 per cent in 2005 (UNDP 2007). Financial repayments continued to flow, and for sub-Saharan Africa aggregate levels of debt remained over half of GDP in 2003 (World Bank 2006c).

Even the relatively few examples of growth highlight how a narrow, technical understanding of development can obscure socially destructive processes. Ghana was one of the continent's success stories, not least through the privatisation of its gold mines in the 1990s. Its annual per capita growth of 2 per cent between 1990 and 2005 was extraordinary by African standards. However, this also involved the destruction of local agriculture and the loss of livelihoods, with particularly dire consequences for many women, an increased incidence of contagious diseases and environmental destruction (Bush 2004). Underdevelopment in Africa, even more than in Latin America, seemed to confirm characterisations of 'accumulation by dispossession' (Harvey 2003, 2005) and dependency analyses.

However, these processes were also vitally conditioned by local relations. Restructuring was not simply imposed by rich countries and the international financial institutions. Local ruling classes supported much of the liberalising agenda and the economic stability and export orientation it brought, as exemplified even by the practice of nominally leftist governments in Brazil and South Africa. Alternatively, countries also had more or less freedom to adopt independent strategies. So, for example, Chile in the early 1990s implemented capital controls rather effectively. In Latin America there were also moves towards regional trading agreements and regional and national production systems less dependent on exports to rich countries. In particular, in the wake of Argentina's crisis, populist governments rejected US plans to develop a free trade area of the Americas. Most significantly, across Latin America there were signs of revolt against the liberal agenda. This went furthest in Venezuela, with the Chavez regime, amongst other things, establishing the Bolivarian Alternative for the Americas, with Cuba and later Bolivia, as a form of regional integration not based on free trade and liberalism. Elsewhere on the continent, more moderately leftist governments were elected, usually on the basis of avowed opposition to the IMF and liberalisation. This remained an uncertain and contested process. Latin American societies, not least Venezuela, remained hugely unequal. The rich and powerful resisted reforms and nationalisation, even as these remained modest by the standards of the 1960s and 1970s. The populist regime in Venezuela survived a coup attempt in 2002, which clearly had US support, but was primarily the product of the domestic opposition.

The Asian 'Miracle' and the Contradictions of Competition

In contrast to the experiences in Latin America and Africa, much of Asia seemed to confound predictions of dependency. The success of several open economies challenged ideas that integration into the global economy necessarily prevented growth. In particular, the Asian 'tigers', South Korea, Taiwan, Hong Kong and Singapore, sustained very high growth rates; see Figure 14.4. Each increased its level of openness to trade and did much better than countries that adopted ISI strategies. The original tigers were followed by a second group of 'tiger cubs' which included Thailand, Malaysia, Indonesia and (somewhat less plausibly given its growth performance) sometimes also the Philippines. Most recently China expanded rapidly.

Predictably, there was a vigorous and unresolved debate about the role of openness in growth. For liberals, these experiences support arguments for the benefits of trade and liberalisation (World Bank 1993; Teranishi 1996). Any enduring problems tended to be read as caused by obstacles to market freedom; and the 1997 crisis, for example, can be attributed to 'crony capitalism'. This interpretation was challenged by institutionalist accounts that stressed the important role of the state rather than the free market in Asian development. In Korea (Amsden 1989) and Taiwan (Wade 1990), in particular, interventionist developmental states implemented ISI policies prior to opening and developed strategic industrial policies to create their successful export industries, rather than relying on factor endowments and comparative advantage (Burkett and Hart-Landsberg 2000a). If the tiger cubs were more open to, and reliant upon, foreign capital and export markets, this was also shown in their vulnerability to the 1997 crash. China's success reaffirmed the importance of a strong state in directing the economy.

These apparently opposing interpretations may actually have much in common (Burkett and Hart-Landsberg 2000a, 2000b; Radice 2008). The states or markets dualism provides the classic counterpoint of mainstream theory, while both sets of interpretations see the successes in Asia as a model for others to follow. There are (at least) two problems with this. Firstly, integration into the global economy, on whatever basis, involves competition – and therefore losers as well as winners. There is a fallacy of composition in suggesting that what the tigers achieved can be easily or indefinitely extended. Secondly, both liberal and statist perspectives typically share the emphasis on 'national' political economies, tending to downplay social conflicts within them – or at best hope for amicable class relations as being most conducive to economic success. Most of these countries, for most of the time, had repressive regimes, and their success was built on the intensity of labour's exploitation.

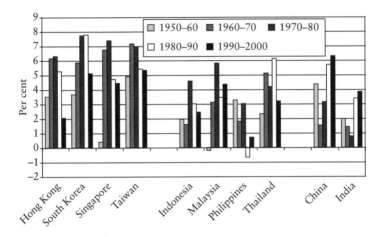

Figure 14.4 Annual average GDP per capita growth (per cent) in selected Asian economies

Source: Maddison 2003

For Taiwan and Korea in particular, their situation within the cold-war global political economy provided the basis for their 'miracle' economies. Korea, a Japanese colony until 1945, was of course then literally the front line in the war against communism in the 1950s. As such, it received massive US aid, perhaps 9 per cent of GDP in the 1950s and still 6 per cent in the following decade (Harris 1987; Heston et al. 2002). US troops provided the majority of overseas earnings. The US army also supported military rule of the Park dictatorship from 1960 until 1979. Taiwan, also previously a Japanese colony and afterwards run by the exiled Guomindang leadership, was rewarded with China's privileged seat at the UN until 1971, and it too received significant US aid until the early 1960s (Harris 1987).

Both Korea and Taiwan also had authoritarian domestic regimes able to repress labour. The long working hours in Korea were particularly brutal, and wages, particularly for women, very low (Amsden 1989; Burkett and Hart-Landsberg 2000a). However, both regimes also enacted many reforms. Land redistribution in particular supported rising agricultural incomes. In Taiwan these provided an important market for manufactured goods; they also encouraged relatively high rates of savings, which could fund investments and the state-directed programmes of industrial development. In both there were high levels of state planning. In Korea this was usually organised through state-directed finance to the privately owned conglomerates or *chaebol*. In Taiwan, at least initially, it was achieved through very high levels of direct state ownership of industry (Burkett and Hart-Landsberg 2000a). A wave of workers' militancy broke the Korean military regime and repressive labour relations in 1987. Higher wages meant exports suffered, but bigger domestic markets helped sustain very strong rates of growth, above 5 per cent a year until 1998 (Heston et al. 2002). In Taiwan, military rule also ended in 1987 and there too exports also declined as the countries came under pressure from the United States to revalue their currencies. There was some bank denationalisation in Korea, under pressure from the IFIs, and in Taiwan direct ownership of industry was gradually reduced, but the state continued to dominate key sectors, particularly in finance.

The city states of Singapore and Hong Kong and the next wave of tiger cubs had less prior ISI and more reliance on foreign capital (Burkett and Hart-Landsberg 2000b). However, there was considerable variation between them. For example, in terms of foreign ownership, Malaysia already had levels of FDI over 20 per cent of GDP in 1980. In Thailand this was just 3 per cent, although it then rose rapidly, to 10 per cent in 1990, 24 per cent in 2000 and 40 per cent in 2005 (UNCTAD 2007b). Like Korea, Malaysia and Thailand both also borrowed heavily, with Japanese capital as the principal lender, particularly to Thailand.

The yen revaluation of the 1980s meant that the Asian NICs, particularly the 'cubs', which pegged their currencies to (or close to) the dollar, were able to capture increasing export markets in the United States. They also attracted FDI, as Japanese MNCs in particular established regional production networks utilising what had become lower costs in these countries. Burkett and Hart-Landsberg describe a 'tidal wave' of FDI from Japan (2000a:229). Firms from the original NICs also followed this logic to some extent. Where Asia had accounted for only 18.5 per cent of Japan's exports in 1985, this grew to 44.0 per cent in 1995. However, with the Japanese recession in the early 1990s, investment declined. Debt levels had to rise to sustain the investment. Fortunately, or so it appeared, higher borrowing was itself possible in Japan at very low interest rates (Kincaid 2001). Low interest rates and booming stock markets in Europe and America also encouraged investors to look for higher returns in Asia. As fast-growing economies they in any case were attractive sites for foreign lenders. A bubble economy developed. The Chinese yuan was devalued in 1994, but then, as the Japanese slump continued, the leading powers reversed the currency moves of Plaza, allowing the yen to devalue in an attempt to stimulate the Japanese economy.

Asian currencies pegged to the dollar became relatively dearer, making it hard to sustain export growth and to attract FDI. The need for foreign borrowing and portfolio capital increased. This eventually provoked speculation that, in the first instance, Thailand would be unable to sustain its link with the dollar. The Thai government spent $54 billion trying to defend its currency peg, buying baht with dollars (Higgott 1998). Once it lost and the baht fell, this meant that assets within Thailand, including those of speculative portfolio investors, were devalued. The Thai experience encouraged similar speculative attacks on other currencies in the region, notably the Malaysian ringgit, Indonesian rupiah and Korean won. The subsequent economic crises were severe, provoking the revolutionary situation which finally overthrew the Suharto dictatorship in Indonesia. However, this was contained. With the notable exception of Malaysia, where the government organised its own restructuring (Burkett and Hart-Landsberg 2000a), IMF-sponsored rescue packages bailed out the lenders and pushed substantial liberalisation onto the affected countries. Large sections of Korean capital, in particular, became available for sale to foreign MNCs in a way not previously possible. Foreign ownership tripled to 41 per cent between 1996 and 2004 (Kho et al. 2006). Domestic austerity made workers pay. Economic growth did soon resume, but on a new and more liberal basis.

Devaluation and domestic recession, which put downward pressure on wages, revived the export performance of the Asian economies. As in Latin America after 1982, increased trade could also pay increased debts. For each of the tiger cubs, debt and debt repayment were higher in 2005 than they had been in 1990, but could be paid through higher export earnings. However, by this time their exports were also facing increased competition in rich-country markets from those of China. The terms of trade for Korea fell by 23 per cent between 2000 and 2004/5 and by smaller margins for most of the other Asian NICs (UNDP 2007).

China's rise was even more remarkable than that of the original tigers, especially in view of its size. Sometimes the official Chinese data might be questionable, but even conservative estimates suggest an annual rise in GDP per capita of 7 per cent between 1978 and 2004 (Naughton 2006). Export volumes, the measurement of which does not depend on Chinese statistics alone, grew even more rapidly, from $18 billion to $761 billion between 1980 and 2005; that is from about 1 per cent to 7.5 per cent of the world total (WTO 2006).

Similar debates about the relative importance of the state and the market and of the domestic and the international are again fought out in relation to China. Processes of capital accumulation and exploitation within China were decisive. China under Mao remained a very poor country, but it did substantially industrialise. It was therefore able to supply vital inputs like electricity and steel. This enabled the subsequent increases, particularly in industrial productivity, where output per employee accelerated from the 1990s, but overall rose almost fivefold between 1978 and 2004 (Dunn 2007). The post-1979 reforms were gradual. In terms of the domestic economy, although large proportions were privatised, effective control could often remain in the hands of the Communist Party. There was not a free market within China. Opening to foreign investment was also relatively slow, with the total net inflow in 2005 amounting to about 3 per cent of GDP. This included mergers and acquisitions and investment from Hong Kong (much of which was recycled from the mainland to take advantage of the more favourable terms offered to foreigners) (Sargeson 1999; OECD 2005). Most investment therefore remained Chinese.

Trade rose rapidly. China's exports and its surplus, particularly with the United States, attracted much attention. The crude export/GDP ratio reached 37 per cent in 2005 (UNDP 2008). This can be somewhat misleading, as the value added in assembly operations, for example, is lower than the value of the finished exports. Consumption within China also rose significantly, albeit very unevenly. Of course, this domestic market was in tension with the need to keep wages low in the export sector. Evidence of wage pressures and sporadic workers' struggles remained some distance from establishing anything close to a 'Fordist' moment of accumulation within China. Nevertheless, China's accumulation was geographically concentrated, and although 'reforms' dislocated elements of the earlier commune- and enterprise-based welfare system, in aggregate China's people did appear to become better off. Life expectancy, for example, rose from 63.2 to 71.5 years between the early 1970s and the 2000s (UNDP 2006).

Nevertheless, whatever its role in producing growth, given its size, China's trade could impact significantly on the rest of the world economy. It contributed to the major US deficits discussed in the previous chapter. It also competed with other countries, particularly its East Asian neighbours. Increasing supply contributed significantly to the general lowering of prices. However, China was also a major importer. This provided a vital part of the changing patterns of trade within Asia. While between 1996 and 2005 a roughly constant 55 per cent share of China's exports went to rich countries, their share of its imports fell from 53 to 38 per cent, displaced particularly by other countries in

East Asia (UN 2006). So for the Asian economies there could be complementarities. Korea lost textile sales to the United States, but gained machinery exports to China. However, this did not promise a stable equilibrium, and China's start-up needs for capital goods may later decline. Korea's strengths lay in a narrow range of industries that could be squeezed from above by Japan and below by lower-wage producers (Burkett and Hart-Landsberg 2000a). Other countries like Indonesia lost exports to Chinese competition without having obvious niches to which to turn. The adjustment costs, even if such areas of comparative advantage could be identified, might be considerable.

China's rise raised the prospect that still others might follow, with India the most likely candidate. India also liberalised after 1991 and became a much more open economy. It grew at a remarkable 4.2 per cent per capita per year between 1990 and 2005 (UNDP 2007). FDI in current-dollar terms jumped 100-fold between 1980 and 2005, reaching $45 billion (UNCTAD 2007b). The export/GDP ratio tripled from 7 to 21 per cent between 1990 and 2005 (UNDP 2007). Neither its restructuring nor its growth matched that of China, but it had advantages in the prevalence of the English language, particularly useful in ICT and in internationally-oriented service sector operations like call centres. Prospects remained unclear. For India itself there were suggestions that internationally-oriented sectors were developing as an enclave economy rather than providing more widespread benefits (Barnes 2008). India provided some of the more critical writing on 'development' and how 'growth' can come at the expense of traditional society and destroy subsistence economies, producing increased poverty, especially for women (Shiva 1989). However, even relatively sensitive measures like the UN's Human Development Index also suggested significant improvements (UNDP 2007). For other countries, India's exports had the potential to add to trade competition, drive down prices and further undermine the position of the export-oriented model.

Liberalisation and Changing Patterns of Global Accumulation

Economic success transformed several countries in East Asia. For the original tigers, the end of the third world is real. Korea, Taiwan, Singapore and Hong Kong face difficulties, but are no longer poor. This understandably encourages emulators. However, it was not obvious whether what was possible for four small economies can be simultaneously sustained by other, bigger economies. The slight dip in overall international inequality noted in the figures at the beginning of this chapter is attributable to the achievements of relatively few countries. China's growth accounted for a third of all poorer-country growth between 1980 and 2005. With the four tigers, the share was 62 per cent. India contributed a further 10 per cent (World Bank 2006c). Without China and India, the World Bank's own figures show a steep rise in both inter- and intra-national inequality after 1980 (2006c:63).

However, the apparent success of a second tier of Asian economies added weight to arguments in favour of export-oriented industrialisation and the demands made by international institutions that other countries should become more open. In crude economic terms, structural adjustment achieved some moderate successes. The size of the formal economy and the proportion of the population 'economically active', particularly of women, tended to grow. Urbanisation almost everywhere proceeded rapidly. However, even the apparent successes worked by redistributing income upwards, without producing anything like the success enjoyed by the Asian tigers. Particularly in Africa, growth remained at best very slow.

Critics can show many economic and social disasters (Stiglitz 2002). Amongst other things, the emphasis on export markets often undermined locally-oriented production. This could mean diminishing production of vital supplies (like food) and economies being made more dependent on volatile international markets, for example in building trades where local supplies and traditional methods had previously predominated (Wells et al. 1998). As mercantilist and dependency theorists had long suggested, export-oriented industries often created fewer multiplier effects within the domestic economy. The suspicion remained that this more liberal world served the interests of powerful states. For example, debt restructuring averted crisis for the global financial system, while developing countries' debt rose from $2107 billion in 1997 to $2800 billion in 2005. Capital increasingly flowed from them to the developed world, especially the United States, as shown in Table 14.2. Accumulation by dispossession here seems clear.

Table 14.2 Global capital flows 1995–2005 ($US billion)

Economy	1995			2000			2005		
	In	Out	Net	In	Out	Net	In	Out	Net
US	439	–352	86	1047	–561	486	1212	–427	785
Japan	157	–269	–112	45	–168	–123	232	–371	–139
Eurozone	n/a	n/a	n/a	988	–949	39	1644	–1523	–121
UK	187	–185	2	792	–776	17	1365	–1306	59
Developing countries	319	–245	74	297	–408	–111	716	–1174	–458

Source: IMF 2007b

However, there were also instances of significant wealth creation in poorer countries, particularly in East Asia. Some of this was produced and appropriated by Japanese or Western capital (Burkett and Hart-Landsberg 2000a). Nevertheless, the major beneficiaries remained the ruling classes within those countries. China's growth in particular introduced considerable tensions for the established rich-country capitalist class. New poles of accumulations also introduced new possibilities of class-based resistance within those countries.

Bukharin (1972) characterised a tension between the tendencies towards nationalisation and internationalisation. The former won out in the drive to inter-imperialist competition that produced the First World War. It seems reasonable to argue that the latter tendency, that towards internationalisation, predominated at the end of the twentieth century (Radice 2008). Growth was stronger in some poorer countries than in established rich ones, some of this involving the movement of capital into new areas. However, both tendencies continued to operate at the same time, with capital and interstate competition producing contradictory and ever changing patterns of accumulation.

Conclusion

The debt crisis and its resolution represented a defeat for poorer countries and allowed their incorporation into the world economy on terms more favourable to the rich. However, it was also supported by powerful interests within the developing world and, particularly in Latin America, met increasing resistance. The success of several Asian economies demonstrated that dependency was not absolute, and despite exploitation, poorer countries can also accumulate successfully. However, in a competitive world system such success is hard to generalise, and new challengers continually threaten those who had earlier succeeded.

15

GLOBAL GOVERNANCE OR THE NEW IMPERIALISM

Chapter 6 discussed the earlier period of globalisation and imperialism. It briefly discussed Marxist theories and argued that despite flaws these captured essential elements of the process. The renewed phase of globalisation and imperialism in the late twentieth century reopened debate about how these should be understood. The term 'imperialism' regained currency amongst both Marxist and non-Marxist commentators, but exactly what this meant in the new context was not always clear. This chapter outlines three sets of theories, organised around a characterisation made by Callinicos (2007). The first set of theories rejects the pertinence of nation-state-centred perspectives and consequently of national imperialism. Questions instead become those of 'global governance', a 'global state' (Robinson 2002, 2007; Robinson and Harris 2000), or of 'empire' (Hardt and Negri 2000), this last perceived in a pervasive and general sense. The second set of theories sees the predominance of the United States and its imperialism as producing a very different world to that of the interstate rivalries that characterised the pre-First World War period (Panitch and Gindin 2005; Hudson 2003; Arrighi 1994, 2003). Finally, there are those who identify enduring interstate rivalries and stronger similarities with the earlier period of classical imperialism (Gowan 1999; Harvey 2003; Callinicos 2007). While sympathetic to this last perspective, this chapter suggests it often leaves underexamined the relation between politics and economics in the contemporary global political economy.

Governance Beyond the Nation State

This section considers arguments that the nation state has been superseded as the appropriate institutional form of governance. Avowed Marxists like Hardt and Negri (2000) and Robinson (2002, 2007) share this broad perspective with more mainstream characterisations of globalisation. However, a historical materialist perspective is able to understand the nation state as a relatively recent and historically specific phenomenon. It cannot be presumed to survive indefinitely in a particular form as capitalism changes. Increasingly transnational systems of production, trade and finance make territorial nation states less adequate as the political form. This does not necessarily mean that nation states are disappearing, but that their authority becomes just one amongst many at the global, national and local level. In Bull's (1977) well-known formulation, the contemporary world should be characterised as neo-medievalism, with overlapping claims to power.

There are numerous powerful statements of state retreat in the face of globalisation. Some of the claims were discussed in the earlier chapters on production, trade and particularly finance. The mobility and therefore power of capital, these interpretations maintain, enabled it to steal a march on territorially-bound nation states. In extremis, states become mere transmission belts into local arenas for global capital (Cox 1996; Cerny 1996, 2000). We experience 'deterritorialisation' (Scholte 2000), 'a borderless world' (Ohmae 1994), even the 'end of geography' (O'Brien 1992). Disclaiming the wilder hyperbole, more qualified versions of the thesis of state retreat became something of an orthodoxy (Held et al. 1999). For many of these accounts, the implication is that the world became more liberal and less 'governed', although for some this was unsustainable and required a new 'great transformation' and new institutional structures (Kapstein 1994; Gray 1998; Cox 2002; Munck 2005). Others saw such institutions of governance as already emerging. However, the realist, state-centred view of international relations and classical Marxist views of imperialism become redundant.

In these debates Marxists appear on both sides. Some Marxist formulations of the state perhaps contribute to a reified view that sees it as a singular 'thing'. Conceiving the state as 'nothing but the executive committee of the whole bourgeoisie' (Marx and Engels 1965:35) usefully dethrones any position of pre-eminence assigned by political theory. States must act in ways at least broadly compatible with capital accumulation within their borders and therefore with the interests of nationally based capitalists. However, this too strongly asserts a unitary and coherent nature. The state also has to be understood as historically constructed and legitimised (Draper 1977). Even at the national level it has to be something more than the capitalist executive. States are shaped by domestic social forces, by class and other struggles. Moreover, as Barker (1978) and von Braunmuhl (1978) have pointed out, the state is manifestly not the executive committee of the whole bourgeoisie, which as a class is inherently international. States also adapt to 'world order' in their 'external' relations, including those with other states (Cox 1981). States may have more autonomy, be more plural and be more changeable than is suggested by the analogy with an executive committee. State sovereignty was always relative and conditional. Even within a given territory it was never the sole legitimate authority. Patriarchal power within the family has long existed alongside – and only relatively recently and in part been challenged by – that of the state. Various community loyalties may have carried as much weight. The invocation of 'legitimacy' to state authority underlies the conservatism inherent in visions of state sovereignty. Owners of communications media, religious leaders and the rich in general are alternative sources of power with whom the state is likely to negotiate. It may take up arms to suppress them – or they it. But only exceptionally.

An interpretation something like this seems to lie behind characterisations of an emerging global state. For Marxists this reflects the rise of a global capitalist class. Capital may, in principle, always have been international, but in practice this increased dramatically as corporations became more highly internationalised over the last 60 years. Capital, this interpretation suggests, also organised beyond the nation state. It went from being a 'class in itself' to being a 'class for itself' (Robinson and Harris 2000; Robinson 2002; Gill 1990; van der Pijl 1998). The language repeats that used by Marx (1978b) and an idea important to later Marxists (Lukács 1974; Thompson 1968) to refer to processes of working-class formation. Exploitation by capital creates a working class 'in itself'. Despite their common objective position, workers can remain divided from each other, and unity is forged only through processes of struggle and solidarity, making the proletariat a class 'for itself'. Marxists have traditionally regarded capitalists as a band of 'hostile brothers' (Marx 1969:29). Inter-capitalist competition provides much of the system's unique dynamic. On the other hand, the capitalist family is united in its opposition to labour, and may also cooperate in formal ways through trusts and cartels, as well as informal and sometimes illegal combinations, 'to defraud the public' (Smith 1997). Robinson (2002) suggests that the fraternity has become stronger and particularly more global, the hostility muted. From the mid 1970s regular organised cooperation became institutionalised. The Trilateral Commission involved explicit cooperation between state and private-sector actors in North America, Europe and Japan (Gill and Law 1988; Gill 1990; Keohane 2005). The World Economic Forum took transnational corporate planning further (Robinson and Harris 2000). Van der Pijl (2007) details the Bilderberg conferences of what he calls an Atlantic ruling class, which were attended by representatives of transnational capital, the 'political formation' and the hegemonic order; this last consisted of international organisations, foundations and planning councils, media and intellectuals. Perhaps somewhat neglected, capital itself provides important institutions of governance; in particular the MNCs directly control the lives of their millions of employees, as well as having more or less direct influence on political- and social-movement institutions. Capital becomes genuinely global and the global state reflects this.

The development of supra-state regimes has for some time been the staple of 'liberal institutionalist' IPE (Keohane and Nye 1977; Keohane 2005). A range of powerful institutions developed, often constituted by nation states, but more than the sum of their parts. The 'surrender' of sovereignty has probably gone furthest with the euro countries of the EU, and many poorer countries of course experience an even harsher version of the liberal policy constraints when borrowing from the IFIs. Interdependence is 'asymmetrical', but even powerful states bind themselves by rules and practices which endure – for example, when governments change or hegemony wanes (Keohane 2005). The institutions have their own power and a considerable degree of autonomy, employing thousands of permanent staff and controlling budgets of billions of dollars. While their views and policies could hardly be considered inimical to US interests, nor for example are the IMF and World Bank necessarily exactly in step, either with each other or with their major contributors (Stiglitz 2002).

However, for many descriptions of global governance and the global state, these supranational institutions comprise only one element. Nation states still matter. Much of political economy is still organised through them and through their inter-relations. This does not necessarily contradict depictions of a global state any more than the real authority of state governments within the US or Australian federal systems contradicts the power of those nation states. These sub-state powers also remain significant. There can be real competition within nation states, between different regions, and between regions in different countries, for example to attract funding from the EU. Moreover, these are not simply concentric layers of policy making. Within the EU, sub-state interests, regions like Catalonia or Scotland, or even small-scale campaigns like that of the 'McLibel Two' against McDonald's, may more or less successfully invoke the supra-state level against 'their own' nation states. An international corporate alliance lobbied successfully for the inclusion of intellectual property protection within the remit of the WTO (Sell 2000), and the social-movement opposition to this in relation to anti-retroviral drugs may at least have contributed to the softening of the position in the Doha declarations of the WTO. Perhaps most contentiously, Islamism raised – and has been raised as a test of – issues of allegiance to the nation state.

Thus governance cannot be reduced to narrowly political institutions. In particular, civil society actors have become an essential component. The idea of civil society is complex and contested. Much of the current usage is derived from Gramsci (1971), who used the term in various slightly different ways, but from whom an understanding of civil society as a terrain between the political and the economic has typically been taken. As such, it is an arena of relatively free ideological contest, within which for Gramsci communists needed to contest ruling-class hegemony to win a 'war of position' prior to any revolutionary 'war of manoeuvre'. Gramsci's conception was implicitly national, but this has been extended to the international or global level in more recent writing (Gills 1993). Similarly, the rise of new social movements was originally conceived as a largely national phenomenon, but Hegedus (1989) in particular characterised a process of their 'planetisation'. Others have subsequently described the explosion of global social or civil society movements (Anheier et al. 2001). This vision of governance is therefore broader than government, and more readily encompasses ideas and agencies alongside formal institutions.

Some of this writing has a clearly liberal and celebratory tone, but it is in many ways similar to that of postmodern Marxists such as Hardt and Negri (2000). 'Empire' is not that of a nation, but one of capital unbound by national or other differences. This all-pervasiveness means that resistance in any part influences the whole. There are innumerable possibilities for creative subjectivities to reshape the world in a positive way.

Critics have suggested there is an element of wishful (liberal or anarchist) thinking in such plural visions. These, sometimes inadvertently, have conservative implications. They fail to identify fully the asymmetry amongst the numerous powers in the world. They offer no identifiable central problem or set of problems or strategic target on which opposition might focus (see, for example, Tilly 2003; Wood 2003; Radice 2008).

There is also a well-known counter-argument to the claims of globalisation and state retreat, which maintains that these are exaggerated, if not completely unfounded (Hirst and Thompson 1999; Weiss 1998). Not only do states retain considerable policy autonomy (Garrett 2000), but the international flows are themselves organised either at the behest of states or with their permission. Most capital remains distinctly national (Doremus et al. 1998). Although absolute sovereignty may always have been something of a 'convenient fiction' (Strange and Tooze 1981), nation states and the state system retain their importance. From a Marxist perspective, the state remains essential for the reproduction of capital, however much the form might change (Burnham 1994).

Nor can civil society be so radically separated from politics and economics. Gramsci was of course aware that it was a realm pervaded by the interests of the already rich and powerful. However, some of his characterisations do lend themselves to a significant break with the earlier understandings of civil society in Hegel and Marx. In these, civil society, or *bürgerliche Gesellschaft* (literally 'bourgeois society'), was something that included the economy, representing everything from the state to private life. As Gramsci makes clear, civil society is also encroached from the other side, as it were, by the state. Indeed, in one unfortunate equation he suggests that the state simply is political society and civil society (1971:263). Of course freedom from economic and political pressures is always a question of degree. There are dangers of too pessimistic a depiction of structural determination, but also of assuming away the interests of the rich and powerful. Many contemporary non-governmental organisations rely on either governments or corporations for their funding, or act more or less directly as subcontractors for governments, as welfare and other formerly state functions are privatised. US encouragement for NGOs in developing countries has long been seen as part of a neo-imperialist project (Leys 1996; Petras 1999).

The Enduring Power of US Imperialism

States, moreover, are very different. State powerlessness, in general, cannot be extrapolated from evidence of one state, or even several states. The United States is not the same as Australia, is not the same as Uruguay, is not the same as Fiji. Conversely, the power to act effectively cannot be attributed universally on the evidence of a few powerful states.

The US state is the largest formal institution the world has ever known. Government income and spending may have fallen slightly as a share of GDP, but levels in 2003 of 27 and 31 per cent respectively were within a few points of highs in the early 1980s. As of 2005, the federal budget was $2.5 trillion. Federal civilian employment was 2.7 million with another 1.1 million in the military. States and local governments within the United States employed a further 5.0 million and 13.7 million respectively (Census 2008). One might also argue that the US state is the most powerful institution, at least in modern history, in relation to its rivals. With respect to overall wealth, in dollar terms it is more than two and a half times the size of Japan, the world's second richest state. In aggregate terms, the EU approaches the United States in total wealth, but its political fragmentation makes such aggregation suspect in any consideration of institutional power. In military terms, since the end of the cold war and the collapse of the USSR, the United States is further ahead of potential rivals than ever. Its unique political and economic position consistently persuaded others to finance its trade deficits and thus its consumption norms and military spending. The role of the dollar gives America a unique, indeed 'super-imperialist' (Hudson 2003) role in the world.

The global institutions were established and continue to operate as tools of a few powerful states, particularly the United States. The veto in the UN Security Council and the voting shares in the IMF and WB leave control in the hands of a few rich countries. This power is symbolised in the nomination of European and American heads of the last two organisations, a practice that seems beyond challenge. Harvey (2003), for example, sees Wall Street and the US Treasury controlling the IMF in their interests. The WTO has a more democratic structure, which perhaps underlies the deadlock in negotiations in the Doha round and some US wariness. However, it too has been criticised as a tool of rich countries, the quad (United States, Canada, Japan and Europe) setting agendas, and the insistence on consensus allowing an effective veto, while the disciplinary mechanisms rely on the power of the rich members.

Other institutions have some autonomy; the UN for example, refused to sanction the US invasion of Iraq. However, few would imagine that the institutions might act directly against the United States. The budgets and staffs of the international organisations are smaller by orders of magnitude than those of the US state. They also lack any independent military force, which remains the preserve of states (and to some extent of private mercenary armies sanctioned by states). Action, which Keohane (2005) acknowledges cannot be against the United States, depends on raising funds from states. This is attested by the deals that 'resolved' the debt crisis of the 1980s and the Asia Crisis in 1997. The US empire, in particular, while undoubtedly conditioned by other institutions, remains the central force in the world (Harvey 2003). Indeed, both its imperial nature and the limited nature of constraint on its power were confirmed by the invasion of Iraq.

US conservatives have explicitly articulated an imperial 'project for the new American century'. However, even those who see US imperialism as a central force in the world usually acknowledge that it works in less direct ways than the classical imperialism of the late nineteenth and early twentieth centuries (Hudson 2003; Arrighi 1994, 2003). For example the role of (neoliberal) ideas (Harvey 2005) and clusters of national and international institutions like 'The Wall Street–Treasury–IMF Complex' (Wade and Veneroso 1998) may be fundamental to securing its role. Nor is the project simply national, but rather that of particular sections of US (finance) capital (Panitch and Gindin 2005; Blackburn 2006). It is concerned with appropriation at home and abroad (Harvey 2003, 2005).

The Persistence of Interstate Competition

A third perspective suggests that the role of nation states either has not or cannot be superseded within capitalism. Empirically, significant interstate competition continues to characterise the global political economy. Some evidence of this was detailed in the previous chapters. The United States, despite its pre-eminent wealth and power, still faces challenges and does not order the world to its design. Domestic forces also constrain the power of leading states. Conceptually, the interstate system is precisely the necessary political form of global capitalism.

Most contemporary theorists acknowledge that earlier theories of imperialism too readily attributed to imperial states the role of agents of emerging national cartels or even of state capitalist trusts. There was already in the early twentieth century a substantial interpenetration of capital, allowing Kautsky (2004) to posit at least the possibility of 'ultra-imperialism' and a peaceful capitalist carve-up of the world. Conversely, more recent increases in capitalist internationalisation might not imply a retreat of the state or the end of imperialism. The relative pressures towards nationalisation and internationalisation vary, but the two tendencies are concurrent (Bukharin 1972; Radice 2008). Nor can the actions of the state be read off too quickly from whichever tendency appears to predominate at a specific time. Nation states are not mere agents of national capital. Indeed, the nation-state system preceded modern capitalism as it has been understood here. Nevertheless, only as capitalism perfected the (apparent) separation of economics and politics could the interstate system take on a distinctly capitalist form (Wood 2002; Callinicos 2007). This separation then precisely made possible the movement of capital across borders without direct political or military intervention (Rosenberg 2006). To see contemporary capital mobility as in some sense the negation of the nation state therefore misunderstands precisely what is distinct about the state form under capitalism.

Earlier chapters outlined a significant economic restructuring, but also suggested strong continuities. There remained significant economic competition, particularly between the rival geographical poles of growth in East Asia, North America and Europe and between the major countries within them. Therefore the likelihood was of significant, ongoing geopolitical struggles (Callinicos 2007). The United States's economic power does not go unchallenged. For example, the rise of the euro threatened dollar seigniorage, while China, rather than simply offering a manufacturing platform for US capital, had its own agenda, much to the concern of various US interest groups. The exploitation of its own working class had social and economic limits. US pre-eminence should not therefore be exaggerated. Its military adventures were not a conspicuous success.

The internationalisation of the state cannot be read off from that of capital. There are, for Harvey, two logics, whose relationship is

> problematic and often contradictory (that is, dialectical) rather than ... one-sided. This dialectical relation sets the stage for an analysis of capitalist imperialism in terms of the intersection of these two distinctive but intertwined logics of power. The difficulty for concrete analyses of actual situations is to keep the two sides of this dialectic simultaneously in motion and not to lapse into either a solely political or a predominantly economic mode of argumentation. (2003:30)

The final 'solely' and 'predominantly' are problematic. They imply priority to the political over the economic mode. Instead, some prioritisation, but of course not sole determination, of the economic would seem almost a defining character of a specifically Marxist analysis. Political power is then conditioned by this. As Pozo-Martin writes, describing dialectical relations is insufficient, unless it defines 'the kind of geopolitical explanation to be called on stage in understanding how the territorial logic unfolds' (2007:553).

Ashman and Callinicos (2006) cite this passage approvingly and Callinicos (2007) suggests that it is necessary to insert a distinct (realist) moment of state intervention into analyses of the global economy. He suggests doing this in a way analogous to Marx's insertion of increasingly concrete determinants into his analysis of capital. The more concrete cannot be deduced from the more abstract concepts. However, the concrete determinants may be discrete, but they are not arbitrary. For example, what we know about capital in general shapes the character of particular capitals in competition. This seems reasonable, on condition that we recall that the realist starting point is not, or is no longer, the state as 'black box' (Cohen 2008). Realists have been willing to open the box to locate an array of domestic social forces shaping state behaviour. The danger in this is of simply replacing the abstract political power with the generalisation of multiple causality. So, as Pozo-Martin (2007) suggests, it is necessary to describe the specifically capitalist logic that this implies. Once again, it is necessary to recall what has been described above as a conceptual 'asymmetry', in which the political and the economic are not reducible to each other, but internally rather than externally related, mutually conditioning, but in ways that may not be equal.

The US state needs to control accumulation within its borders. To do this it struggles both with domestic social relations and with international competitors. Its limited ability to achieve this accumulation provides the basis for understanding contemporary political as well as economic rivalry.

Conclusion

A historical materialist analysis undermines perspectives which, perceiving state power in the past to have been greater than it actually was, attribute states' contemporary limits to the sweeping force of globalisation. For some, economic change has nevertheless led to a change in political forms and a decline in states' relative significance. They operate alongside other powers at supra-state and sub-state level, their functions incorporated into what as yet exists as a 'network', lacking a centralised institutional form (Robinson and Harris 2002). However, this may overstate the plurality and the importance of non-state actors and institutions. The US state in particular remains powerful, but in ways that are potentially undermined, as it struggles to maintain its economic base against domestic and foreign challengers.

CONCLUSIONS: WHAT PROSPECTS FOR THE STATE, CAPITAL AND LABOUR?

1st Gent.   Our deeds are fetters that we forge ourselves.
2nd Gent.   Ay, truly: but I think it is the world that brings the iron.

George Eliot, *Middlemarch*

This book has attempted to provide a Marxist critique of the global political economy, interpreting the world from a materialist but anti-determinist perspective. It has described the dramatic transformation of the world, achieved in little more than 200 years since the industrial revolution, and significant if less epochal shifts in more recent times. The changes of the last 30 years seem comprehensible and transmutable if not simply reversible. There has been 'progress', in the sense of changing material ways of production and a preclusion of alternatives.

The introduction cited Cox's (1981) famous statement to the effect that theory is always strategic, always connected to particular interests. The various theories discussed in the first part of this book – the liberal emphasis on markets, the institutional-ist emphasis on states, the insistence of critical perspectives on incorporating or prioritising ideas, gender and the environment – were criticised as partial rather than wrong. They identify real and often important aspects of the global political economy, but their partiality militates against providing a basis for a thoroughgoing comprehension or systematic challenge. Marxism too is partial, if distinct in acknowledging this. Even what is in principle a holistic perspective cannot say everything and must necessarily prioritise. Marxism bases its priorities on the strategic if momentous goal of labour emancipation. In doing this it stresses the centrality of questions of work and attempts to identify structures of political economy, in order to identify likely fault lines and politically effective strategies of change. Marxism makes no pretensions to being an objective social science, although some have argued that it more than holds its own by conventional standards of predictive and explanatory power (Murray 1997).

Precisely because Marxism is not deterministic, it can interpret the relationship between economic change and the behaviour of states and labour in a relatively optimistic manner. The adoption of liberal policies and the weakness of labour organisation need not be read back as structurally determined and immutable. This, of course, is not to suggest that labour's conditions can simply be remade, regardless of the conditions of political economy. In particular, the analysis here contested the idea of sweeping changes often characterised as globalisation.

Some labour supporters have accepted this vision and see it as undermining local bases of resistance. Orientations and organisations which seek power in a national arena from which it has vanished become redundant. Globalisation is like a force of nature, which workers cannot and should not attempt to oppose. Instead they need strategies for harnessing it. Both Marxism and conventional social democratic politics are precluded (Giddens 1995, 1998). More positively, labour can continue to play a role if it changes direction and competes at the same scale as global capital (Tilly 1995; Radice 1999; Mazur, 2000). Globalisation may then be a necessary concept for labour, not because it tells us that resistance is futile (however severe labour's problems might be), but because (or in as far as) it tells us of the need for a strategic reorientation, an 'up-scaling' of action. However, the evidence discussed here suggests that this overstates change and misreads the appropriate arenas for labour action.

Capital's reorganisation was in many respects rather modest and its movements highly patterned. There were significant differences and tensions in capital's transformation, depending on what was considered. For example, levels of international investment, trade and financial movement all increased, but unevenly. Structure and restructuring depended on what sector or commodity was considered, over time and between places. Overall, there were significant new growth poles in East Asia, particularly in China.

There was also significant stagnation in Japan and Europe. However, the vast majority of economic output remained highly concentrated in familiar rich countries.

Restructuring was also crucially dependent on, and patterned by, the actions of powerful states. Chapter 5 discussed the important observation that in pre-capitalist societies there was not the separation between politics and economics that would develop later. However, it cautioned against reading this distinction too strictly. There were elements of independent economic power within feudal societies. Conversely, within capitalism the separation is always only conditional. State autonomy from capital is always relative, and to see the power of states as disappearing misreads the relationship between states and capital. It is more complementary than antagonistic. However, states are not reducible to executives of a national capitalist class: this class is inherently international (Barker 1978), and states are also always historically conditioned by domestic social relations. States continued to play an important and to some extent independent role in shaping economic processes.

The reality of state autonomy made possible the Keynesian compromises and the real gains made by workers in the post-war period. However, this autonomy's relative nature meant that these gains were always limited, and the variety of social-democratic and Stalinist strategies which looked to the state to secure change were always insufficient. Indeed, much recent restructuring was implemented either through deliberate state design or at least with states' willing compliance. Labour's defeats might be more political than economic (Walker 1999). Anti-labour laws continue to be pursued at the national level. Capital and its supporters seem unaware that dull economic compulsion is sufficient to keep labour in its place. It therefore seems particularly inappropriate for labour strategies to abandon the national level.

Similarly there is little to suggest that the global scale of capital precludes labour action at local scales. Indeed, there might be reasons to believe that integrated production systems become more vulnerable to local action. There is at least some evidence for this local power being utilised (Thelen and Kume 1999; Castree 2000;

Herod 2000). Capitalism remains a global system and is ultimately able to subvert local and national opposition. However, this happens as an ever contested social process, not an immediately accomplished fact. Similarly, labour can, and ultimately must, act at the global level. But the different scales of action are potentially complementary rather than exclusionary alternatives.

REFERENCES

Ackers, P., Smith, C. and Smith, P. (1996) 'Against all odds?', in P. Ackers, C. Smith and P. Smith (eds) *The New Workplace and Trade Unionism*, London, Routledge

Aglietta, M. (1987) *The Theory of Capitalist Regulation*, London, Verso

Alesina, A. and Weder, B. 'Do corrupt governments receive less foreign aid?', *The American Economic Review*, 92(4)

Allen, L. (2005) *The Global Economic System Since 1945*, London, Reaktion Books

Allen, R. C. (1998) 'Agricultural output and productivity in Europe, 1300–1800', Discussion Paper No. 98–14, Department of Economics, The University of British Columbia, Vancouver, September

Althusser, L. (1969) *For Marx*, London, Allen Lane

—— and Balibar, É. (1970) *Reading Capital*, London, New Left Books

Altschuler, A., Anderson, M., Jones, D., Roos, D. and Womack, J. (1984) *The Future of the Automobile*, London, George Allen & Unwin

Amsden, A. (1989) *Asia's Next Giant: South Korea and Late Industrialization*, New York, Oxford University Press

Anderson, B. (1991) *Imagined Communities*, London, Verso

—— (2000) *Doing the Dirty Work?* London, Zed Books

Anderson, P. (1979a) *Lineages of the Absolutist State*, London, Verso

—— (1979b) *Considerations of Western Marxism*, London, Verso

Anderson, T. (2004) 'Some thoughts on method in political economy', *Journal of Australian Political Economy*, 54

Anheier, H., Glasius, M. and Kaldor, M. (eds) (2001) *Global Civil Society*, Oxford, Oxford University Press

Archibugi, D. and Michie, J. (1997) *Technology, Globalisation and Economic Performance*, Cambridge, Cambridge University Press

Armstrong, P., Glyn, A. and Harrison, J. (1984) *Capitalism Since World War II*, London, Fontana

Arrighi, G. (1994) *The Long Twentieth Century*, London, Verso

—— (2003) 'The social and political economy of global turbulence', *New Left Review 20*

—— (2005a) 'Hegemony unravelling – 1', *New Left Review*, 32

—— (2005b) 'Hegemony unravelling – 2', *New Left Review*, 33

Arthur, C. (1997) 'Against the logical–historical method', in F. Moseley and M. Campbell (eds) *New Investigations of Marx's Method*, New Jersey, Humanities Press

Ashley, R. K. (1986) 'The poverty of neorealism', in R. O. Keohane (ed.) *Neorealism and Its Critics*, New York, Columbia University Press

Ashman, S. and Callinicos, A. (2006) 'Capital accumulation and the state system: assessing David Harvey's *The New Imperialism*', *Historical Materialism*, 14(4)

Atkinson, R. D. (2006) 'Is the next economy taking shape?', *Issues in Science and Technology*, 22(2)

Avineri, S. (1968) *The Social and Political Thought of Karl Marx*, Cambridge, Cambridge University Press

—— (1972) *Hegel's Theory of the Modern State*, Cambridge, Cambridge University Press

Babson, S. (1999) 'Ambiguous mandate: lean production and labor relations in the United States', in H. J. Núñez and S. Babson (eds) *Confronting Change: Auto Labor and Lean Production in North America*, second edition, Mexico, Beneméita Universidad de Puebla

Backhaus, H.-G. (1992) 'Between philosophy and science', in W. Bonefeld, R. Gunn and K. Psychopedis (eds) *Open Marxism, Vol. 1: Dialectics and History*, London, Pluto Press

Baily, M. N. (2004) 'Recent productivity growth: the role of information technology and other innovations', *Federal Reserve Bank of San Francisco Economic Review*

Balaam, D. N. and Veseth, M. (2001) *Introduction to International Political Economy*, New Jersey, Prentice Hall

Banaji, J. (2007) 'Islam, the Mediterranean and the rise of capitalism', *Historical Materialism*, 15(1)

Baran, P. A. and Sweezy, P. M. (1966) *Monopoly Capital*, Harmondsworth, Penguin

Barker, C. (1978) 'A note on the theory of capitalist states', *Capital and Class*, 4

—— (2006) 'Beyond Trotsky: extending combined and uneven development', in B. Dunn and H. Radice (eds) *100 Years of Permanent Revolution*, London, Pluto Press

Barnes, T. (2008) 'Is the Indian IT industry an example of an enclave economy? evidence from sociological research', unpublished paper

Barratt Brown, M. (1974) *The Economics of Imperialism*, Harmondsworth, Penguin

Beck, U. (1992) *Risk Society*, Newbury Park, Sage

Bell, D. (1974) *The Coming of Post-Industrial Society*, London, Heinemann Educational

Beneria, L. (1999) 'The enduring debate over unpaid labour', *International Labour Review*, 138(3)

Berger, T. (1996) 'Norms, identity, and national security in Germany and Japan', in P. J. Katzenstein (ed.) *The Culture of National Security*, New York, Columbia University Press

Berle, A. A. and Means, G. C. (1991) *The Modern Corporation and Private Property*, New Brunswick, Transaction Publishers

Bernstein, E. (1961) *Evolutionary Socialism*, New York, Schocken

Best, J. (2005) *The Limits of Transparency: Ambiguity and the History of International Finance*, New York, Cornell University Press

Bhagwati, J. (2002) *Free Trade Today*, Princeton, Princeton University Press

—— (2005) 'Reshaping the WTO', *Far Eastern Economic Review*, January/February

Bieler, A. and Morton, A. D. (2004) 'Unthinking materialism?', *The British Journal of International Relations*, 6(2)

Birdsall, N. (2006a) 'Rising inequality in the new global economy', *International Journal of Development Issues*, 5(1)

—— (2006b) 'Stormy days on an open field: asymmetries in the global economy', Centre for Global Development, Working Paper no. 81

BIS (2007) *77th Annual Report*, Bank for International Settlements, Basel, available at www.bis.org

Blackburn, R. (1988) *The Overthrow of Colonial Slavery*, London, Verso

—— (1997) *The Making of New World Slavery*, London, Verso

—— (2006) 'Finance and the fourth dimension', *New Left Review*, 39

Blackledge, P. (2006a) *Reflections on the Marxist Theory of History*, Manchester, Manchester University Press

—— (2006b) 'Karl Kautsky and Marxist historiography', *Science and Society*, 70(3)

Blanchard, I. (2001) 'International capital markets and their users, 1450–1750', in M. Prak (ed.) *Early Modern Capitalism: Economic and Social Change in Europe, 1400–1800*, London, Routledge

Block, F. (2001) 'Introduction', in K. Polanyi *The Great Transformation*, Boston, Beacon Press

Block, W. E. (1990) 'Environmental problems, private property rights solutions', in W. E. Block (ed.) *Economics and the Environment: A Reconciliation*, Vancouver, Fraser Institute

BLS (2007) Bureau of Labor Statistics, US Department of Labor, available at www.bls.gov/cpi

Bois, G. (1985) 'Against neo-Malthusian orthodoxy', in T. H. Aston and C. H. E. Philpin (eds) *The Brenner Debate*, Cambridge, Cambridge University Press

Boltho, A. (2003) 'What's wrong with Europe', *New Left Review*, 22

—— and Corbett, J. (2000) 'The assessment: Japan's stagnation – can policy revive the economy?', *Oxford Review of Economic Policy*, 16(2)

Bond, P. (2004) 'Bankrupt Africa: imperialism, sub-imperialism and the politics of finance', *Historical Materialism*, 12(4)

Bonefeld, W. (2004) '"Critical economy" and social constitution', *British Journal of International Relations*, 6(2)

Bourdieu, P. (1977) *Outline of a Theory of Practice*, Cambridge, Cambridge University Press

—— (1984) *Distinction: A Social Critique of the Judgement of Taste*, London, Routledge & Kegan Paul

—— (1998) *Acts of Resistance*, New York, New Press

Bourguignon, F. and Morrison, C. (2002) 'Inequality among world citizens: 1820–1992', *American Economic Review*, 92(4)

Boyer, R. (1990) *The Regulation School: A Critical Introduction*, New York, Columbia University Press

Braudel, F. (1974) *Capitalism and Material Life: 1400–1800*, Glasgow, Fontana/Collins

—— (1985) *Civilization and Capitalism 15th–18th Century, Vol. 3: The Perspective of the World*, London, Fontana

—— (1995) *A History of Civilizations*, Harmondsworth, Penguin

Braunmuhl, C. von (1978) 'On the analysis of the bourgeois nation state within the world market context', in J. Holloway and S. Picciotto (eds) *State and Capital*, London, Arnold

Braverman, H. (1974) *Labour and Monopoly Capital*, New York, Monthly Review

Brenner, R. (1977) 'The origins of capitalist development: a critique of neo-Smithian Marxism', *New Left Review*, 104

—— (1985a) 'Agrarian class structure and economic development in pre-industrial Europe', in T. H. Ashton and C. H. E. Philpin (eds) *The Brenner Debate*, Cambridge, Cambridge University Press

—— (1985b) 'The agrarian roots of European capitalism', in T. H. Ashton and C. H. E. Philpin (eds) *The Brenner Debate*, Cambridge, Cambridge University Press

—— (1998) 'The economics of global turbulence', *New Left Review*, 229

—— (2003) *The Boom and the Bubble*, London, Verso

—— (2006) 'The origins of capitalism', transcript of the discussion with Chris Harman, London, 2004, *International Socialism*, 111

Brewer, A. (1990) *Marxist Theories of Imperialism*, London, Routledge

Bromley, S. (1999) 'The space of flows and timeless time', *Radical Philosophy*, 97

Bronfenbrenner, K. (2003) 'The American labour movement and the resurgence in union organizing', in P. Fairbrother and C. A. B. Yates (eds) *Trade Unions in Renewal: A Comparative Study*, London, Continuum

Brunhoff, S. de (1976) *Marx on Money*, New York, Urizen

—— (1978) *The State, Capital and Economic Policy*, London, Pluto Press

Bryan, D. (2003) 'Bridging differences: value theory, international finance and the construction of global capital', in R. Westra and A. Zuega (eds) *Value and the World Economy Today*, Basingstoke, Palgrave Macmillan

—— and Rafferty, M. (2006) *Capitalism with Derivatives*, New York, Palgrave Macmillan

Bukharin, N. (1972) *Imperialism and World Economy*, London, Merlin

Bull, H. (1977) *The Anarchical Society*, New York, Columbia University Press

Burawoy, M. (1985) *The Politics of Production*, London, Verso

Burch, K. (1997) 'Introduction', in K. Burch and R. A. Denemark (eds) *Constituting International Political Economy*, Boulder, Col., Lynne Rienner

Burkett, P. and Hart-Landsberg, M. (2000a) *Development, Crisis, and Class Struggle*, New York, St. Martin's Press

—— (2000b) 'Alternative perspectives on late industrialisation in East Asia', *Review of Radical Political Economics*, 32(2)

Burnham, P. (1991) 'Neo-Gramscian hegemony and international order', *Capital and Class*, 45

—— (1994) 'Open Marxism and vulgar international political economy', *Review of International Political Economy*, 1(2)

Bush, R. (2004) 'Undermining Africa', *Historical Materialism*, 12(4)

Butler, J. (1990) *Gender Trouble*, London, Routledge

Callinicos, A. (1983) *The Revolutionary Ideas of Karl Marx*, London, Bookmarks

—— (1989) 'Bourgeois revolutions and historical materialism', *International Socialism*, 43

—— (1999) *Social Theory*, Cambridge, Polity

—— (2007) 'Does capitalism need the state system?', *Cambridge Review of International Affairs*, 20(4)

Cammack, P. (1990) 'Statism, new institutionalism, and Marxism', *Socialist Register*, 1990

Campling, L. (2004) 'Editorial introduction to the symposium on Marxism and African realities', *Historical Materialism*, 12(4)

Carchedi, G. (1986) 'Two models of class analysis', *Capital and Class*, 29

Cardoso, F. H. and Falleto, E. (1979) *Dependency and Development in Latin America*, Berkeley, University of California Press

Carver, T. (1975) 'Commentary', in *Karl Marx: Texts on Method*, Oxford, Blackwell

Castells, M. (1997) *The Information Age: Economy, Society and Culture, Vol. 2*, Oxford, Blackwell

—— (2000) *The Information Age: Economy, Society and Culture, Vol. 1*, Blackwell, Oxford Census (2007)

Castree, N. (2000) 'Geographic scale and grassroots internationalism', *Economic Geography*, 76(3)

Census (various years) *Statistical Abstract of the United States*, available at www.census.gov

Cerny, P. G. (1993) 'The deregulation and re-regulation of financial markets in a more open world', in P. G. Cerny (ed.) *Finance and World Politics: Markets, Regimes and States in the Post-hegemonic Era*, Aldershot, Edward Elgar

—— (1996) 'International finance and the erosion of state policy capacity', in P. Gummett (ed.) *Globalization and Public Policy*, Cheltenham, Edward Elgar

—— (2000) 'Restructuring the political arena: globalization and the paradoxes of the competition state', in R. D. Germain (ed.) *Globalization and its Critics*, Basingstoke, Palgrave Macmillan

Chang, H.-J. (2002) *Kicking Away the Ladder: Policies and Institutions for Development in Historical Perspective*, London, Anthem Press

Chester, E. (1978) 'Military spending and capitalist stability', *Cambridge Journal of Economics*, 2

Chomsky, N. (2003) *Understanding Power*, London, Vintage

Chon, S. (1997) 'Destroying the myth of vertical integration in the Japanese electronics industry', *Regional Studies*, 31(1)

Clarke, L. (1997) 'Changing work systems, changing social relations?', *Industrial Relations*, 52(4)

Clarke, S. (1992) 'What in the F——'s name is Fordism?', in N. Gilbert, R. Burrows and A. Pollert (eds) *Fordism and Flexibility: Divisions and Change*, Basingstoke, Macmillan

—— (1994) *Marx's Theory of Crisis*, Basingstoke, Macmillan

Cliff, T. (1957) 'Perspectives on the permanent war economy', *Socialist Review*, March

—— and Gluckstein, D. (1986) *Marxism and Trade Union Struggle*, London, Bookmarks

Cloud, K. and Garrett, N. (1996) 'A modest proposal for inclusion of women's household human capital production in analysis of structural transformation', *Feminist Economics*, 2(3)

Coase, R. H. (1937) 'The theory of the firm', available at www.cerna. ensmp.fr/Enseignement/CoursEcoIndus/SupportsdeCours/COASE. pdf

Coates, D. (2000) *Models of Capitalism: Growth and Stagnation in the Modern Era*, Polity, Cambridge

Cohen, B. J. (1998) *The Geography of Money*, Ithaca, NY and London, Cornell University Press

—— (2008) *International Political Economy*, Princeton, Princeton University Press

Cohn, T. H. (2005) *Global Political Economy*, New York, Pearson

Coleman, L. (2007) 'The gendered violence of development', *British Journal of Politics and International Relations*, 9(2)

Comtrade (various years), available at comtrade.un.org

Cooper, J. P. (1985) 'In search of agrarian capitalism', in T. H. Ashton and C. H. E. Philpin (eds) *The Brenner Debate*, Cambridge, Cambridge University Press

Cox, J. (1998) 'An introduction to Marx's theory of alienation', *International Socialism*, 79

Cox, R. W. (1981) 'Social forces, states and world orders', *Millennium: Journal of International Studies*, 10(2)

—— (1987) *Production, Power and World Order*, New York, Columbia University Press

—— (1996) *Approaches to World Order*, Cambridge, Cambridge University Press

—— (2002) *The Political Economy of a Plural World*, London, Routledge

Croot, P. and Parker, D. (1985) 'Agrarian class structure and the development of capitalism', in T. H. Aston and C. H. E. Philpin (eds) *The Brenner Debate*, Cambridge, Cambridge University Press

Crouzet, F. (1990) *Britain Ascendant*, Cambridge, Cambridge University Press

Dauvergne, P. (2008) 'Globalization and the environment', in J. Ravenhill, *Global Political Economy*, Oxford, Oxford University Press

Davidson, N. (2006a) 'From uneven to combined development', in B. Dunn and H. Radice (eds) *100 Years of Permanent Revolution*, London, Pluto Press

—— (2006b) discussion contribution in 'The origins of capitalism', transcript of the discussion between Chris Harman and Robert Brenner, London, 2004, in *International Socialism*, 111

Delbridge, R. and Lowe, J. (1997) 'Manufacturing control: supervisory systems on the "new" shopfloor', *Sociology*, 31(3)

Deléage, J.-P. (1994) 'Eco-Marxist critique of political economy', in M. O'Connor (ed.) *Is Capitalism Sustainable?*, New York, Guilford Press

Delphy, C. (1977) *The Main Enemy*, London, Women's Research and Resources Centre Publications

Deranyiagala, S. (2005) 'Neoliberalism in international trade', in A. Saad-Fihlo and D. Johnston (eds) *Neoliberalism: A Critical Reader*, London, Pluto Press

—— and Fine, B. (2001) 'New trade theory versus old trade policy: a continuing enigma', *Cambridge Journal of Economics*, 25(6)

Desai, M. (2004) *Marx's Revenge*, London, Verso

Dicken, P. (2003) *Global Shift*, London, Sage

Dobb, M. (1963) *Studies in the Development of Capitalism*, New York, International Publishers

—— (1976) 'A reply', in R. Hilton (ed.) *The Transition from Feudalism to Capitalism*, London, New Left Books

Doremus, P. N., Keller, W. W., Pauly, L. W. and Reich, S. (1998) *The Myth of the Global Corporation*, Princeton, Princeton University Press

Dos Santos, T. (1970) 'The Structure of Dependence', *The American Economic Review*, 60

Dowd, D. (2004) *Capitalism and its Economics*, London, Pluto Press

Draper, H. (1966) 'The two souls of socialism', *New Politics*, 5(1)

—— (1977) *Karl Marx's Theory of Revolution, Vol. 1: State and Bureaucracy*, New York, Monthly Review Press

Dunkley, G. (2004) *Free Trade: Myth, Reality and Alternatives*, London, Zed Books

Dunn, B. (2004a) *Globalisation and the Power of Labour*, Basingstoke, Palgrave Macmillan

—— (2004b) 'Capital movements and the embeddedness of labour', *Global Society*, 18(2)

—— (2004c) 'The regionalisation of international contracting', *Construction Management and Economics*, 22(1)

—— (2007) 'Accumulation by dispossession or accumulation of capital?', *Journal of Australian Political Economy*, 60

Dunne, P. (1990) 'The political economy of military expenditure', *Cambridge Journal of Economics*, 14(4)

Dunning, J. H. (1993) *Multinational Enterprises and the Global Economy*, Wokingham, Addison-Wesley

Eatwell, J. (1996) *International Financial Liberalization*, New York, UNDP Office of Development Studies

Ehrlich, P. (1968) *The Population Bomb*, New York, Sierra Club

Elekdag, S. and Lall, S. (2008) 'Global growth estimates trimmed after PPP revisions', *IMF Survey Magazine: IMF Research*, IMF Research Department, 8 January

Emmanuel, A. (1972) *Unequal Exchange: A Study of the Imperialism of Trade*, London, New Left Books

Endres, A. M. (2007) 'Choice in currency: A Hayekian perspective on international financial integration', proceedings of the sixth conference of the Australian Society of Heterodox Economists, 10–11 December, University of New South Wales, Sydney

Engels, F. (1934) *Herr Eugen Duhring's Revolution in Science*, London, Martin Lawrence

Epstein, S. R. (2001) 'The late medieval crisis as an "integration crisis"', in M. Prak (ed.) *Early Modern Capitalism: Economic and Social Change in Europe, 1400–1800*, London, Routledge

Ereira, A. (1981) *The Invergordon Mutiny*, London, Routledge & Kegan Paul

Evans, P. B., Rueschemeyer, D. and Skocpol, T. (eds) (1985) *Bringing the State Back In*, Cambridge, Cambridge University Press

Federal Reserve (2007) 'Statistics: releases and historical data, foreign exchange rates', available at federalreserve.gov/releases/ on 30 May 2007

Ferguson, N. (2002) *Empire: the Rise and Demise of the British World Order and the Lessons for Global Power*, New York, Basic Books

Ferguson, Y. H. and Mansbach, R. W. (1996) 'The past as prelude to the future?', in Y. Lapid and F. Kratochwil *The Return of Culture and Identity in IR Theory*, Boulder, Col., Lynne Rienner

Feyerabend, P. (1988) *Against Method*, London, Verso

Fieldhouse, D. K. (1973) *Economics and Empire 1830–1914*, London, Weidenfeld & Nicolson

Fine, B. (1984) *Marx's Capital*, London, Macmillan

—— (2003) 'Value theory and the study of contemporary capitalism: a continuing commitment', in R. Westra and A. Zuega (eds) *Value and the World Economy Today*, Basingstoke, Palgrave Macmillan

—— (2004) 'Examining the ideas of globalisation and development critically', *New Political Economy*, 9(2)

—— and Harris, L. (1979) *Rereading Capital*, London, Macmillan

Folbre, N. (1982) 'Exploitation comes home: a critique of the Marxian theory of family labour', *Cambridge Journal of Economics*, 6

Foley, D. (1986) *Understanding Capital: Marx's Economic Theory*, Cambridge, Mass., Harvard University Press

Foreman-Peck, J. (1983) *A History of the World Economy*, Brighton, Wheatsheaf

Foster, J. B. (2000) *Marx's Ecology*, New York, Monthly Review Press

Foucault, M. (1980) *Power/Knowledge*, New York, Pantheon
Frank, A. G. (1970) 'The development of underdevelopment', in R. I. Rhodes (ed.) *Imperialism and Underdevelopment*, New York, Monthly Review
—— (1978) *Dependent Accumulation and Underdevelopment*, London, Macmillan
Frieden, J. A. (1991) 'Invested interests: the politics of national economic policies in a world of global finance', *International Organization*, 45(4)
Friedman, M. (1953) *Essays in Positive Economics*, Chicago, University of Chicago Press
—— (1962) *Capitalism and Freedom*, Chicago, University of Chicago Press
—— and Friedman, R. (1980) *Free to Choose*, London, Secker & Warburg
Fröbel, F., Heinrichs, J. and Kreye, O. (1980) *The New International Division of Labour*, Cambridge, Cambridge University Press
Fukuyama, F. (1992) *The End of History and the Last Man*, London, Hamish Hamilton
Fusfeld, D. R. (2002) *The Age of the Economist*, Boston, Addison Wesley
Galbraith, J. K. (1995) *Money: Whence it Came, Where it Went*, Harmondsworth, Penguin
Garrett, G. (2000) 'Shrinking states? Globalization and national autonomy', in N. Woods (ed.) *The Political Economy of Globalization*, Basingstoke, Palgrave Macmillan
Gereffi, G., Humphrey, J. and Sturgeon, T. (2005) 'The governance of global value chains', *Review of International Political Economy*, 12(1)
Germain, R. D. (1997) *The International Organization of Credit*, Cambridge, Cambridge University Press
Gerschenkron, A. (1962) *Economic Backwardness in Historical Perspective*, Cambridge, Mass., Belknap Press
Gibson-Graham, J. K. (1996) *The End of Capitalism (As We Knew It)*, Cambridge, Mass., Blackwell
Giddens, A. (1979) *Central Problems in Social Theory*, Berkeley, University of California Press
—— (1991) *The Consequences of Modernity*, Cambridge, Polity
—— (1995) *A Contemporary Critique of Historical Materialism*, Basingstoke, Macmillan
—— (1998) *The Third Way*, London, Polity
Gill, S. (1990) *American Hegemony and the Trilateral Commission*, Cambridge, Cambridge University Press

—— (1993) 'Global finance, monetary policy and cooperation among the Group of Seven, 1944–92', in P. G. Cerny (ed.) *Finance and World Politics: Markets, Regimes and States in the Post-hegemonic Era*, Aldershot, Edward Elgar

—— and Law, D. (1988) *The Global Political Economy*, New York, Harvester

—— —— (1993) 'Global hegemony and the structural power of capital', in S. Gill (ed.) *Gramsci, Historical Materialism and International Relations*, Cambridge, Cambridge University Press

Gills, B. (1993) 'The hegemonic transition in East Asia: a historical perspective', in S. Gill (ed.) *Gramsci, Historical Materialism and International Relations*, Cambridge, Cambridge University Press

Gilpin, R. (1986) 'The richness of the tradition of political realism', in R. O. Keohane (ed.) *Neorealism and Its Critics*, New York, Columbia University Press

—— (1987) *The Political Economy of International Relations*, Princeton, Princeton University Press

—— (2001) *Global Political Economy*, Princeton, Princeton University Press

Glyn, A. (2006) *Capitalism Unleashed: Finance, Globalization, and Welfare*, Oxford, Oxford University Press

Goldstein, J. S. (1997) 'Taking off the gender blinders in IPE', in K. Burch and R. A. Denemark (eds) *Constituting International Political Economy*, Boulder, Col., Lynne Rienner

Gordon, D. M. (1978) 'Up and down the long roller coaster', in Union for Radical Political Economics (ed.) *US Capitalism in Crisis*, New York, Union for Radical Political Economics

Gordon, R. J. (2000) 'Does the "new economy" measure up to the great inventions of the past', National Bureau of Economic Research, Working Paper no. 7833

Gorz, A. (1982) *Farewell to the Working Class*, London, Pluto Press

Gowan, P. (1999) *The Global Gamble*, London, Verso

Gramsci, A. (1971) *Prison Notebooks*, London, Lawrence & Wishart

Gray, J. (1998) *False Dawn: The Delusions of Global Capitalism*, London, Granta

Green, F. and Nore, P. (eds) (1977) *Economics: An Anti-Text*, London, Macmillan

Gunn, R. (1992) 'Against historical materialism', in W. Bonefeld, R. Gunn and K. Psychopedis (eds) *Open Marxism, Vol. 2: Theory and Practice*, London, Pluto Press

Guzzini, S. (1998) *Realism in International Relations and International Political Economy*, London, Routledge

—— (1999) 'The use and misuse of power analysis in international threory', in R. Palan (ed.) *Global Political Economy*, London, Routledge

Habermas, J. (1976) *Legitimation Crisis*, London, Heinemann

Halevi, J. and Kriesler, P. (2004) 'Stagnation and economic conflict in Europe', *International Journal of Political Economy*, 34(2)

—— and Lucarelli, B. (2002) 'Japan's stagnationist crisis', *Monthly Review*, 59

Hamilton, A. (1997) 'Report on manufactures', in G. T. Crane and A. Amawi (eds) *The Theoretical Evolution of International Political Economy*, New York, Oxford University Press

Hardin, G. (1968) 'The tragedy of the commons', *Science*, 168(3859)

Hardt, M. and Negri, A. (2000) *Empire*, Cambridge, Mass.: Harvard University Press

Harman, C. (1984) *Explaining the Crisis*, London, Bookmarks

—— (1986) *How Marxism Works*, London, Bookmarks

—— (1989) 'From feudalism to capitalism', *International Socialism*, 45

—— (1999) *A People's History of the World*, London, Bookmarks

—— (2007) 'The rate of profit and the world today', *International Socialism*, 115

—— (2008) 'From the credit crunch to the spectre of global crisis', *International Socialism*, 118

Harris, N. (1981) 'Crisis and the core of the world system', *International Socialism*, 10

—— (1987) *The End of the Third World: Newly Industrializing Countries and the Decline of an Ideology*, Harmondsworth, Penguin

Harrod, J. (1987) *Power, Production, and the Unprotected Worker*, New York, Columbia University Press

Hartmann, H. (1981) 'The unhappy marriage of Marxism and feminism', in L. Sargent (ed.) *The Unhappy Marriage of Marxism and Feminism*, London, Pluto Press

Harvey, D. (1982) *The Limits of Capital*, Oxford, Basil Blackwell

—— (1990) *The Condition of Postmodernity: An Enquiry into the Origins of Cultural Change*, Oxford, Blackwell

—— (2003) *The New Imperialism*, Oxford, Oxford University Press

—— (2005) *A Brief History of Neoliberalism*, Oxford, Oxford University Press

Harvey, M. (2001) *Undermining Construction: The Corrosive Effects of False Self-Employment*, London, Institute of Employment Rights

Hayek, F. A. (1962) *The Road to Serfdom*, London, Routledge & Kegan Paul

Hayter, T. (1971) *Aid as Imperialism*, Harmondsworth, Penguin

Heaton, H. (1948) *Economic History of Europe*, New York, Harper & Brothers

Hegedus, Z. (1989) 'Social movements and social change in self-creative society', *International Sociology*, 4(1)

Hegel, G. W. F. (1991) *Elements of the Philosophy of Right*, Cambridge, Cambridge University Press

Heilbroner, R. (2000) *The Worldly Philosophers*, Harmondsworth, Penguin

—— and Milberg, W. (1995) *The Crisis of Vision in Modern Economic Thought*, Cambridge, Cambridge University Press

Held, D. (1990) *Introduction to Critical Theory: Horkheimer to Habermas*, Cambridge, Polity

—— McGrew, A., Goldblatt, D. and Perraton, J. (1999) *Global Transformations*, Cambridge, Polity

Helleiner, E. (1993) 'American hegemony and global economic structure: from closed to open financial relations in the postwar world', thesis submitted for the Ph.D. degree, London School of Economics, University of London

—— (1994) *States and the Reemergence of Global Finance*, Ithaca, NY, Cornell University Press

—— (2000) 'New voices in the globalisation debate: green perspectives on the world economy', in R. Stubbs and G. R. D. Underhill (eds) *Political Economy and the Changing Global Order*, Oxford, Oxford University Press

—— (2005) 'The evolution of the international financial and monetary system', in J. Ravenhill (ed.) *Global Political Economy*, Oxford, Oxford University Press

Hensman, R. (2001) 'World trade and workers' rights', *Antipode*, 33

Henwood, D. (1998) *Wall Street*, London, Verso

—— (2003) *After the New Economy*, New York, New Press

Herod, A. (2000) 'Implications of just-in-time production for union strategy', *Annals of the Association of American Geographers*, 90(3)

Heston, A., Summers, R. and Aten, B. (2002) Penn World Table, version 6.1, Center for International Comparisons at the University of Pennsylvania (CICUP), October, available at http://pwt.econ.upenn. edu/ on 31 January 2007

—— —— —— (2006) Penn World Table, version 6.2, Center for International Comparisons of Production, Income and Prices at the University of Pennsylvania, September, available at http://pwt.econ. upenn.edu/ on 31 January 2007

Higgot, R. (1991) 'Towards a non-hegemonic IPE', in C. N. Murphy and R. Tooze (eds) *The New International Political Economy*, Boulder, Col., Lynne Rienner

—— (1998) 'The Asian economic crisis', *New Political Economy*, 3(3)

Hilferding, R. (1981) *Finance Capital: A Study of the Latest Phase in Capitalist Development*, London, Routledge & Kegan Paul

Hill, C. (1993) *A Nation of Novelty and Change*, London, Bookmarks

Hilton, R. H. (1985a) 'Introduction', in T. H. Aston and C. H. E. Philpin (eds) *The Brenner Debate*, Cambridge, Cambridge University Press

—— (1985b) 'A crisis of feudalism', in T. H. Aston and C. H. E. Philpin (eds) *The Brenner Debate*, Cambridge, Cambridge University Press

—— (1990) *Class Conflict and the Crisis of Feudalism*, London, Verso

Himmelweit, S. (1977) 'The individual as the basic unit of analysis', in F. Green and P. Nore (eds) *Economics: An Anti-Text*, London, Macmillan

—— (2002) 'Making visible the hidden economy: the case for gender impact analysis of economic policy', *Feminist Economics*, 8(1)

—— and Mohun, S. (1977) 'Domestic labour and capital', *Cambridge Journal of Economics*, 1

Hines, C. (2000) *Localization: A Global Manifesto*, London, Earthscan

Hirst, P. and Thompson, G. (1999) *Globalization in Question*, Cambridge, Polity

Hobbes, T. (1991) *Leviathan*, Cambridge, Cambridge University Press

Hobsbawm, E. J. (1962) *The Age of Revolution: Europe 1789–1848*, London, Weidenfeld & Nicolson

—— (1969) *Industry and Empire*, Harmondsworth, Penguin

—— (1975) *The Age of Capital: 1848–1875*, New York, Mentor

—— (1987) *The Age of Empire: 1975–1914*, London, Weidenfeld & Nicolson

—— and Ranger, T. (eds) (1984) *The Invention of Tradition*, Cambridge, Cambridge University Press

Hobson, J. A. (2007) *Imperialism: A Study*, available at www.marxists.org/archive/hobson/1902/imperialism/ on 21 March 2007

Hobson, J. M. (2000) *The State and International Relations*, Cambridge, Cambridge University Press

—— (2007) 'Back to the future of "one logic or two"?', *Cambridge Review of International Affairs*, 20(4)

Hodgkin, T. (1972) 'Some African and third world theories of imperialism', in R. Owen and B. Sutcliffe (eds) *Studies in the Theory of Imperialism*, London, Longman

Hodgson, G. M. (1993) *Economics and Evolution*, Cambridge, Polity

Holloway, J. (1994) 'Global capital and the nation state', *Capital and Class*, 51

—— (1995a) 'Capital moves', *Capital and Class*, 57

—— (1995b) 'From scream of refusal to scream of power', in W. Bonefeld, R. Gunn, J. Holloway and K. Psychopedis (eds) *Open Marxism, Vol. 3: Emancipating Marx*, London, Pluto Press

Horlings, E. (2001) 'Pre-industrial economic growth and the transition to an industrial economy', in M. Prak (ed.) *Early Modern Capitalism: Economic and social change in Europe, 1400–1800*, London, Routledge

Hoskyns, C. and Rai, S. M. (2007) 'Recasting the global political economy', *New Political Economy*, 12(3)

Hudson, M. (2003) *Super Imperialism*, London, Pluto Press

Hummels, D. L. and Stern, R. M. (1994) 'Evolving patterns of North American merchandise trade and foreign direct investment, 1960–1990', *The World Economy*, 17(1)

Humphries, J. (1977) 'Class struggle and the persistence of the working-class family', *Cambridge Journal of Economics*, 1

Hunt, E. K. (1992) *History of Economic Thought*, second edition, New York, HarperCollins

—— and Sherman, H. J. (1981) *Economics: An Introduction to Traditional and Radical Views*, New York, Harper & Row

Hutton, W. (1995) *The State We're in*, London, Jonathan Cape

—— (2006) *The Writing on the Wall*, London, Little, Brown

Hyman, R. (1999) 'Imagined Solidarities: Can Trade Unions Resist Globalization?', in P. Leisink (ed.) *Globalization and Labour Relations*, Cheltenham, Edward Elgar

ILO (2008) 'Employment: yearly statistics', available at http://laborsta.ilo.org on 6 March 2008

IMF (1992) *International Financial Statistics Yearbook*, New York, IMF

—— (2005) *World Economic Outlook*, Washington, DC, IMF

—— (2006) *International Financial Statistics Yearbook*, New York, IMF

—— (2007a) 'Currency composition of official exchange reserves', COFER, available at www.imf.org/external/np/sta/cofer/eng/index.htm on 14 May 2007

—— (2007b) *Global Financial Stability Report 2007*, Washington, DC, IMF

Itoh, M. and Lapavitsas, C. (1999) *Political Economy of Money and Finance*, Basingstoke, Macmillan

Jones, B. (1982) 'Destruction or redistribution of engineering skills?', in S. Wood (ed.) *The Degradation of Work?* London, Unwin Hyman

Jones, E. (2005) 'Liquor retailing and the Woolworths/Coles juggernaut', *Journal of Australian Political Economy*, 55

Jones, G. (1993) 'Introduction', in G. Jones (ed.) *Transnational Corporations: A Historical Perspective*, London, Routledge

—— (2005) *Multinationals and Global Capitalism*, Oxford, Oxford University Press

Kant, I. (1993) *Critique of Pure Reason*, London, Everyman

Kapstein, E. B. (1994) *Governing the Global Economy: International Finance and the State*, Cambridge, Mass., Harvard University Press

Katzenstein, P. J. (ed.) (1996) *The Culture of National Security*, New York, Columbia University Press

—— (1998) *Cultural Norms and National Security*, New York, Cornell University Press

—— (2003) 'Same war: different views', *International Organization*, 57

Kautsky, K. (1983) *Selected Writings*, London, Macmillan

—— (2004) 'Ultra-imperialism', available at www.marxists.org/archive/kautsky/1914/09/ultra-imp.htm on 13 November 2006

Keane, C. (2007) 'Whatever happened to the recession?', paper presented to the conference on 'Examining the foundations of the Australian boom', organised by the *Journal of Australian Political Economy*, University of Sydney, December 12

Keily, R. (2003) 'On Maghnad Desai's *Marx's Revenge*', *Historical Materialism*, 11(3)

Kenwood, A. G. and Lougheed, A. L. (1992) *The Growth of the International Economy: 1820–1990*, London, Routledge

Keohane, R. O. (1986) 'Realism, neorealism and the study of world politics', in R. O. Keohane (ed.) *Neorealism and Its Critics*, New York, Columbia University Press

—— (2005) *After Hegemony*, Princeton, Princeton University Press

—— and Nye, J. S. (1977) *Power and Independence: World Politics in Transition*, Boston, Little, Brown

Keynes, J. M. (1973) *The General Theory of Employment, Interest and Money*, London, Macmillan

Kho, B.-C., Stulz, R. M. and Warnock, F. E. (2006) 'Financial globalisation, governance and the evolution of the home bias', BIS Working Paper no. 220, available at www.bis.org

Kidron, M. (1970) *Western Capitalism since the War*, Harmondsworth, Penguin

—— (1974) *Capitalism and Theory*, London, Pluto Press

Kincaid, J. (2001) 'Marxist political economy and the crises in Japan and East Asia', *Historical Materialism*, 8

Kinder, H. and Hilgemann, W. (1978) *Atlas of World History, Vol. 2*, Harmondsworth, Penguin

Kindleberger, C. P. (1973) *The World in Depression 1929–39*, London, Allen Lane

—— (1975) 'The rise of free trade in Western Europe', *Journal of Economic History*, 35(1)

Kirshner, J. (1999) 'The political economy of realism', in E. B. Kapstein and M. Mastanduno (eds) *Unipolar Politics: Realism and State Strategies after the Cold War*, New York, Columbia University Press

Kitching, G. N. (2001) *Seeking Social Justice Through Globalization*, University Park, Pennsylvania State University Press

Kobrin, S. J. (1984) 'Expropriation as an attempt to control foreign firms in LDCs', *International Studies Quarterly*, 28(3)

Kolm, S.-C. (1968) 'Review: Léon Walras' correspondence and related papers', *American Economic Review*, 58(5)

Kotz, D. M. (1994) 'The regulation theory and the social structure of accumulation approach', in D. M. Kotz, T. McDonough and M. Reich (eds) *Social Structures of Accumulation: The Political Economy of Growth and Crisis*, Cambridge, Cambridge University Press

—— McDonough, T. and Reich, M. (eds) (1994) *Social Structures of Accumulation: The Political Economy of Growth and Crisis*, Cambridge, Cambridge University Press

Kovel, J. (2002) *The Enemy of Nature*, Nova Scotia, Fernwood Publishing

Krasner, S. D. (1976) 'State power and the structure of international trade', *World Politics*, 28(3)

—— (1999) *Sovereignty: Organized Hypocrisy*, Princeton, Princeton University Press

Kreps, D. M. (1989) 'Nash equilibrium', in J. Eatwell, M. Milgate and P. Newman (eds) *Game Theory*, London, Macmillan

Krugman, P. R. and Obstfeld, M. (2003) *International Economics*, Boston, Addison-Wesley

Laclau, E. and Mouffe, C. (1985) *Hegemony and Socialist Strategy*, London, Verso

Ladurie, E. L. R. (1985) 'A reply to Robert Brenner', in T. H. Ashton and C. H. E. Philpin (eds) *The Brenner Debate*, Cambridge, Cambridge University Press

Lairson, T. D. and Skidmore, D. (2003) *International Political Economy*, Belmont, Thomson

Lake, D. A. (2000) 'British and American hegemony compared', in J. A. Frieden and D. A. Lake (eds) *International Political Economy: Perspectives on Global Power and Wealth*, fourth edition, London, Routledge

Landry, B. J. L., Mahesh, S. and Hartman, S. (2005) 'The changing nature of work in the age of e-business', *Journal of Organizational Change Management*, 18(2)

Lapavitsas, C. (1988) 'Financial crisis and the stock exchange crash', *International Socialism*, 38

Lapid, Y. (1996) 'Culture's ship: returns and departures in international relations theory', in Y. Lapid and F. Kratochwil (eds) *The Return of Culture and Identity in IR Theory*, Boulder, Col., Lynne Rienner

Lash, S. and Urry, J. (1987) *The End of Organized Capitalism*, Cambridge, Polity

—— —— (1994) *Economies of Signs and Space*, Sage, London

Lawson, T. (1997) *Economics and Reality*, London, Routledge

Lenin, V. I. (1950) *Selected Works*, Moscow, Foreign Languages Publishing House

—— (1961) *Collected Works, Vol. 38: Philosophical Notebooks*, London, Lawrence & Wishart

—— (1965) *Imperialism: The Highest Stage of Capitalism*, Peking, Foreign Languages Press

—— (1976) *The State and Revolution*, Peking, Foreign Languages Press

Levi-Faur, D. (1997) 'Economic nationalism: from Friedrich List to Robert Reich', *Review of International Studies*, 23(3)

Leys, C. (1996) *The Rise and Fall of Development Theory*, Nairobi, East African Educational Publishers

Leyshon, A. and Thrift, N. (1997) *Money/Space*, London, Routledge

Lipietz, A. (1985) 'A Marxist Approach to Urban Ground Rent: The Case of France', in M. Ball, V. Bentivegna, M. Edwards and M. Folin (eds) *Land Rent, Housing and Urban Planning: A European Perspective*, London, Croom Helm

—— (1987) *Mirages and Miracles: The Crisis of Global Fordism*, London, Verso

List, F. (1983) *The National System of Political Economy*, London, Frank Cass

—— (1997) 'Political and cosmopolitical economy', in G. T. Crane and A. Amawi (eds) *The Theoretical Evolution of International Political Economy: A Reader*, New York, Oxford University Press

Locke, J. (1991) *Locke on Money*, Oxford, Oxford University Press

—— (1993) *Political Writings*, Harmondsworth, Penguin

Lomborg, B. (2001) *The Skeptical Environmentalist*, Cambridge, Cambridge University Press

Lukács, G. (1974) *History and Class Consciousness*, London, Merlin

Lukes, S. (1974) *Power: A Radical View*, London, Macmillan

Luxemburg, R. (1963) *The Accumulation of Capital*, London, Routledge & Kegan Paul
—— (1970) 'The Mass Strike', in M.-A. Waters (ed.) *Rosa Luxemburg Speaks*, New York, Pathfinder
—— (1989) *Reform or Revolution*, London, Bookmarks
Lyotard, J.-F. (1984) *The Postmodern Condition: A Report on Knowledge*, Minneapolis, University of Minnesota Press
MacEwan, A. and Tabb, W. K. (1989) 'Instability and change in the world economy', in A. McEwan and W. K. Tabb (eds) *Instability and Change in the World Economy*, New York, New York University Press
Mackintosh, M., Brown, V., Costello, N., Dawson, G., Thompson, G. and Trigg, A. (eds) (1996) *Economics and Changing Economies*, Milton Keynes, Open University
MacLean, J. (2000) 'Philosophical roots of globalization and philosophical routes to globalization', in R. D. Germain (ed.) *Globalization and its Critics*, Basingstoke, Palgrave Macmillan
Maddison, A. (1991) *Dynamic Forces in Capitalist Development: A Long-Run Comparative View*, Oxford, Oxford University Press
—— (2003) *The World Economy: Historical Statistics*, Paris, OECD
Magdoff, H. (1969) *The Age of Imperialism*, New York, Monthly Review Press
Magnusson, L. (2004) *The Tradition of Free Trade*, Abingdon, Routledge
Makuwira, J. (2006) 'Development? Freedom? Whose development and freedom?' *Development in Practice*, 16(2)
Malthus, T. R. (1970) *An Essay on the Principle of Population*, Harmondsworth, Penguin
Mandel, E. (1968) *Marxist Economic Theory*, London, Merlin
Mann, M. (1986) *The Sources of Social Power*, Cambridge, Cambridge University Press
Manning, B. (1992) *1649: The Crisis of the English Revolution*, London, Bookmarks
—— (1994) 'The English revolution and the transition from feudalism to capitalism', *International Socialism*, 63
Marchand, M. H. and Runyon, A. S. (2000) *Gender and Global Restructuring*, London, Routledge
Marris, R. (1964) *The Economic Theory of 'Managerial' Capitalism*, London, Macmillan
Marshall, A. (1961) *Principles of Economics*, London, Macmillan
Martinez Alier, J. (1994) 'Ecological economics and ecosocialism', in M. O'Connor (ed.) *Is Capitalism Sustainable?* New York, Guilford Press

Marx, K. (1969) *Theories of Surplus Value, Part 2*, London, Lawrence & Wishart
—— (1970) *A Contribution to the Critique of Political Economy*, Moscow, Progress Publishers
—— (1973a) *Grundrisse*, New York, Random House
—— (1973b) *Surveys from Exile*, Harmondsworth, Penguin
—— (1974) *The First International and After*, New York, Vintage Books
—— (1975) *Early Writings*, Harmondsworth, Penguin
—— (1976) *Capital: A Critique of Political Economy, Vol. 1*, Harmondsworth, Penguin
—— (1977) *Selected Writings*, ed. D. McLellan, Oxford, Oxford University Press
—— (1978a) *Capital: A Critique of Political Economy, Vol. 2*, Harmondsworth, Penguin
—— (1978b) *The Poverty of Philosophy*, Peking, Foreign Languages Press
—— (1981) *Capital: A Critique of Political Economy, Vol. 3*, Harmondsworth, Penguin
—— and Engels, F. (1965) *Manifesto of the Communist Party*, Beijing, Foreign Languages Press
—— —— (1974) *The German Ideology*, London, Lawrence & Wishart
Masterson, T. (1998) 'Household labour, the value of labour-power and capitalism', paper prepared for the 1998 Eastern Economic Association Conference's International Working Group on Value Theory
Mazur, J. (2000) 'Labor's new internationalism', *Foreign Affairs*, 79(1)
McCormack, G. (2002) 'Breaking the iron triangle', *New Left Review*, 13
McGarr, P. (2000) 'Why green is red', *International Socialism*, 88
McGrew, A. (1992) 'The state in advanced capitalist societies', in J. Allen, P. Braham and P. Lewis (eds) *Political and Economic Forms of Modernity*, Cambridge, Polity
McNally, D. (1988) *Political Economy and the Rise of Capitalism: A Reinterpretation*, Berkeley, University of California Press
Middlebrook, K. J. (1996) 'The politics of industrial restructuring', in F. C. Deyo (ed.) *Social Reconstructions of the World Automotive Industry*, Basingstoke, Macmillan
Mill, J. S. (1994) *Principles of Political Economy*, Oxford, Oxford University Press
Milward, A. and Saul, S. B. (1977) *The Development of the Economies of Continental Europe: 1850–1914*, London, George Allen & Unwin

Mitchell, B. R. (1998) *International Historical Statistics: The Americas 1750–1993*, London, Macmillan
—— (2003) *International Historical Statistics: Africa, Asia and Oceania 1750–2000*, Basingstoke, Palgrave Macmillan
Mohun, S. (1977) 'Consumer sovereignty', in F. Green and P. Nore (eds) *Economics: An Anti-Text*, London, Macmillan
Molyneux, J. (1995) 'Is Marxism deterministic?', *International Socialism*, 68
Moran, M. (1991) *The Politics of the Financial Services Revolution*, Basingstoke, Macmillan
Morgenthau, H. J. (1963) *Politics among Nations*, New York, Alfred A. Knopf
Moseley, F. (1999) 'The decline of the rate of profit in the post-war United States economy', *Historical Materialism*, 4
Munck, R. (2005) *Globalization and Social Exclusion*, Bloomfield, Kumarian Press
Mundell, R. (1963) 'Capital mobility and stabilization policy under fixed and flexible exchange rates', *Canadian Journal of Economics and Political Science*, 29(4)
Murphy, R. T. (2000) 'Japan's economic crisis', *New Left Review*, 1
Murray, P. (1997) 'Redoubled empiricism', in F. Moseley and C. Campbell (eds) *New Investigations of Marx's Method*, Atlantic Highlands, NJ, Humanities Press
Naughton, B. (2006) *The Chinese Economy*, Cambridge, Mass., MIT Press
Nayyar, D. (2007) 'Globalization and free trade: theory, history and reality', in A. Shaikh (ed.) *Globalization and the Myths of Free Trade*, London, Routledge
NBSC (2005) 'Statistical data', National Bureau of Statistics of China, available at www.stats.gov.cn on 9 February 2007
Nelson, B (1996) 'The triumph and "Tragedy" of Walter Reuther', *Reviews in American History*, 24(3)
Núñez, H. J. (1999) 'Introduction', in H. J. Núñez and S. Babson (eds) *Confronting Change: Auto Labor and Lean Production in North America*, second edition, Mexico, Beneméita Universidad de Puebla
Nunnenkamp, P. (2004) 'To what extent can foreign direct investment help achieve international development goals?', *World Economy*, 27(5)
Nye, J. S. (2004) *Soft Power: The Means to Success in World Politics*, New York, PublicAffairs
Nygaard, B. (2006) 'Bourgeois revolution: the genesis of a concept', paper presented to the Historical Materialism Conference, London, December 8–10

Ó hUllacháin, B. (1997) 'Restructuring the American semiconductor industry', *Annals of the Association of American Geographers*, 87(2)

O'Brien, R. (1992) *Global Financial Integration: The End of Geography*, London, Pinter

—— and Williams, M. (2004) *Global Political Economy*, Basingstoke, Palgrave Macmillan

O'Connor, M. (1994a) 'Introduction: liberate, accumulate – and bust?', in M. O'Connor (ed.) *Is Capitalism Sustainable?* New York, Guilford Press

—— (1994b) 'Codependence and indeterminacy', in M. O'Connor (ed.) *Is Capitalism Sustainable?* New York, Guilford Press

OECD (2005) *OECD Economic Surveys: China*, Paris, OECD

—— (2008) 'OECD.Stat Extracts', available at http://webnet4.oecd.org/wbos/ on 17 January 2008

Ohmae, K. (1994) *The Borderless World: Power and Strategy in the Global Marketplace*, London, HarperCollins

Onuf, N. (1997) 'A constructivist manifesto', in K. Burch and R. A. Denemark (eds) *Constituting International Political Economy*, Boulder, Col., Lynne Rienner

Oxfam (2002) *Rigged Rules and Double Standards*, available at www.oxfam.org.uk on 2 March 2007

Panitch, L. (2001) 'Class and Inequality: Strategy for Labour in the Era of Globalization', paper presented to the International Studies Association, Chicago, 23 Febuary

—— and Gindin, S. (2005) 'Finance and American empire', *Socialist Register*, 2005

Parker, M. and Slaughter, J. (1988) *Choosing Sides: Unions and the Team Concept*, Boston, South End Press

Pearce, J. (1982) *Under the Eagle*, London, Latin American Bureau

Perraton, J. (2000) 'What are global markets', in R. D. Germain (ed.) *Globalization and its Critics*, Basingstoke, Palgrave Macmillan

Petras, J. (1999) 'NGOs: in the service of imperialism', *Journal of Contemporary Asia*, 29

Pettman, J. J. (1996) *Worlding Women*, St Leonards, NSW, Allen & Unwin

Pijl, K. van der (1998) *Transnational Classes and International Relations*, London, Routledge

—— (2007) 'Capital and the state system: a class act', *Cambridge Review of International Affairs*, 20(4)

Pilat, D., Cimper, A., Olsen, K. and Webb, C. (2006) 'The changing nature of manufacturing in OECD economies', STI Working Paper no. 2006/9, OECD Directorate for Science, Technology and Industry

Pilkington, J. (2006) 'Saline straightjacket: a political economy examination of the supposed intractability of salinity', MA thesis, University of Sydney

Pilling, G. (1986) 'The law of value in Ricardo and Marx', in B. Fine (ed.) *The Value Dimension*, London, Routledge & Kegan Paul

Piore, M. and Sabel, C. (1984) *The Second Industrial Divide: Possibilities for Prosperity*, New York, Basic Books

Platt, D. C. M. (1972) 'Economic imperialism and the businessman', in R. Owen and B. Sutcliffe (eds) *Studies in the Theory of Imperialism*, London, Longman

Polanyi, K. (2001) *The Great Transformation*, Boston, Beacon Press

Pollert, A. (1988) 'The flexible firm: fiction or fact?', *Work, Employment and Society*, 2(4)

Popper, K. R. (1961) *The Poverty of Historicism*, London, Routledge & Kegan Paul

—— (1962) *The Open Society and its Enemies, Vol. 2: The High Tide of Prophecy: Hegel, Marx and the Aftermath*, London, Routledge & Kegan Paul

Portes, R., Rey, H. and Oh, Y. (2001) 'Information and capital flows: the determinants of transactions in financial assets', *European Economic Review*, 45

Postan, M. M. and Hatcher, J. (1985) 'Population and class relations in feudal society', in T. H. Ashton and C. H. E. Philpin (eds) *The Brenner Debate*, Cambridge, Cambridge University Press

Poulantzas, N. (1978) *Classes in Contemporary Capitalism*, London, Verso

Pozo-Martin, G. (2007) 'Autonomous or materialist geopolitics?', *Cambridge Review of International Affairs*, 20(4)

Prebisch, R. (1950) *The Economic Development of Latin America and its Principal Problems*, New York, United Nations

—— (1971) *Change and Development: Latin America's Great Task*, New York, Praeger

Psychopedis, K. (1995) 'Emancipating explanation', in W. Bonefeld, R. Gunn, J. Holloway and K. Psychopedis (eds) *Open Marxism, Vol. 3: Emancipating Marx*, London, Pluto Press

Radice, H. (1999) 'Taking globalization seriously', *Socialist Register*, 1999

—— (2008) 'The developmental state under global neoliberalism', unpublished manuscript

Raff, D. M. G. (1988) 'Wage determination theory and the five-dollar day at Ford', *Journal of Economic History*, 48(2)

Ram, R. and Zhang, K. H. (2002) 'Foreign direct investment and economic growth: evidence from cross-country data for the 1990s', *Economic Development and Cultural Change*, 51(1)

Rees, J. (1998) *The Algebra of Revolution: The Dialectic and the Classical Marxist Tradition*, London, Routledge

Reich, R. B. (1991) *The Work of Nations*, London, Simon & Schuster

Reinert, E. S. (2005) 'German economics as development economics', in K. S. Jomo and E. S. Reinert (eds) *The Origins of Development Economics*, London, Zed Books

—— and Reinert, S. A. (2005) 'Mercantilism and economic development', in K. S. Jomo and E. S. Reinert (eds) *The Origins of Development Economics*, London, Zed Books

Reus-Smit, C. (2001) 'Constructivism', in S. Burchill, R. Devetak, A. Linklater, M. Paterson, C. Reus-Smit and J. Tait (eds) *Theories of International Relations*, Basingstoke, Palgrave Macmillan

Ricardo, D. (1951) *On the Principles of Political Economy and Taxation*, Cambridge, Cambridge University Press

Rinehart, J. (1999) 'The International Motor Vehicle Program's lean production benchmark: a critique', *Monthly Review*, January

—— Huxley, C. and Robertson, D. (1997) *Just Another Car Factory: Lean Production and its Discontents*, Ithaca, NY, ILR Press

Robinson, J. (1964) *Economic Philosophy*, Harmondsworth, Pelican

Robinson, R. (1972) 'Non-European foundation of European imperialism', in R. Owen and B. Sutcliffe (eds) *Studies in the Theory of Imperialism*, London, Longman

Robinson, W. I. (2002) 'Capitalist globalization and the transnationalization of the state', in M. Rupert and H. Smith (eds) *Historical Materialism and Globalization*, London, Routledge

—— (2007) 'The pitfalls of a realist analysis of global capitalism', *Historical Materialism*, 15(3)

—— and Harris, J. (2000) 'Towards a global ruling class?', *Science and Society*, 64(1)

Rodriguez, F. and Rodrik, D. (2000) 'Trade policy and economic growth', Working Paper no. 9912, http://ksghome.harvard.edu/~drodrik/skeptic1299.pdf

Rodrik, D. (2001) 'The global governance of trade: as if development really mattered', New York, United Nations Development Programme, www.undp.org/bdp

Rogowski, R. (1989) *Commerce and Coalitions: How Trade Affects Domestic Political Alignments*, Princeton, Princeton University Press

Rosdolsky, R. (1980) *The Making of Marx's Capital*, London, Pluto Press

Rosenberg, J. (1994) *The Empire of Civil Society*, London, Verso

—— (2000) *The Follies of Globalisation Theory*, London, Verso

—— (2006) 'Why is there no international historical sociology?' *European Journal of International Relations*, 12(3)

Rostow, W. (1960) *The Stages of Growth*, Cambridge, Cambridge University Press

Rousseau, J.-J. (1968) *The Social Contract*, Harmondsworth, Penguin

Rowthorn, R. and Ramaswamy, R. (1997) 'Deindustrialization: its causes and implications', International Monetary Fund, Washington, DC

Roxborough, I. (1979) *Theories of Underdevelopment*, Basingstoke, Macmillan

Rubenstein, J. M. (1992) *The Changing US Auto Industry*, London, Routledge

Rubin, I. I. (1973) *Essays on Marx's Theory of Value*, Montreal, Black Rose Books

—— (1979) *A History of Economic Thought*, London, Ink Links

Ruggie, J. G. (1998) *Constructing the World Polity*, London, Routledge

Runyon, A. S. and Marchand, M. H. (2000) 'Conclusion', in M. H. Marchand and A. S. Runyon (eds) *Gender and Global Restructuring*, London, Routledge

Rupert, M. (1995) *Producing Hegemony: The Politics of Mass Production and American Global Power*, Cambridge, Cambridge University Press

—— (2000) *Ideologies of Globalization: Contending Visions of a New World Order*, London, Routledge

Russett, B. (1985) 'The mysterious case of vanishing hegemony: or, is Mark Twain really dead?', *International Organization*, 39(2)

Rustin, M. (1989) 'The politics of post-Fordism: or, the trouble with "New Times"' *New Left Review*, 175

Samuelson, P. A. (2004) 'Where Ricardo and Mill rebut and confirm arguments of mainstream economists supporting globalization', *Journal of Economic Perspectives*, 18(3)

—— Hancock, K. and Wallace, R. (1975) *Economics*, Sydney, McGraw-Hill

Sargeson, S. (1999) *Reworking China's Proletariat*, Basingstoke, Macmillan

Sassen, S. (1996) *Losing Control? Sovereignty in an Age of Globalization*, New York, Columbia University Press

Sau, R. (1978) *Unequal Exchange, Imperialism and Underdevelopment*, Calcutta, Oxford University Press

Saxenian, A. (1994) *Regional Advantage: Culture and Competition in Silicon Valley and Route 128*, Cambridge, Mass., Harvard University Press

Sayer, D. (1987) *The Violence of Abstraction*, Oxford, Blackwell

Scholte, J. A. (2000) *Globalization: A Critical Introduction*, Basingstoke, Palgrave Macmillan

Schumpeter, J. A. (1954) *Capitalism, Socialism, and Democracy*, London, Unwin University Books

—— (1994) *History of Economic Analysis*, London, Routledge

Seccombe, W. (1974) 'The housewife and her labour under capitalism', New Left Review, 83

—— (1975) 'Domestic labour: reply to critics', New Left Review, 94

Sell, S. K. (2000) 'Big Business and the New Trade Agreements', in R. Stubbs and G. R. D. Underhill (eds) *Political Economy and the Changing Global Order*, Oxford, Oxford University Press

Shaikh, A. (2007a) 'Introduction', in A. Shaikh (ed.) *Globalization and the Myths of Free Trade*, London, Routledge

—— (2007b) 'Globalization and the myths of free trade', in A. Shaikh (ed.) *Globalization and the Myths of Free Trade*, London, Routledge

Shiva, V. (1989) *Staying Alive: Women, Ecology, and Development*, London, Zed Books

Simon, H. A. (1982) *Models of Bounded Rationality*, Cambridge, Mass., MIT Press

—— (1991) 'Organizations and markets', *Journal of Economic Perspectives*, 5(2)

Sinclair, T. J. (2005) *The New Masters of Capital*, Ithaca, NY, Cornell University

Singer, H. W. (1950) 'The distribution of gains between investing and borrowing countries', *American Economic Review*, 40(2)

Skocpol, T. (1977). 'Wallerstein's World Capitalist System: a theoretical and historical critique', *American Journal of Sociology*, 82(5)

Sloman, J. and Norris, K. (1999) *Economics*, Australia, Prentice Hall

Smith, A. (1853) *An Inquiry into the Nature and Causes of the Wealth of Nations, Vol. 2*, Edinburgh, Adam & Charles Black

—— (1997) *The Wealth of Nations, Books 1–3*, Harmondsworth, Penguin

Smith, N. (1984) *Uneven Development*, Oxford, Basil Blackwell

—— (2006) 'The geography of uneven development', in B. Dunn and H. Radice (eds) *100 Years of Permanent Revolution*, London, Pluto Press

Smith, T. (1993) 'Marx's *Capital* and Hegelian dialectical logic', in F. Moseley (ed.) *Marx's Method in* Capital: *A Re-examination*, Atlantic Highlands, NJ, Humanities Press

—— (2000) *Technology and Capital in the Age of Lean Production: A Marxian Critique of the 'New Economy'*, Albany, State University of New York

Snidal, D. (1985) 'The Limits of Hegemonic Stability Theory', *International Organization*, 39(4)

Solow, B. L. and Engerman, S. L. (eds) (1987) *British Capitalism and Caribbean Slavery*, New York, Cambridge University Press

Spero, J. E. (1982) *The Politics of International Economic Relations*, second edition, London, George Allen & Unwin

Squires, J. and Weldes, J. (2007) 'Beyond being marginal', *British Journal of Politics and International Relations*, 9(2)

Stiglitz, J. (2002) *Globalization and its Discontents*, London, Penguin

Stilwell, F. (2006) *Political Economy*, Oxford, Oxford University Press

Stopford, J. and Strange, S. (1991) *Rival, States, Rival Firms*, Cambridge, Cambridge University Press

Storper, M. and Walker, R. (1989) *The Capitalist Imperative*, New York, Basil Blackwell

Strange, S. (1985) 'Protectionism and world politics', *International Organization*, 39(2)

—— (1986) *Casino Capitalism*, Oxford, Oxford University Press

—— (1988) *States and Markets: An Introduction to Political Economy*, New York, Basil Blackwell

—— (1991) 'An eclectic approach', in C. N. Murphy and R. Tooze (eds) *The New International Political Economy*, Boulder, Col., Lynne Rienner

—— (1996) *The Retreat of the State: Diffusion of Power in the World Economy*, Cambridge, Cambridge University Press

—— (1998) *Mad Money*, Manchester, Manchester University Press

—— and Tooze, R. (1981) 'States and Markets in Depression: Managing Surplus Industrial Capacity in the 1970s', in S. Strange and R. Tooze (eds) *The International Politics of Surplus Capacity: Competition for Market Shares in the World Recession*, London, George Allen & Unwin

Sweezy, P. (1976) 'A critique', in R. Hilton (ed.) *The Transition from Feudalism to Capitalism*, London, New Left Books

Sylvester, C. (2002) *Feminist International Relations*, Cambridge, Cambridge University Press

Tabb, W. K. (1999) *Reconstructing Political Economy*, London, Routledge

Takahashi, K. (1976) 'A contribution to the discussion', in R. Hilton (ed.) *The Transition from Feudalism to Capitalism*, London, New Left Books

Takemae, E. (2003) *The Allied Occupation of Japan*, New York, Continuum

Taylor, G. (2002) 'Labour and subjectivity', in A. Dinerstein and M. Neary (eds) *The Labour Debate: An Investigation into the Theory and Reality of Capitalist Work*, Aldershot, Ashgate

Teranishi, J. (1996) 'Shared growth and the East Asian miracle', *Journal of Japanese and International Economics*, 10(3)

Teschke, B. and Heine, C. (2002) 'The dialectic of globalisation: a critique of Social Constructivism', in M. Rupert and H. Smith (eds) *Historical Materialism and Globalization*, London, Routledge

Thatcher, M. (1987) interview for *Woman's Own*, 23 September, available at www.margaretthatcher.org/speeches/displaydocument.asp?docid=106689, on 29 April 2008

Thelen, K. and Kume, I. (1999) 'The effects of globalization on labor revisited', *Politics and Society*, 27(4)

Thieblot, A. J. (2002) 'Technology and labor relations in the construction industry', *Journal of Labor Research*, 23(4)

Thompson, E. P. (1968) *The Making of the English Working Class*, Harmondsworth, Penguin

—— (1978) *The Poverty of Theory and Other Essays*, London, Merlin

Thun, E. (2008) 'The globalization of production', in J. Ravenhill, *Global Political Economy*, Oxford, Oxford University Press

Tickner, J. A. (1996) 'Identity in international relations theory: feminist perspectives', in Y. Lapid and F. Kratochwil, *The Return of Culture and Identity in IR Theory*, Boulder, Col., Lynne Rienner

Tilly, C. (1978) *From Mobilization to Revolution*, Reading, Mass., Addison-Wesley

—— (1995) 'Globalization threatens labor's rights', *International Labor and Working-Class History*, 47(1)

—— (2003) 'A nebulous empire', in G. Balakrishnan (ed.) *Debating Empire*, London, Verso

Touraine, A. (1971) *The Post-Industrial Society*, New York, Random House

Trotsky, L. (1969) *The Permanent Revolution and Results and Prospects*, New York, Pathfinder

—— (1977) *The History of the Russian Revolution*, London, Pluto Press

UN (various years) *United Nations International Trade Statistics Yearbook*, New York, UN

UNCTAD (2006a) 'World investment directory: FDI country profiles', available at www.unctad.org/Templates/Page.asp?intItemID=3198&lang=1

—— (2006b) *World Investment Report 2006*, available at www.unctad. org

—— (2007a) *Handbook of Statistics 2006–07*, New York, United Nations Commission on Trade and Development

—— (2007b) *World Investment Report 2007*, available at www.unctad. org

Underhill, G. R. D. (1993) 'Negotiating financial openness', in P. G. Cerny (ed.) *Finance and World Politics*, Aldershot, Edward Elgar

UNDP (2006) *Human Development Report 2006*, New York, United Nations Development Programme

—— (2007) *Human Development Report 2007/2008*, New York, United Nations Development Programme

Vance, T. N. (1951) 'The permanent war economy', *New International*, 17(1), available at www.marxists.org/history/etol/writers/vance/1950/ permwar

Veblen, T. (1964) *What Veblen Taught: Selected Writings*, ed. W. C. Mitchell, New York, Kelley

—— (1998) *The Theory of the Leisure Class*, Amherst, NY, Prometheus Books

Venables, A. J. (1996) 'International trade', in M. Mackintosh, V. Brown, N. Costello, G. Dawson, G. Thompson and A. Trigg (eds) *Economics and Changing Economies*, Milton Keynes, Open University

Vernon, R. (1966) 'International investment and international trade in the product cycle', *Quarterly Journal of Economics*, 80

Viner, J. (1948) 'Power versus plenty as objectives of foreign policy in the seventeenth and eighteenth centuries', *World Politics*, 1(1)

Wade, R. (1990) *Governing the Market*, Princeton, Princeton University Press

—— (2005) 'Globalization, poverty, and inequality', in J. Ravenhill (ed.) *Global Political Economy*, Oxford, Oxford University Press

—— and Veneroso, F. (1998) 'The Asian crisis', *New Left Review*, 228

Walby, S. (1986) *Patriarchy at Work*, Cambridge, Polity

Walker, R. A. (1999) 'Putting capital in its place: globalization and the prospects for labor', *Geoforum*, 30

Wallerstein, I. (1974) *The Modern World-System*, New York, Academic Press

—— (2000) *The Essential Wallerstein*, New York, The New Press

—— (2002) *The Decline of American Power*, New York, The New Press

Walter, A. (1993) *World Power and World Money*, Hemel Hempstead, Harvester Wheatsheaf

Waltz, K. N. (1959) *Man, the State and War*, New York, Columbia University Press

—— (1979) *Theory of International Politics*, Reading, Mass., Addison-Wesley

Warren, B. (1980) *Imperialism, Pioneer of Capitalism*, London, New Left Books

Watson, T. J. (1995) *Sociology, Work and Industry*, London, Routledge

Weber, M. (1930) *The Protestant Ethic and the Spirit of Capitalism*, London, Unwin University Books

—— (1968) *Economy and Society*, New York, Bedminster Press

Weeks, J. (1981) *Capital and Exploitation*, London, Edward Arnold

Weiss, L. (1998) *The Myth of the Powerless State*, Ithaca, NY, Cornell University Press

—— (2006) 'The business of buying American: government procurement as trade strategy in the United States', *Review of International Political Economy*, 13(5)

Wells, J., Sinda, S. H. and Haddar, F. (1998) 'Housing and building materials in low-income settlements in Dar es Salaam', *Habitat International*, 22(4)

Wendt, A. (1987) 'The agent–structure problem in international relations theory', *International Organization*, 41(3)

—— (1992) 'Anarchy is what states make of it: the social construction of power politics', *International Organization*, 46(2)

—— (1999) *Social Theory of International Politics*, Cambridge, Cambridge University Press

Went, R. (2000) *Globalization*, London, Pluto Press

Wheelock, J. (1996) 'People and households in economic analysis', in M. Mackintosh, V. Brown, N. Costello, G. Dawson, G. Thompson and A. Trigg (eds) *Economics and Changing Economies*, Milton Keynes, Open University

Whitworth, S. (2000) 'Theory and exclusion: gender, masculinity, and international political economy', in R. Stubbs and G. R. D. Underhill (eds) *Political Economy and the Changing Global Order*, Oxford, Oxford University Press

Williams, E. E. (1964) *Capitalism and Slavery*, London, Deutsch

Williamson, O. E. (1975) *Markets and Hierarchies*, New York, Free Press

Winch, G. (1994) 'The search for flexibility: the case of the construction industry', *Work, Employment and Society*, 8(4)

Wolf, M. (2005) *Why Globalization Works*, New Haven, Yale Nota Bene

Wolf, W. (1996) *Car Mania*, London, Pluto Press

Womack, J. P., Jones, D. T. and Roos, D. (1990) *The Machine That Changed the World: The Story of Lean Production*, New York, Rawson Associates

Wood, A. (1994) *North–South Trade, Employment and Inequality: Changing Fortunes in a Skill-Driven World*, Oxford, Clarendon Press

—— (1998) 'Globalisation and the rise in labour market inequalities', *Economic Journal*, 108

Wood, E. M. (1998) 'Modernity, postmodernity, or capitalism?', in R. W. McChesney, E. M. Wood and J. B. Foster (eds) *Capitalism and the Information Age*, New York, Monthly Review Press

—— (2002) *The Origin of Capitalism: A Longer View*, London, Verso

—— (2003) 'A manifesto for global capitalism?', in G. Balakrishnan (ed.) *Debating Empire*, London, Verso

Wood, S. (ed.) (1982) *The Degradation of Work?* London, Unwin Hyman

Wootton, D. (1993) 'Introduction', in John Locke, *Political Writings*, edited by D. Wootton, Harmondsworth, Penguin

World Bank (1993) *The East Asian Miracle*, Oxford, Oxford University Press

—— (2006a) 'World development indicators 2006', available at www.worldbank.org on 23 May 2007

—— (2006b) *Global Development Finance*, Washington, DC, IBRD/World Bank

—— (2006c) *World Development Report 2006: Equity and Development*, Washington, DC, World Bank

Wright, E. O. (1983) 'Giddens' critique of Marxism', *New Left Review*, 138

WTO (2006) *International Trade Statistics 2006*, World Trade Organisation, available at www.wto.org on 1 December 2006

—— (2007) 'International trade and tariff data', available at www.wto.org/english/res_e/statis_e/statis_e.htm on 28 May 2007

Wunder, H. (1985) 'Peasant organization and class conflict in Eastern and Western Germany', in T. H. Ashton and C. H. E. Philpin (eds) *The Brenner Debate*, Cambridge, Cambridge University Press

Yearley, S. (1996) *Sociology, Environmentalism, Globalization: Reinventing the Globe*, London, Sage

Young, L. (1996) *Fear of the Dark*, London, Routledge

INDEX

Numbers in Italics indicate tables

thermodynamics, second law of
66
Thirty Years War 127–31
Thompson, E.P. 50, 81–2, 117
Thucydides 39
total factor productivity 229
see also productivity
towns, rise of markets and 101–4
see also urbanisation
trade 5
post World War II 144–5
rise of, urbanisation and
101–4
state monopolies and
mercantilism 32–5
see also international trade
trade deficits 201, 211
Britain 209
US 212–13, 220–3, 226, 301
trade theory 183–90, 274
see also trade
trade unions 22, 45
Europe *v* US capital 234
financial regulation and
209–11
Fordism and 226, 234, 257
Japan 267–8
pay levels 243
post-Fordism and 231–3
post-war militancy and
compromise 134–40, 251
restructuring and 241–4,
279–80, 282–3
social welfare and 251
threat to capitalist order 130
US attack on 279
see also labour; working class
Transnationality Index 170
Trilateral Commission 309
Trotsky, L. 78, 289–90

unemployment 130
Japan 272
technological change and 227

United Auto Workers (UAW) 134
United Nations 313, 314
United States of America (US)
challenges to 315–16
defeat of organised labour and
finance 213–14, 278–9
deficits 215, 220–3
economic growth after 1870
119–20, 125, 266
enduring clout of 312–14
financial system and 211–13,
215, 221
Great Depression and New
Deal 128, 129–31, 187
post-war boom and labour
134–6
relative decline 180, 263–5,
278–9
trade and 35, 180–1, 188, 195,
201
trade deficits 212–13, 220–3,
226, 301
world economy and post
Bretton Woods 278–82
US dollar
devaluation 280–1
international finance and 143,
148–50, 210–13, 221,
281–2
US War of Independence 112
urbanisation 101–4, 303
use value 248, 250, 255
utilitarianism 15–16, 19

value 19
labour theory of 250
metals and money 205
use *v* exchange 248, 250,
260–2
Vance, T.N. 140
Veblen, T. 44, 45
Venezuela 173, 295
Vernon, R. 168
Volcker, P. 213, 215, 279, 291